THE LEGAL CONSISTENCY OF TECHNOLOGY REGULATION IN EUROPE

By bringing together fundamental rights, economic law, and recent legislation in the areas of digital platforms, data, and AI, this open access book gives a comprehensive picture of the state of play in technology regulation in the EU.

Risks of regulatory fragmentation are on the rise with ever more legislative instruments becoming applicable to the technology sector. This book explores the prospects and challenges of ensuring legal consistency in a period of transition in which new legislation is being implemented and the interpretation of existing laws is being challenged by the use of data, AI, and platform technologies.

The book analyses the legal consistency of technology regulation from three perspectives: (1) the relationship between the EU and the Council of Europe; (2) the relationship among EU regulatory frameworks; and (3) the relationship between EU and Member State law. By covering issues of fundamental rights protection, the free flow of data, consumer protection, competition, and innovation, the book gives a unique and extensive outlook into the state of the art in academic and policy discussions.

Unravelling the relationship between legal fields, the book is an essential resource for academics, practitioners and students wishing to understand the increasingly complex landscape of technology regulation in Europe.

The Legal Consistency of Technology Regulation in Europe

Edited by
Inge Graef
and
Bart van der Sloot

•HART•
OXFORD • LONDON • NEW YORK • NEW DELHI • SYDNEY

HART PUBLISHING

Bloomsbury Publishing Plc

Kemp House, Chawley Park, Cumnor Hill, Oxford, OX2 9PH, UK

1385 Broadway, New York, NY 10018, USA

29 Earlsfort Terrace, Dublin 2, Ireland

First published in Great Britain 2024

A catalogue record for this book is available from the British Library.

A catalogue record for this book is available from the Library of Congress.

Library of Congress Control Number: 2024931650

ISBN: HB: 978-1-50996-802-2
ePDF: 978-1-50996-804-6
ePub: 978-1-50996-803-9

Typeset by Compuscript Ltd, Shannon

TABLE OF CONTENTS

PART IV
LEGAL CONSISTENCY BETWEEN EU AND MEMBER STATE LAW

PART V
LESSONS LEARNED AND FUTURE PERSPECTIVES

LIST OF CONTRIBUTORS

Mark D Cole is Professor of Media and Telecommunications Law at the University of Luxembourg and Director for Academic Affairs at the Institute of European Media Law (EMR) in Saarbruecken, Germany. He also works at the Interdisciplinary Centre Security, Reliability and Trust (SnT) and the Institute of Advanced Studies (IAS) at the University of Luxembourg as well as being a member of the Advisory Committee of the Luxembourgish Audiovisual Regulatory Authority. He is founding and co-editor of the European Data Protection Law Review.

Ana Maria Corrêa is a senior researcher and lecturer at KU Leuven in Belgium. She is the vice-president of IVR Belgium. She recently published her book *Discrimination in Online Platforms: A Comparative Law Approach to Design, Intermediation and Data Challenges* focused on the legal governance and liability of online platforms on the matter of discrimination against protected classes. She is a regularly invited speaker on the intersection of technology and non-discrimination law and the author of various articles on the field.

Léon Dijkman, PhD (European University Institute), LLM (University of California, Berkeley, School of Law), LLM, LLB, BA (Utrecht University), is senior associate at the Amsterdam office of Hoyng Rokh Monegier and an assistant professor at the Erasmus School of Law in Rotterdam, where he teaches intellectual property law and legal method. His first book, *The Proportionality Test in European Patent Law*, was published with Hart in November 2023.

Christina Etteldorf is Senior Research Scientist at the Institute of European Media Law (EMR) in Saarbruecken, Germany. She studied law at the University of Saarland with German and International Media and Information Law as her area of specialisation and holds the academic degree of Assessor iuris. She is a self-employed consultant in the field of data protection law since 2016 and, since 2020, lecturer at the University of Saarland teaching in the field of intellectual property and media law.

Catalina Goanta is an Associate Professor of Private Law and Technology at Utrecht University, and Principal Investigator of the ERC HUMANads Starting Grant, focused on understanding the impact of content monetisation on social media and on reinterpreting private law fairness in the context of platform governance. This research was supported by the ERC Starting Grant research project HUMANads (2022–2027), ERC-2021-StG No 101041824.

Inge Graef is Associate Professor of Competition Law at Tilburg University, Netherlands. She is affiliated to the Tilburg Institute for Law, Technology, and Society (TILT) and the Tilburg Law and Economics Center (TILEC). Inge holds expertise in the areas of competition law, platform regulation and the governance of data-driven innovation. She holds a PhD in law from KU Leuven.

Maria Lillà Montagnani is Associate Professor of Commercial Law at Bocconi University in Milan, Italy. Additionally, she directs the Bocconi LL.M. Program in European and Social Law and is Transatlantic Technology Law Fellow at Stanford Law School.

Laurens Naudts is postdoctoral researcher at the AI, Media and Democracy Lab and Institute for Information Law (University of Amsterdam in the Netherlands) and affiliated senior researcher at the KU Leuven Centre for IT & IP Law in Belgium. He is working on the political philosophy and governance of AI, focusing on relational dynamics and structural injustice within a digitally mediated society. His doctoral research examined the concepts of equality and non-discrimination and their function in the regulation of automated decision-making.

Bart van der Sloot is an Associate Professor at the Tilburg Institute for Law, Technology, and Society in the Netherlands. He was awarded two highly prestigious research stipends by the Dutch Scientific Organisation. The Top Talent Research Grant fully covered his PhD project and the Veni grant (2021–2025) covers a research project called: the right to be let alone … by yourself. In 2023, he was awarded the Early Career Award by the Royal Netherlands Academy of Arts and Sciences.

Andreas Wiebe, LL.M. (Virginia) is a professor of competition law, intellectual property law and media law at the University of Göttingen, Germany, and Director of the LL.M. Programme in European and Transnational ICT and IP Law at the University of Göttingen.

Laura Zoboli is Assistant Professor of Commercial Law at the University of Brescia, Italy. She also serves as the Scientific Coordinator of the Centre for Antitrust and Regulatory Studies at the University of Warsaw and Co-Director of the ASCOLA (Academic Society for Competition Law) Centre Europe Chapter.

TABLE OF CASES

Court of Justice of the European Union

Opinions of the Court of Justice of the European Union

Opinions of Advocates General of the Court of Justice of the European Union

Decisions of the European Commission

Decisions of the European Data Protection Board

European Court of Human Rights

National Cases

TABLE OF LEGISLATION

Treaties

EU Legislation

EU Legislative Proposals

Council of Europe

National Legislation

PART I

Setting the Stage

1

Introduction

INGE GRAEF AND BART VAN DER SLOOT

The field of technology regulation finds itself in a period of transition. New legislation has been or is about to be adopted (such as the Digital Services Act (DSA), Digital Markets Act (DMA), Data Act, e-Privacy Regulation and Artificial Intelligence (AI) Act). Contemporary data technologies and Artificial Intelligence typically trigger the application of several legal regimes in parallel.

For example, the profiling of consumers for the purposes of targeted advertising is subject to the European Union (EU) data protection and consumer rules as well as the proposed AI Act. Although the EU aims for harmonisation, these laws typically entail different standards and requirements and the legal evaluation of a technology or data processing operation may vary according to which regime is applied. Similarly, data-driven systems can raise concerns about equality and discrimination that are subject to the European Convention on Human Rights in the context of the Council of Europe (CoE) as well as to the EU's legal framework. Again, it matters for the outcome of a case whether it is scrutinised under the CoE's or the EU's legal acquis. Finally, the relationship between EU and Member State law can be unclear at times, because of the complex interaction between legal requirements, with partial overlap and at times divergencies.

I. Background

The parallel application of legal regimes at the level of the CoE, the EU and the Member States is not necessarily a problem. Useful complementarities may exist when sets of rules target different concerns or protect different values, and when tasks for enforcement or resolving of disputes can be divided among the competent authorities and courts. However, with the EU and national legislators as well as the Court of Justice of the European Union and the European Court of Human Rights (ECtHR) becoming increasingly active in the field of technology regulation, the risk of inconsistencies and incongruities between legal frameworks rises. This may create legal uncertainty and lead to either under- and overregulation due to the fragmentation of the regulatory framework.

Against this background, the objective of this book is to reflect on the consistency of the overall legal framework in selected fields of technology regulation by mapping complementarities, gaps and tensions, and by drawing lessons for the future development of the law.

II. Approach

The book focuses on the legal consistency of technology regulation from three perspectives:

(1) the relationship between the EU and CoE frameworks;
(2) the relationship between various EU frameworks;
(3) the relationship between EU and Member State law.

For each of these perspectives, several domains of technology regulation are discussed in the different parts of the book. The selection of these fields or topics aims at giving a comprehensive picture of the state of play in technology regulation, combining issues of fundamental rights protection, internal market integration, competition and innovation in the private as well as public sector.

Each of the chapters discusses what the state of affairs is regarding the consistency of the legal framework in the respective area and pays attention to the impact of regulatory fragmentation in the respective field and how possible inconsistencies can be resolved.

III. Outline of the Book

Part II focuses on the relationship between CoE and EU law as regards two topics.

In chapter two, Laurens Naudts and Ana Maria Corrêa pay attention to how discrimination law is scattered throughout Europe. In the CoE, there is the general prohibition of discrimination, contained in Article 14 ECHR, and several supplementary articles and documents, setting out broad principles that apply to any governmental action or inaction. The EU, by contrast, has opted for sector-specific regulation and has provided more detailed guidelines, applicable to both governmental and private organisations. Both institutions fill potential regulatory gaps of the other, but it is equally clear that the jurisprudence of the ECtHR and the Court of Justice is significantly different, especially when dealing with algorithmic decision-making and profiling.

In chapter three, Bart van der Sloot examines the differences and overlaps between the right to privacy and the right to data protection. While the right to privacy is primarily the domain of the ECtHR, the EU is dominant in the field of data protection. Despite their different starting points, the ECtHR and the Court of Justice have mostly interpreted both rights in a complementary manner, closely following each other's footsteps.

Part III deals with the consistencies and inconsistencies of EU legislation. The EU has adopted a wide array of rules and principles in the technology domain. While several regimes may be applicable to the same matter, the EU often simply resolves this tension by providing that a legal instrument 'shall be without prejudice to the application' of another legal instrument.

In chapter four, Catalina Goanta pays attention to the interaction between the proposed AI Act and EU consumer regulation, in particular the Unfair Commercial Practices Directive. The AI Act sets out rules applicable to AI technologies with the aim of protecting consumers, for instance against behavioural distortions and the exploitation of vulnerabilities. EU consumer rules apply in parallel to such practices, which gives rise to questions about which regime will prevail as the AI Act may not be stricter than the existing consumer rules on all accounts.

In chapter five, Maria Lillà Montagnani and Laura Zoboli explore potential conflicts between the data protection framework and the rules on the re-use of public sector information and the push for open data, such as those laid down in particular in the Open Data Directive. Although data can be anonymised and aggregated, it is clear that data can often also be de-anonymised and re-identified, so that the General Data Protection Regulation (GDPR) would apply. While the re-use and open data regimes push for data to be as open and available as possible, the GDPR finds that personal data should be treated as safely, securely and confidentially as possible.

In chapter six, Andreas Wiebe discusses the regulation of machine-generated data. The EU tries to find a balance between protecting investments into the collection of machine-generated data and ensuring a sufficient level of access to such data in order to stimulate follow-on innovation. As such, machine-generated data is subject to several regimes at the same time, including the Data Governance Act, the Data Act and intellectual property regimes. The parallel application of these legal instruments raises questions about the scope of protection of machine-generated data and the interpretation of existing exceptions and limitations of intellectual property rights.

Part IV addresses the potential tensions between EU legislation and their implementation by Member States.

In chapter seven, Mark Cole and Christina Etteldorf discuss the implementation of the GDPR in Member State law. Although the GDPR is officially a Regulation, it is often described as a 'Regulation light' because it leaves it to Member States to set rules on quite a number of topics. This means that there are still legal inconsistencies and divergencies between the various implementations.

In chapter eight, Inge Graef pays attention to EU and national regimes regulating digital platforms. The DMA complements the existing EU competition rules by imposing additional obligations on a set of particularly powerful platforms, referred to as gatekeepers, with the aim of ensuring contestable and fair markets in the digital sector. The DMA does not fully preclude Member States from imposing further obligations on gatekeepers for other objectives beyond ensuring contestable and fair markets. However, the boundaries of these objectives are not easy to draw. For this reason, the interaction between EU and national rules targeting digital platforms gives rise to questions regarding substantive overlaps and division of tasks between the European Commission as the enforcer of the DMA and national competition authorities that are becoming increasingly proactive.

In chapter nine, Léon Dijkman explores the functioning of the patent system in light of the interaction between the different layers of patent protection at the international, regional and national levels. With the Unified Patent Court having become operational, the already fragmented patent system will need to evolve towards yet another reality in the EU in the future.

Finally, Part V concludes by giving an overview of the main findings of this book in the form of three common trends to be kept in mind for ensuring legal consistency in technology regulation.

IV. Acknowledgements

The editors would like to acknowledge that this work was undertaken in the context of the Digital Legal Studies research initiative, which is funded through the Law Sector Plan of the Dutch Ministry of Education, Culture and Science (OCW). Bart van der Sloot would like to acknowledge the Dutch Scientific Organisation (NWO)'s Veni Grant (VI.Veni.201R.082).

Finally, the editors would like to thank Paolo Belloni for his help with formatting and preparing the manuscript.

PART II

Legal Consistency between the EU and CoE Frameworks

2

Data-Driven Inequality and Discrimination: Challenges and Opportunities for Regulating AI Systems in the CoE and EU

LAURENS NAUDTS AND ANA MARIA CORRÊA

I. Introduction

The principles of equality and non-discrimination are a cornerstone of the Council of Europe (CoE) and the European Union (EU) legal orders. It should come as no surprise that AI governance initiatives have positioned equality and non-discrimination as navigational beacons for future technological advancements. This chapter investigates whether the legal approach to equality and non-discrimination is sufficiently robust to take up the mantle.[1]

In the first phase, the chapter examines how adverse differential and discriminatory treatment imposed by AI systems threatens to introduce and reinforce socio-relational and socio-economic inequality (Section II). In the second phase, the contribution investigates whether the legal interpretation of equality and non-discrimination within the CoE and the EU are sufficiently robust to capture the distinct harms AI systems might generate. To do so, a multi-tiered approach is followed. The contribution first identifies how the legal principle of equality and

[1] For references to the notions of equality and non-discrimination in regulatory initiatives concerning AI, see among others: CoE: Ad Hoc Committee on Artificial Intelligence (CAHAI), 'Possible elements of a legal framework on artificial intelligence, based on the Council of Europe's standards on human rights, democracy and the rule of law' (3 December 2021) available at rm.coe.int/cahai-2021-09rev-elements/1680a6d90d, paras 27–28; Ad Hoc Committee on Artificial Intelligence (CAHAI), 'Feasibility Study' (17 December 2020) available at rm.coe.int/cahai-2020-23-final-eng-feasibility-study-/1680a0c6da, 32. For EU: Proposal of the Commission for a Regulation of the European Parliament and of the Council laying down harmonised rules on Artificial Intelligence (Artificial Intelligence Act) and amending certain Union Legislative Acts, COM(2021) 206 final (Proposed AI Act); Proposal of the Commission for a Regulation of the European Parliament and of the Council on a Single Market for Digital Services (Digital Services Act) and amending Directive 2000/31/EC, COM(2020) 825 final. For its analysis, this chapter builds, in part, upon the research performed within L Naudts, *Fair or Unfair Differentiation? Reconsidering the Concept of Equality for the Regulation of Algorithmically Guided Decision-Making* (Doctoral Dissertation, KU Leuven, 2023).

non-discrimination might perform distinct functions and goals within the CoE and the EU systems (Section III).[2] This foundational exploration into the legal nature of equality and non-discrimination is the point of departure for a deeper comparative analysis between both orders. More specifically, the chapter investigates how different institutional (Section IV) and conceptual dynamics (Sections V and VI) further determine the specific harms the legal principle of equality and non-discrimination is able to address.[3] This comparative analysis serves a dual purpose. First, it helps locate areas of divergence and convergence, inconsistency and complementarity between the two systems. Second, it helps highlight each system's respective strengths and weaknesses in their response to address AI-driven harm.[4] When considered in unison, this exercise reveals what areas of debate will be most pertinent for the future regulation of AI systems (Section VII).

II. Challenges to Equality and Non-discrimination in the AI Environment

Consider the now-abolished Austrian public employment sorting system (AMS algorithm).[5] This system automatically allocated scores to job seekers. Depending

[2] Specific concepts that are relevant to AI governance debate, including the definition of harassment, the protection against discrimination via speech norms, and the prohibition to instruct discriminatory actions, are left outside the scope of this analysis.

[3] In studying the position of equality and non-discrimination within both orders, this chapter draws upon a rich body of comparative scholarship. See among others: O De Schutter, 'Three Models of Equality and European Anti-Discrimination Law' (2006) 57 *Northern Ireland Legal Quarterly* 1; S Haverkort-Speekenbrink, *European Non-Discrimination Law: A Comparison of EU Law and the ECHR in the Field of Non-Discrimination and Freedom of Religion in Public Employment with an Emphasis on the Islamic Headscarf Issue* (Intersentia, 2012); C Tobler, 'Equality and Non-Discrimination under the ECHR and EU Law – A Comparison Focusing on Discrimination against LGBTI Persons' (2014) ZaöRV 74, 521–61 available at www.zaoerv.de/74_2014/74_2014_3_a_521_562.pdf; J Gerards, 'Non-Discrimination, the European Court of Justice and the European Court of Human Rights: Who Takes the Lead?' in T Giegerich (ed), *The European Union as Protector and Promoter of Equality* (Springer International Publishing, 2020), available at link.springer.com/chapter/10.1007/978-3-030-43764-0_7; J Gerards, 'Systeemverklaringen voor verschillen tussen de gelijkebehandelingsrechtspraak van het HvJ EU en het EHRM' (2021) 12 *SEW, tijdschrift voor Europees en economisch recht* 571; A Rosas, 'The Court of Justice of the European Union: A Human Rights Institution?' (2022) 14 *Journal of Human Rights Practice* 204.

[4] See among others: R Xenidis, 'Tuning EU Equality Law to Algorithmic Discrimination: Three Pathways to Resilience' (2020) 27 *Maastricht Journal of European and Comparative Law* 736; J Gerards and F Zuiderveen Borgesius, 'Protected Grounds and the System of Non-Discrimination Law in the Context of Algorithmic Decision-Making and Artificial Intelligence' (2022) 20 *Colorado Technology Law Journal* 56; J Gerards and R Xenidis, *Algorithmic Discrimination in Europe: Challenges and Opportunities for Gender Equality and Non Discrimination Law* (Publications Office of the European Union, 2021), available at op.europa.eu/en/publication-detail/-/publication/082f1dbc-821d-11eb-9ac9-01aa75ed71a1/language-en; S Wachter, B Mittelstadt and C Russell, 'Why Fairness Cannot Be Automated: Bridging the Gap between EU Non-Discrimination Law and AI' (2021) 41 *Computer Law & Security Review* 105567; Naudts (n 1).

[5] N Kayser-Bril, 'Austria's Employment Agency Rolls out Discriminatory Algorithm, Sees No Problem' (*AlgorithmWatch*, 6 October 2019), available at algorithmwatch.org/en/austrias-employment-agency-ams-rolls-out-discriminatory-algorithm/; D Allhutter et al, 'Algorithmic Profiling of Job

on their outlook of finding employment, job seekers were placed into one of three categories: high job prospects in the short term, mediocre prospects, and low prospects in the long term.[6] The goal was to raise the efficiency of counselling and resource allocation of labour market programs. Financial focus and investment were placed on the group with mediocre prospects. Under one model, however, women, disabled people and people over 30 would be weighed negatively by the system. Regardless of their qualifications or experience, unemployed persons possessing those traits were more likely to be classified into the lowest-level group. They would receive less support from the AMS and instead be assigned to external agencies to improve their job prospects. The system was met with criticism and disapproval. Allhutter and others note how the system's design and functioning was liable to reinforce the cumulative disadvantages already faced by vulnerable and marginalised groups in the labour market.[7] Moreover, 'classifying job seekers as "hopeless" can trigger a process in which resource deprivation can lead to the realisation and validation of the prediction'.[8]

The AMS example illustrates how AI interferes with two related yet distinct egalitarian aspirations: relational and distributive equality.[9] First, as a relational ideal, equality represents a societal commitment to ensure persons have equal social status within relationships maintained with their peers, institutions, and private corporations.[10] People should be heard and recognised; allowed to express themselves in socially meaningful ways.[11] Following this paradigm, equality also stands opposed to acts and structures of oppression and domination that arise within societies characterised by unequal distributions of power. These acts may include psychological and economic exploitation and stereotyping individuals and social groups. The latter might occur, for example, when certain groups of job

Seekers in Austria: How Austerity Politics Are Made Effective' (2020) 3 *Frontiers in Big Data* 5; P Lopez, 'Reinforcing Intersectional Inequality via the AMS Algorithm in Austria' (2019) *Proceedings of the STS Conference Graz*; P Lopez, 'Bias Does Not Equal Bias: A Socio-Technical Typology of Bias in Data-Based Algorithmic Systems' (2021) 10 *Internet Policy Review*, available at policyreview.info/articles/analysis/bias-does-not-equal-bias-socio-technical-typology-bias-data-based-algorithmic.

[6] Allhutter et al (n 5).

[7] ibid 7. In reference to: OH Gandy, *Coming to Terms with Chance: Engaging Rational Discrimination and Cumulative Disadvantage* (Routledge, 2016).

[8] Allhutter et al (n 5) 7.

[9] See also: Naudts (n 1); S Viljoen, 'A Relational Theory of Data Governance' (2021) 131 *The Yale Law Journal* 573; S Barocas, M Hardt and A Narayanan, 'Fairness and Machine Learning', available at fairmlbook.org/pdf/fairmlbook.pdf 253; A Birhane, 'Algorithmic Injustice: A Relational Ethics Approach' (2021) 2 *Patterns* 100205, available at www.sciencedirect.com/science/article/pii/S2666389921000155?via%3Dihub; A Kasirzadeh, 'Algorithmic Fairness and Structural Injustice: Insights from Feminist Political Philosophy' (2022) *Proceedings of the 2022 AAAI/ACM Conference on AI, Ethics, and Society*, available at arxiv.org/abs/2206.00945.

[10] ES Anderson, 'What Is the Point of Equality?' (1999) 109 *Ethics* 287; C Schemmel, 'Distributive and Relational Equality' (2011) 11 *Politics, Philosophy & Economics* 123, available at journals.sagepub.com/doi/10.1177/1470594X11416774; C Fourie, F Schuppert and I Walliman-Helmer (eds), *Social Equality: On What It Means to Be Equals* (Oxford University Press, 2015); Birhane (n 9).

[11] See for instance: IM Young, *Justice and the Politics of Difference* (Princeton University Press, 1990); N Fraser and A Honneth, *Redistribution Or Recognition?: A Political-Philosophical Exchange* (Verso, 2003).

seekers are assumed and labelled as more hopeless. Second, equality can be viewed as a distributive or outcome-oriented ambition. Every person should have a fair share of prized public goods. To realise social equality, people should have equal access to certain publicly prized or justice-relevant goods, such as fundamental rights, education, or employment benefits. By barring specific categories of job seekers from enjoying a particular financial help, the AMS system reduced their ability to meaningfully participate in other areas of social life.

Discriminatory acts, like the adverse differential treatment imposed by the AMS algorithm, can be particularly inimical to relational and distributive equality. In this case, individuals were treated disadvantageously due to their demographic aspects. Discrimination, then, is understood as an adverse action. It refers to disadvantageous differential treatment unjustifiably imposed upon, or an unjustifiable adverse impact or result experienced by, a person (or group of persons) due to their possession of an ascriptive characteristic or membership of a socially salient group.

Systems like the AMS algorithm are not anomalies. In our digital society, people are continuously classified, categorised, and ranked on various features or attributes, such as their characteristics, preferences, or other measurable actions or behaviours. Based upon the commonalities people allegedly share, these systems create profiles whereby the members of one group are treated differently from the members of another group.[12] Yet, do these systems impose AI-specific challenges concerning people's claim to equality and non-discrimination that non-automated decisions do not? While the promise AI holds remains untapped, there are several characteristics these technologies exhibit and offer decision-makers that regulators should consider ensuring their regulatory initiatives are future-proof. Four of these, relevant to the discussion at hand, are highlighted here.

First, by having access to vast amounts of data, decision-makers can now differentiate between individuals based on a more significant number of traits.[13] A financial institution may profile creditors based on traditional criteria, such as income and age. Still, they might also discover other relevant attributes. Some attributes may be more laborious to measure and map with non-automated means, such as people's behaviours, preferences, or other monitorable actions. Moreover, these traits may not always share an intuitive connection to the domain in which they are used. For instance, data-driven analytics may uncover how people's keystroke patterns when filing an online credit application indicate their trustworthiness.[14] Second, AI-driven decision-making systems derive and

[12] See also F Schauer, *Profiles, Probabilities and Stereotypes* (Belknap Harvard, 2006) 1–25; M Hildebrandt, 'Defining Profiling: A New Type of Knowledge?' in M Hildebrandt and S Gutwirth (eds), *Profiling the European Citizen: Cross-Disciplinary Perspectives* (Springer Netherlands, 2008), available at doi.org/10.1007/978-1-4020-6914-7_2.

[13] S Wachter, 'The Theory of Artificial Immutability: Protecting Algorithmic Groups under Anti-Discrimination Law' (2022) 97 Tul. L. Rev. 149, available at: www.tulanelawreview.org/pub/artificial-immutability.

[14] For an example of strange correlations, see: SF DeAngelis, Solutions Enterra, 'Artificial Intelligence: How Algorithms Make Systems Smart' (2014) *Wired*, available at www.wired.com/insights/2014/09/artificial-intelligence-algorithms-2/.

apply group-level generalisations. While individuals may be the final recipient of an outcome produced by AI systems, the statements about these individuals are often statements about the groups they are a member of. Third, the instructions underlying these systems can be uniformly applied and streamlined with less administrative costs. Finally, the AI environment is highly interconnected and data easily exchangeable; decisions taken in one domain may inform decisions in another: consumption behaviour derived for marketing purposes might be relevant for credit and insurance institutions. When decision-makers exploit these characteristics of complexity and scale, differential treatment imposed by these systems can be distinctive in form and content. In turn, associated inequalities become distinctive in content and form too.

AI-driven decisions may replicate and *reinforce* structural and institutional forms of existing social and economic disparities. Profiles can act as a proxy for traits that reflect histories of disadvantage, such as a person's ethnicity, religion, or gender. For these social groups, the digital environment is another institutional layer they must challenge. At the same time, when decisions are reliant upon less tangible characteristics, such as (the totality of) a person's (monitorable) attributes, behaviours, or actions, which do not share a connection with histories of disadvantage, decisions may introduce inequality alongside novel dimensions. Entire groups of people, and their members, may suddenly find themselves excluded from areas of social life deemed critical for their personal, relational, and socio-economic development based on strange correlations.[15] Due to the large-scale effects, these actions could potentially restructure society alongside novel strata.[16] Assuming equality represents specific relational and economic interests all citizens share, AI systems are indiscriminate in their threat thereto.[17] That is not to say that the regulatory response should be the same for all: the needs of underrepresented and vulnerable groups differ from those who experience singular bad AI-driven outcomes. Legislation should account for these differences.

Whether the law can challenge these AI-driven harms depends on the tools it currently has in its availability. As part of this toolset, the legal principles of equality and non-discrimination perform a crucial function. These principles have found expression within human rights and non-discrimination laws. They govern the conditions under which differential treatment – or vice versa, similar treatment – can be justifiably imposed. In this context, laws prohibiting discriminatory behaviour are an unquestioned ally to equality. It is, therefore, necessary to

[15] Creel and Hellman refer to these domains as 'realms of opportunity'. Areas of life that are connected to other paths of opportunities. The money a person gains from employment may affect their ability to pursue different hobbies. K Creel and D Hellman, 'The Algorithmic Leviathan: Arbitrariness, Fairness, and Opportunity in Algorithmic Decision Making Systems', *Proceedings of the 2021 ACM Conference on Fairness, Accountability, and Transparency* (Association for Computing Machinery, 2021), available at doi.org/10.1145/3442188.3445942.

[16] A Vedder and L Naudts, 'Accountability for the Use of Algorithms in a Big Data Environment' (2017) 31 *International Review of Law, Computers & Technology* 206.

[17] Naudts (n 1). See also: Creel and Hellman (n 15); Wachter (n 13).

investigate whether the legal conceptualisation of equality and non-discrimination is sufficiently robust to accommodate AI-driven social and economic injustice.

III. Equality and Non-discrimination in the CoE and EU

The European legal landscape is multi-layered and scattered, a complexity which this chapter cannot capture.[18] To help identify areas of divergence within this complexity, the conceptual and regulatory building blocks that characterise the role of equality and non-discrimination in the CoE and EU will be highlighted. First, it examines the historical evolution and relationship between both legal notions. Second, both orders' critical equality and non-discrimination provisions and their respective scope of application are analysed.

A. Equality and Non-discrimination: Formal or Substantive?

Scholars have categorised equality's historical evolution alongside various models of equality.[19] Under the historical first model – equality before the law – equality can be likened to a principle of good governance. It is then a vertical or institutional check against irrational public action. Like situations should be treated alike (or different cases differently). Failure to do so constitutes discrimination unless there is a reasonable justification for doing otherwise. Equality, then, is procedural, an instrument to gauge the rationality of the explanation provided.

Under the second model, equality transitions to a human right with clear normative ambitions: to combat certain forms of differential treatment experienced as denigrating, exclusionary, or otherwise harmful. Within Europe, this approach to equality is typified by identifying a series of protected characteristics, such as a person's gender or ethnicity, whose use will be subject to heightened scrutiny.[20] Additionally, the law might identify certain publicly prized or justice-relevant

[18] See among others: D Schiek, 'From European Union Non-Discrimination Law towards Multidimensional Equality Law for Europe' in D Schiek and V Chege (eds), *European Union Non-Discrimination Law: Comparative Perspectives on Multidimensional Equality Law* (Routledge-Cavendish Taylor & Francis Group, 2008); Tobler (n 3); Gerards, 'Non-Discrimination, the European Court of Justice and the European Court of Human Rights' (n 3); Gerards, 'Systeemverklaringen voor verschillen tussen de gelijkbehandelingsrechtspraak van het HvJ EU en het EHRM' (n 3).

[19] See for instance: C McCrudden and H Kountouros, 'Human Rights and European Equality Law' in H Meenan (ed), *Equality Law in an Enlarged European Union: Understanding the Article 13 Directives* (Cambridge University Press, 2007), available at www.cambridge.org/core/books/equality-law-in-an-enlarged-european-union/human-rights-and-european-equality-law/66198EDD0522813DC16A689 8DBDA68A9; S Sottiaux, 'Het Gelijkheidsbeginsel: Langs Oude Paden En Nieuwe Wegen' (2008) 72 *Rechtskundig Weekblad* 690.

[20] Sottiaux (n 19); McCrudden and Kountouros (n 19).

goods where discrimination is met with additional caution due to the function these goods hold for social or economic participation. For instance, every person should have equal access to *fundamental rights* or an *equal opportunity to enter the job market*. Importantly, this model applies not only to institutional dynamics. It also governs interpersonal or private relationships.

Under its final evolutionary step, equality calls for societal transformation. Rather than prohibiting certain discriminatory behaviours, this approach acknowledges that additional and proactive measures are needed to effectuate institutional and collective change, social inclusivity and cultural diversity.[21] Although these interests benefit society as a whole, these goals can only be attained when heightened visibility and protection are given to those who, for various reasons, are underrepresented or historically disadvantaged. Correcting historical disadvantages may necessitate positive or affirmative action, for example.

This evolutive transition represents a shift from formal to substantive equality.[22] Equality evolved from a purely procedural notion mandating rational and consistent application of the law to a substantive concept aiming for social and cultural inclusivity, diversity, and tolerance that also protects personal dignity and autonomy.[23] As part of this evolution, the law gradually incorporated more socio-relational and distributive egalitarian ambitions, and the legal tools to realise those ambitions expanded. Whereas equality as rationality represents formal equality and transformative equality represents substantive equality, the human-rights model sits between both narratives.[24] Yet, the dividing line between these models should not be sharply drawn: they co-exist and mutually inform one another.[25] The following section identifies how these models operate within the CoE and EU. Importantly, however, depending on the model of equality at play, the principle of equality and non-discrimination might represent a specific legal tradition and function.

B. The European Convention on Human Rights

The Council of Europe's foundational non-discrimination clause is Article 14 of the European Convention on Human Rights (ECHR). Article 14 ECHR stipulates

[21] Sottiaux (n 19) 691.

[22] S Fredman, 'Substantive Equality Revisited' (2016) 14 *International Journal of Constitutional Law* 712.

[23] McCrudden and Kountouros (n 19); Sottiaux (n 19); S Prechal, '"Non-Discrimination Does Not Fall Down From Heaven": The Context and Evolution of Non-Discrimination in EU Law' (Eric Stein, Working Paper No. 4, 2009) 17.

[24] Sottiaux (n 19); De Schutter (n 3); McCrudden and Kountouros (n 19); OM Arnardóttir, 'Discrimination as a Magnifying Lens: Scope and Ambit under Article 14 and Protocol No. 12' in E Brems and J Gerards (eds), *Shaping Rights in the ECHR: The Role of the European Court of Human Rights in Determining the Scope of Human Rights* (Cambridge University Press, 2014) 331, available at www.cambridge.org/core/books/shaping-rights-in-the-echr/discrimination-as-a-magnifying-lens/7D456DA527C1D513A0093DA19611610A.

[25] See also: Sottiaux (n 19); M Spinoy, 'Discriminatie in Het Gelijkekansendecreet? Reflecties Bij GwH Nr. 110/2019' (2020) *Tijdschrift voor Bestuurswetenschappen en Publiekrecht* 317.

that the enjoyment of the rights and freedoms set forth in the ECHR shall be secured without discrimination on any ground, such as sex, race, colour, language, religion, political or other opinion, national or social origin, association with a national minority, property, birth or other status. Article 14 ECHR is thus positioned as an accessory rather than an independent, fundamental right: it must be invoked with another substantive Convention right. Still, for the ECtHR to find a violation of Article 14 ECHR, it is not necessary for there to be a violation of that other right. Instead, it is sufficient for a case of differential treatment to fall within the wider ambit of one or more Convention rights.[26]

The Convention does not have a direct interpersonal or private scope.[27] The ECHR acts as an institutional check against the (in)action of State bodies. In this sense, Article 14 ECHR also represents the vertical and procedural ideal of equality before the law. For example, in the case of Moraru versus Romania, the Court had to consider the legitimate use of height and size requirements as entrance criteria for potential candidates for the country's military educational programs.[28] The Court went on to examine whether the reasons put forward by the authorities to justify differential treatment were relevant and sufficient. The ECtHR did not argue against selection criteria but found that the Romanian authorities failed to provide evidence connecting the selection requirements (in this case, size) to their justification (a necessary degree of strength). Due to this lack of rationality, the ECtHR found a violation of Article 14 ECHR.[29]

Though the latter case exemplifies a formal equality assessment, Article 14 ECHR has been given more normative substance over the years. For instance, the ECtHR is particularly cautious when differential treatment can conflict with democratic values, personal dignity and autonomy. Likewise, in their anti-stereotyping and vulnerability case law, the ECtHR recognises how inequality may come about through social dynamics.[30] As part of this evolution, the ECtHR started to identify certain ascriptive traits, such as being of a particular gender or having an intellectual and mental disability, as symbolic representations of certain types of social injustice. When these traits are a basis for differential treatment, the ECtHR will heighten its level of scrutiny because they are more likely to produce a negative

[26] Protocol No. 12 to the Convention for the Protection of Human Rights and Fundamental Freedoms (ECHR) [2000] ETS 177, did establish a general prohibition of discrimination but has seen limited case law due to a lack of ratification. For a case concerning Protocol 12 to the ECHR, see *Sejdic and Finci v Bosnia and Herzegovina* App nos 27996/06 and 34836/06 (ECtHR Grand Chamber, 22 December 2009) para 55.

[27] Though private actors are (in principle) not obliged to respect the ECHR, States can be condemned for their inaction to sufficiently guard people against unjustified unequal treatment in their relationships with private actors. Gerards, 'Systeemverklaringen voor verschillen tussen de gelijkebehandelingsrechtspraak van het HvJ EU en het EHRM' (n 3) 572. See for instance: *Pla and Puncernau v Andorra* App no 69498/01 (ECtHR, 15 December 2004); *Garcia Mateos v Spain* App no 38285/09 (ECtHR, 19 May 2013).

[28] *Moraru v Romania* App no 64480/19 (ECtHR, 8 November 2022).

[29] ibid para 55.

[30] See eg *Konstantin Markin v Russia* App no 30078/06 (ECtHR Grand Chamber, 22 March 2012); *Alajos Kiss v Hungary* App no 38832/06 (ECtHR Second Section, 20 May 2010, final 20 August 2010).

societal impact.[31] By articulating the conditions under which unjustifiable social inequality occurs, the Court can indirectly influence personal or horizontal social relationships.

On a related note, the ECtHR has also specified that fundamental rights have clear social and or economic implications even though the Convention essentially covers civil and political rights.[32] Or in the words of the ECtHR, there is no 'water-tight division' between the public and private domains.[33] As part of this transition, the ECtHR now recognises that States can have an active or transformative duty to correct factual inequalities and structural deficiencies. For example, in matters relating to education, the ECtHR has recognised how applicants with a history of direct discrimination may need proactive assistance, including structured involvement on the part of social services.[34]

C. The European Union

Equality has long been foundational in the European Union as a general principle of EU law. Its history is rich and complex. Equality's initial function as a procedural tool to evaluate and govern internal market regulation and integration were complemented by a fundamental rights narrative aimed to combat specific status-based inequalities.[35] Over the decades, both functions gained increased constitutional anchorage.[36]

Two landmark moments relevant to the current AI legal landscape are discussed here. The first concerns the addition of Article 13 EC (Article 19 TFEU) to the Treaty establishing the European Community following the 1997 Treaty of Amsterdam. This provision enabled the EU legislator to combat discrimination based on sex, racial or ethnic origin, religion or belief, disability, age, or sexual

[31] OM Arnardóttir, 'The Differences That Make a Difference: Recent Developments on the Discrimination Grounds and the Margin of Appreciation under Article 14 of the European Convention on Human Rights' (2014) 14 *Human Rights Law Review* 647.

[32] *Airey v Ireland* App no 6289/73 (ECtHR, 9 October 1979) para 26.

[33] ibid; *Jurčić v Croatia* App no 54711/15 (ECtHR, 4 May 2021) para 64. See however also Council of Europe, *European Social Charter*, 7th edn (Collected Texts, January 2015).

[34] See eg *Horváth and Kiss v Hungary* App no. 11146/11 (ECtHR, 29 January 2013) paras 101–104.

[35] For cases concerning equality as an economic imperative, reference can be made to the CJEU's case law on EU agricultural policies and tax discrimination. The CJEU also invoked economic considerations to condemn certain status-based inequalities. For instance, discrimination based on nationality can conflict with the ideal of free movement within the market. Similarly, gender-based equality standards were initially developed from economic labour law considerations aimed to avoid unfair competitive disadvantages in the market. See T Tridimas, *The General Principles of EU Law*, 2nd edn (Oxford University Press, 2006); Prechal (n 23); E Ellis and P Watson, 'Essential Characteristics of EU Law' in E Ellis and P Watson (eds), *EU Anti-Discrimination Law*, 2nd edn (Oxford University Press, 2012), available at oxford.universitypressscholarship.com/10.1093/acprof:oso/9780199698462.001.0001/acprof-9780199698462-chapter-002.

[36] For an in-depth overview of the various manifestations of equality as a general principle of EU law: E Muir, 'The Essence of the Fundamental Right to Equal Treatment: Back to the Origins' (2019) 20 *German Law Journal* 817.

orientation. This provision served as the basis for the EU Equality Directives, which significantly enhanced the position of equality and non-discrimination as a legislative tool to govern public and private relationships and behaviours in the EU. The role of equality and non-discrimination as fundamental rights was further strengthened by their incorporation into the Charter of Fundamental Rights of the European Union (CFR), which came into force in 2009.[37] Given the Charter's status as primary law, it will be discussed first.

Article 20 CFR protects equality before the law. This provision is traditionally seen as a wide-ranging and open-ended institutional benchmark: formal equality in creating and applying EU law. Article 21(1) CFR gives expression to Article 20 CFR.[38] The latter is modelled after Article 14 ECHR and formulated as a prohibition to discriminate. In this context, the explanations to Article 21(1) CFR note that in so far as the Charter corresponds to Article 14 of the ECHR, it applies in compliance with it.[39]

According to Bell, 'Article 21 emerges as a type of *lex specialis* in contrast to the *lex generalis* found in Article 20'. Under this view, Article 21 CFR functions as an institutional lens for evaluating status-based differential treatment linked to socially significant characteristics or traits that signal histories of disadvantage that bring about or are associated with social inequality.[40] Unlike Article 20 CFR, the CJEU has given – albeit in a limited set of cases – a direct horizontal effect to Article 21 CFR.[41] Article 21 CFR reflects equality as a human right that mitigates legal and social exclusion based on ascriptive categories.[42] Article 20 CFR represents the traditional view of equality as a neutral standard of good governance to evaluate the rationality of non-ascriptive differentiation grounds as a motivational basis for the application of different legal standards to comparable situations.[43] This view has somewhat been

[37] ibid 818.

[38] Case C-356/12 *Wolfgang Glatzel v Freistaat Bayern* ECLI:EU:C:2014:350, [2014] 3 CMLR 52, para 43. See also Case C-190/16 *Werner Fries v Lufthansa CityLine GmbH* ECLI:EU:C:2017:513, [2017] 7 WLUK 56, para 29; and Case C-243/19 *A v Veselības ministrija* ECLI:EU:C:2020:872, [2021] 2 CMLR 2, para 35. See also: A Ward, 'The Impact of the EU Charter of Fundamental Rights on Anti-Discrimination Law: More a Whimper than a Bang?' (2018) 20 *Cambridge Yearbook of European Legal Studies* 32, 33.

[39] However, as seen in the previous Section, Article 14 ECHR has been used in a more traditional, rationality-oriented sense. The question can thus be raised, to what extent does Article 14 ECHR inform Article 20 of the Charter of Fundamental Rights of the European Union [2012] OJ C 326/391 (CFR)? See also Explanations relating to the Charter of Fundamental Rights [2007] OJ C303/17, under Article 52(3) CFR.

[40] M Bell, 'Article 20: Equality Before the Law' in S Peers et al (eds), *The EU Charter of Fundamental Rights: A Commentary* (Hart Publishing, 2014) 565. See also: H Eklund and C Kilpatrick, 'Article 21 EU Charter of Fundamental Rights' in S Peers et al (eds), *The EU Charter of Fundamental Rights: A Commentary* (Hart Publishing, 2021).

[41] The CJEU laid down the horizontal direct effect of Article 21 CFR on the basis of religion and age-based differentiation. Case C-414/16 *Egenberger v Evangelisches Werk Fur Diakonie und Entwicklung eV* ECLI:EU:C:2018:257, [2019] 1 CMLR 9, paras 76–77. Case C-144/04 *Werner Mangold v Rüdiger Helm* ECLI:EU:C:2005:709, [2005] ECR I-9981, paras 74–78.

[42] R Xenidis, 'Transforming EU Equality Law? On Disruptive Narratives and False Dichotomies' (2019) 38 *Yearbook of European Law* e2.

[43] Such a reading may follow from *Glatzel* (n 38). First, the CJEU analysed EU law concerning the minimum standards for drivers of specific vehicles. The CJEU considered the compatibility of visual

confirmed by the CJEU. For instance, in its case law, the CJEU clarified that the EU Equality Directives give specific expression to Article 21(1) CFR.[44] Even though Article 21 CFR has been given a limited degree of interpersonal range, its status as an all-encompassing human right remains limited: it primarily addresses discrimination by the institutions and bodies of the Union themselves when exercising powers conferred to them and by the Member States in their implementation of Union law.[45] Moreover, the explanations to the Charter further clarify how Article 21 CFR does not impose a sweeping ban on discrimination.

The EU Equality Directives then protect EU citizens against specific types of status-based discrimination in decisions relating to publicly prized goods or domains, such as employment, education, and the provision of goods and services.[46] Moreover, the Directives extend explicitly to both public and private actors. In addition, they also incorporate more substantive and transformative ambitions. Among others, the EU Equality Directives prohibit the socio-relational harm of harassment and establish the conditions under which positive action measures are possible. The Directives have a clear scope of application and offer a heightened level of protection. Their personal and material range of application is relatively narrow, however. In case an act of differentiation does not occur within one of the protected domains and cannot be linked directly or indirectly to a prohibited (personal) characteristic, the Directives do not offer protection.

The Charter and the EU Equality Directives symbolise equality's shift from an institutional benchmark meant to constrain public bodies during the dawn of the EU and to realise internal market objectives (equality as a means) to a concept that is concerned with personal autonomy, social inclusion and cultural diversity (equality as an end).[47] A transformation the CJEU has contributed to in its

acuity requirements, and whether these constitute discrimination on the grounds of disability, under Article 21 CFR. The CJEU then examined whether the law could justifiably impose different exception regimes depending on the category of driver. The EU law in question created two groups of drivers depending on the size of the vehicle, the number of passengers carried and the responsibilities involved in driving such vehicles. In other words, the CJEU evaluated the rightful use of a status-based differentiation criterion (visual acuity) via Article 21 CFR, whereas it applied Article 20 CFR on a non-status-based difference (type of driver). Unfortunately, the CJEU's case law is not always as consistent or coherent in its application of the Charter, making the respective scope of application and mutual relationship between both provisions unclear.

[44] See for instance: Case C-83/14 *CHEZ Razpredelenie Bulgaria AD v Komisia za zashtita ot diskriminatsia* ECLI:EU:C:2015:480, [2016] 1 CMLR 14, para 42.

[45] CFR, Article 51(1).

[46] Directive 2000/43/EC of the Council implementing the principle of equal treatment between persons irrespective of racial or ethnic origin (Racial Equality Directive) [2000] OJ L180/22; Directive 2000/78/EC of the Council establishing a general framework for equal treatment in employment and occupation [2000] OJ L303/16; Directive 2006/54/EC of the European Parliament and of the Council on the implementation of the principle of equal opportunities and equal treatment of men and women in matters of employment and occupation (recast) [2006] OJ L204/23; Directive 2004/113/EC of the Council implementing the principle of equal treatment between men and women in the access to and supply of goods and services [2004] OJ L373/37.

[47] Prechal (n 23) 2; M Bell, 'The Transformation of EU Anti-Discrimination Law' in M Bell (ed), *Anti-Discrimination Law and the European Union* (Oxford University Press, 2002), available at

interpretation of these instruments. Still, this is an evolutive process in motion. In this context, the economic origins of the EU's equality and non-discrimination concepts remain present. As observed by Xenidis, EU law remains a 'pragmatic compromise that guarantees a form of citizenship as socio-economic participation, in line with a transnational European proto-society that heavily revolves around market structures and interactions'.[48] For example, the Directives offer individual non-discrimination rights against differential treatment based on ascriptive traits. While those traits have been chosen due to their close link with historical and social disadvantage, the associated rights are primarily granted in economic domains characterised by unbalanced market opportunities (eg, employment, social protection, and access to goods and services).[49]

IV. Institutional Divergence and Convergence

On a foundational conceptual level, both orders evolve towards alignment. The general principles of equality and non-discrimination transitioned from an institutional and procedural constraint to one that is more normatively rich, interpersonal and transformative. This transition, however, is subject to various institutional dynamics. In this context, this section first analyses areas of institutional divergence between the CoE and EU. Differences can be linked to the (material) scope and competencies each order covers and the procedures to trigger an investigation into differential treatment. In the second step, this section looks a specific area of institutional alignment. In particular, the CoE and EU follow a distributive paradigm to equality. In turn, they might fail to capture the relational egalitarian harm AI technologies generate. These institutional dynamics may feed into how both orders approach the justification of differential treatment. The latter, and the repercussions thereof for AI, this chapter will touch upon later.

A. Competences and Procedures

Given the central role performed by the ECtHR and CJEU in interpreting equality as a legal principle, discrepancies in the interpretation and function of equality can be partly explained due to differences in their respective interpretative reach and

oxford.universitypressscholarship.com/10.1093/acprof:oso/9780199244508.001.0001/acprof-9780199244508-chapter-8; E Muir, 'The Transformative Function of EU Equality Law' (2013) 21 *European Review of Private Law* 1231, available at kluwerlawonline.com/journalarticle/European+Review+of+Private+Law/21.5/ERPL2013075; E Muir, *EU Equality Law: The First Fundamental Rights Policy of the EU* (Oxford University Press, 2018) available at oxford.universitypressscholarship.com/10.1093/oso/9780198814665.001.0001/oso-9780198814665.

[48] Xenidis (n 42) 37.

[49] This model is not absolute, however. EU law for example prohibits race- and ethnicity-based discrimination in the field of education.

procedure. The ECtHR exercises an external check on States' adherence to human rights. The CJEU is tasked to govern the internal constitutional order of the EU, including the respect to fundamental rights therein.[50] The CJEU not only monitors Member States and EU institutions' abidance to EU law, but it also ensures consistent interpretation and application. Moreover, unlike the ECtHR, which develops its equality and non-discrimination concept from a single source, the CJEU does so through its interpretation of multiple legal sources, including, but not limited to, the Charter and Equality Directives. The CJEU's interpretative reach thus expands alongside the EU's competencies and legislative actions.

Within this broader context, it is also essential to consider the particular interpretative power given to the CJEU. The CJEU can enforce and annul EU law. Its most distinctive characteristic, however, is the preliminary ruling procedure: Member State judges can issue preliminary questions regarding the interpretation and application of EU law. It was not until recently, through the adoption of Protocol 16 to the ECHR, that the highest courts and tribunals of contracting parties could request the ECtHR an advisory opinion concerning the interpretation and application of Convention Rights.[51] The adoption of the CFR and the status of equality as a foundational and stand-alone rather than accessory principle further contributed to the CJEU's interpretative leadership in equality law.[52] Due to the accessory nature of Article 14 ECHR, there was often less opportunity nor the need to conceptualise equality and non-discrimination.[53]

Given that the EU's legal system exhibits greater complexity, some additional observations concerning the CJEU's interpretative reach are in order. First, and although questions have been raised concerning the EU and the CJEU's (political) legitimacy to enter the human-rights debate, it is unmistakable that this shift has been gradually taking place. True, the CJEU is not a human rights court in the strict sense. It remains bound by the limitations set out by Article 51(1) CFR. Still, the CJEU can operationalise Articles 20 and 21 CFR to evaluate unequal treatment by Union institutions and Member States when implementing EU law. Due to the Charter's pivotal position, the CJEU could remain a frontrunner of European equality law in technology-related fields. Given the plethora of AI-relevant legislation that has been, and will be, adopted by the EU legislator, the interpretative potential of Articles 20 and 21 CFR is undeniable.[54] For example, the CJEU has

[50] Rosas (n 3) 211.

[51] Protocol No. 16 to the Convention for the Protection of Human Rights and Fundamental Freedoms [2013] CETS 214.

[52] See among others: Gerards, 'Non-Discrimination, the European Court of Justice and the European Court of Human Rights' (n 3) 138; Gerards, 'Systeemverklaringen voor verschillen tussen de gelijkebehandelingsrechtspraak van het HvJ EU en het EHRM' (n 3) 574.

[53] In her analysis, however, Gerards observes that the dominant narrative that sees the CJEU as leading European equality law must be nuanced. See: Gerards, 'Non-Discrimination, the European Court of Justice and the European Court of Human Rights' (n 3) 137; Gerards, 'Systeemverklaringen voor verschillen tussen de gelijkebehandelingsrechtspraak van het HvJ EU en het EHRM' (n 3) 574.

[54] As an example of such legislation, reference can be made, among others, to: Regulation (EU) 2016/679 of the European Parliament and of the Council on the protection of natural persons

relied upon Article 21(1) CFR to interpret and evaluate the PNR Directive's profiling provisions.[55] Where there is room for interpretation, the CJEU can take a formal, substantive, conservative, or progressive approach to equality. The power of the CJEU to take on this position legitimately has been questioned, however.[56]

As a result of these regulatory interventions at the EU level, the CJEU's interpretative reach might also expand to civil and political domains where the ECtHR typically held a greater range of influence. For instance, the proposed AI Act covers a series of public fields, such as welfare, education, border control and law enforcement. Though the Charter must be interpreted in light of the ECHR where they align, divergence is still possible. First, the Charter can offer a higher level of protection than the Convention. Second, the Charter contains civil and political as well as social and economic rights. Consequently, equality might compete with a different set of interests while balancing rights. For example, the ECHR does not explicitly foresee the right to conduct a business. Yet, considering the EU's economic origins, this right will likely become an important counterpoint to equality when the legality of AI-driven decision-making practices is subject to evaluation.

The ECtHR and CJEU historically governed different domains of life: equality in the enjoyment of civil and political fundamental rights in institutional settings on the one hand and equal treatment vis-à-vis socio-economic opportunities in specifically enumerated public and private domains on the other hand. Rather than viewing this divergence negatively, Gerards believes one could focus on their complementarity: inequalities not addressed via one system might find redress in another.[57] The ECtHR has been quite prolific in addressing inequality within the public domain, as demonstrated by its case law on ethnic profiling within law

with regard to the processing of personal data and on the free movement of such data, and repealing Directive 95/46/EC (General Data Protection Regulation) [2016] OJ L119/1; Regulation (EU) 2022/2065 of the European Parliament and of the Council on a Single Market For Digital Services and amending Directive 2000/31/EC (Digital Services Act) [2022] OJ L277/1; Regulation (EU) 2022/1925 of the European Parliament and of the Council on contestable and fair markets in the digital sector and amending Directives (EU) 2019/1937 and (EU) 2020/1828 (Digital Markets Act) [2022]OJ L265/1; Proposal of the Commission for a Regulation of the European Parliament and of the Council laying down harmonised rules on Artificial Intelligence (Artificial Intelligence Act) and amending certain Union Legislative Acts, COM(2021) 206 final (Proposed AI Act).

[55] Opinion of Advocate General Pitruzella, Case C-817/19 *Ligue des Droits Humains v Conseil des Ministres* ECLI:EU:C:2022:65, para 227; Case C-817/19 *Ligue des Droits Humains v Conseils des Ministres* ECLI:EU:C:2022:491, [2022] 3 CMLR 25, paras 197–199. Directive (EU) 2016/681 of the European Parliament and of the Council on the use of passenger name record (PNR) data for the prevention, detection, investigation and prosecution of terrorist offences and serious crime [2016] OJ L119/132.

[56] M Dawson, 'The Political Face of Judicial Activism: Europe's Law-Politics Imbalance' (Maastricht Faculty of Law Working Paper No. 1, 2012) available at papers.ssrn.com/abstract=1984636; Muir, 'The Transformative Function of EU Equality Law' (n 47); M Dawson, 'The Court of Justice in the Governance of EU Fundamental Rights' (*The Governance of EU Fundamental Rights*, February 2017), available at www.cambridge.org/core/books/governance-of-eu-fundamental-rights/court-of-justice-in-the-governance-of-eu-fundamental-rights/DAA872147BBBA7F3193BAEA791F82224.

[57] See also Gerards, 'Systeemverklaringen voor verschillen tussen de gelijkebehandelingsrechtspraak van het HvJ EU en het EHRM' (n 3) 581.

enforcement and social exclusion in education.[58] The CJEU, for its part, has a rich history of cases concerning specific types of ascriptive inequality in economic areas, such as the employment sector and the provision of goods and services. Moreover, through judicial dialogue, and in case of overlap, both Courts could turn to one another for mutual inspiration regarding AI systems imposed in areas that touch upon their respective area of expertise.[59] For instance, the law enforcement directive adopted in 2016 has a principled prohibition on ethnic profiling. The proposed AI Act identifies as high-risk the use of enrolment algorithms for educational institutes. As aforementioned, in so far as the Charter corresponds to rights guaranteed by ECHR, the meaning and scope of those rights should be the same.[60] At the same time, the CJEU's position to interpret, via the Charter, the discriminatory nature of novel technologies captured under EU law might give it a prime place to be first in tackling renewed questions regarding the function of equality and non-discrimination. And in certain areas, this is already the case. For example, a mutual and bi-directional judicial dialogue exists between both Courts in matters concerning the legality of data-driven systems for mass surveillance.[61]

Institutional dynamics might explain divergence, but they do not rule out convergence. Moreover, divergence need not be problematic where it does not lead to immediate conflict but can be anticipated and accommodated. For instance, Gerards suggests that national actors could ask the European Courts via prejudicial ruling or advisory opinion procedures for further clarification.[62] These options give national courts a tool to find alignment when supranational caselaw appears inconsistent.

B. Social Ambitions, Distributive Constraints?

Within each order, the realisation of egalitarian aspirations might face internal constraints due to how equality protection is framed. More specifically, relational egalitarian ambitions can be curbed when they must be realised within a distributive framework that focuses on individual instances of discrimination.

When equality is viewed as a distributive ideal, people's socio-economic position is assessed in terms of their possession of certain justice-relevant goods. These goods can be material, such as wealth and income, as well as immaterial, such as

[58] See for instance: *Lingurar v Romania* App no 48474/14 (ECtHR, 16 April 2019); *D.H. and Others v the Czech Republic* App no 57325/00 (ECtHR Grand Chamber, 13 November 2007).

[59] See also: Gerards, 'Systeemverklaringen voor verschillen tussen de gelijkebehandelingsrechtspraak van het HvJ EU en het EHRM' (n 3) 581.

[60] CFR, Article 52(3).

[61] See *Big Brother Watch and Others v The United Kingdom* App nos 58170/13, 62322/14 and 24960/15 (ECtHR First Section, 13 September 2018) paras 516–518. See: Joined Cases C-293/12 and C-594/12 *Digital Rights Ireland Ltd v Minister for Communications, Marine and Natural Resources and Others and Kärntner Landesregierung and Others* ECLI:EU:C:2014:238, [2014] 3 CMLR 44.

[62] Gerards, 'Systeemverklaringen voor verschillen tussen de gelijkebehandelingsrechtspraak van het HvJ EU en het EHRM' (n 3) 581.

fundamental rights and opportunities. People's position as social equals can be measured through an evaluation of their distributive shares. Likewise, acts, rules, and practices are considered discriminatory when they interfere with the desired distribution of these justice-relevant goods.

The ECHR and the EU legal frameworks have been constructed around a distributive paradigm. In the case of the ECHR, the human right to non-discrimination guarantees individuals the equal enjoyment of the Convention rights. In the case of the EU, the fundamental right to non-discrimination governs people's access before and to the market.[63] The EU Equality Directives are a prime example of this distributive approach. In her analysis, Xenidis observes how 'the substance of non-discrimination rights is made of distributive opportunities, the recognition [in our wording *socio-relational*] paradigm informs the grammar of their allocation'. Socio-relational considerations are of course important for the law's evolution. Still, interferences with relational equality might be insufficiently recognised as stand-alone harm. For instance, while discrimination takes place as part of people's relationships, it becomes a contestable wrong when it denies people access to fundamental rights or domains of life deemed critical for social and economic participation. The EU's proposed AI Act follows a similar approach. Data quality standards aimed to reduce societal biases are imposed onto AI systems defined as high-risk, which is an assessment coupled to the context and area of life in which they will be used.[64] The central focus therefore lies squarely on the outcome of differential treatment: how does it affect people's enjoyment of fundamental rights and social and economic opportunities? Real social equality, however, may only be realised when certain forms of treatment, such as prejudice, stereotypes and stigma, are sufficiently acknowledged as being wrongful in and of themselves.

Relational inequality moreover arises through social and institutional processes, rather than singular events. Take the example of gender stereotypes perpetuated by recommender systems. The presence of stereotypes is not only condemnable when they limit women's access to a given economic opportunity. More generally, one can condemn their existence because they help maintain existing societal power dynamics. Suppose a society's core concern is the limitation of social inequality regardless of its source of origin. In that case, the law should address these stereotypes wherever they appear and not only when they occur in critical areas of social life. As previously mentioned, an AI system may introduce inequality in one non-critical area of life, such as a movie recommender system, while its actual impact occurs in another. This problem also takes place when equality functions as an accessory human right. Of course, people's genuine enjoyment of fundamental human rights acts as a valuable benchmark to assess whether they are one another's social equals. Still, not every AI-driven act actually deprives people of the

[63] Xenidis (n 42).

[64] See Annexes to the Proposed AI Act, available at eur-lex.europa.eu/resource.html?uri=cellar:e0649735-a372-11eb-9585-01aa75ed71a1.0001.02/DOC_2&format=PDF, Annex III Proposed AI Act: High-Risk AI Systems Referred to in Article 6(2).

immediate enjoyment of a human right. Instead, the cumulative effect of a series of minor breaches can substantially impact a person or group's socio-economic position.

By evaluating AI-driven decisions in isolation and concerning particular (non-material) goods only, laws may overlook how various interweaving relational and economic actions, behaviours, and practices affect people's lives. Social egalitarians would argue that investigating how people are treated within and as part of social, institutional, and relational processes is an intrinsic and self-standing component of equality deserving of attention.[65] The equality approach proposed by the CoE's Ad Hoc Committee on Artificial Intelligence (CAHAI) is willing to break down certain distributive boundaries. Though limited to the public sector, the approach suggests that vulnerable groups should be part of a multi-stakeholder dialogue during the procurement phase.[66] Their involvement would necessitate institutional actors to actively consider how they treat persons in a vulnerable position rather than guarantee those who find themselves in that position a specific outcome. More importantly, this approach illustrates how equality cannot be realised solely by prohibiting the harmful act of discrimination.

V. Conceptual Boundaries I: Grounds-based Limitations

The previous section demonstrated how the disparity between the CoE and EU arises from differences in competencies, (material) scope and procedure. Within those confines, both orders also diverge – and some of this divergence can be explained by the aforementioned institutional dynamics – in their interpretation and evaluation of equality and non-discrimination. Consequently, the notions of equality and non-discrimination also have differing conceptual boundaries.

In this context, it is essential to first note that the CoE and EU both have a grounds-based approach to equality. They assess the discriminatory nature of a given measure by examining the feature or attribute a differentiating action was based on. These grounds, therefore, define the law's scope. They determine who can issue a discrimination claim. The latter is an important observation. The differentiation grounds generated by AI-driven technologies capture groups of people and their group members. Put differently, whether a person or group can contest AI-generated discriminatory harm will depend upon the law's acceptance of making differential treatment based upon the ground subject to

[65] Young (n 11); N Fraser, 'Social Justice in the Age of Identity Politics. Redistribution, Recognition, Participation.' (The Tanner Lectures on Human Values, Stanford University, 30 April–2 May 1996) 29; tannerlectures.utah.edu/_resources/documents/a-to-z/f/Fraser98.pdf; Fourie, Schuppert and Walliman-Helmer (n 10).

[66] Ad Hoc Committee on Artificial Intelligence (CAHAI), 'Possible elements of a legal framework on artificial intelligence' (n 1) para 59.

evaluation. In effect, grounds govern the protective boundaries of equality in the AI environment.

How equality and non-discrimination clauses and legislation are structured is critical to this disparity.[67] Within this grounds-based approach, open models do not limit the possible grounds of discrimination nor define what constitutes discrimination *a priori*. Any form of differentiation can become the subject of evaluation. Closed models, either made so by lawmakers or the judiciary, impose limitations on what can constitute discrimination or may count as an objective justification.

Considering the aforementioned, equality's conceptual boundaries and differences between the CoE and EU therein can be further specified alongside two axes: first, by examining, via limitations placed on the discrimination grounds, the law's protective scope *ratione personae* (discussed in this section), and second, by investigating how the law, or the judiciary, evaluates the justification provided by decision-makers once it is clear that a differentiation ground falls within the law's protective ambit (discussed in the following Section VI).

A. Closed or Open? A Priori Limitations in Defining Discrimination

1. Council of Europe

Article 14 ECHR provides for the enjoyment of rights without discrimination on any ground. Despite this open-ended nature, the ECtHR limited this clause's protective scope. In its interpretation of the discrimination notion, the ECtHR has maintained a divergent and sometimes conflicting case law.[68] On the one hand, it has defined discrimination as an entirely open-ended concept whereby any act of differentiation is liable to violate Article 14 ECHR. On the other hand, there are cases where the Court took a restrictive stance, mandating the differentiating trait to be immutable or closely related to the grounds explicitly mentioned in Article 14 ECHR.[69] In recent years, the ECtHR seemingly settled on an interpretation that views Article 14 ECHR as covering not all differences in treatment but only those based on an identifiable, objective or personal characteristic or 'status' by which

[67] OM Arnardóttir, *Equality and Non-Discrimination under the European Convention on Human Rights* (Brill Nijhoff, 2021) 33, available at brill.com/view/title/8988; Gerards and Zuiderveen Borgesius (n 4).

[68] See for an in-depth discussion: Arnardóttir (n 31); J Gerards, 'The Discrimination Grounds of Article 14 of the European Convention on Human Rights' (2013) 13 *Human Rights Law Review* 99.

[69] For an overview of the case-law, see: Gerards (n 68). See also: Arnardóttir (n 31). See for instance divergence in: *Engel and Others v The Netherlands* App nos 5100/71, 5101/71, 5102/71, 5354/72, 5370/72 (ECtHR, 8 June 1976) para 72; *Rasmussen v Denmark* App no 8777/79 (ECtHR, 28 November 1984) para 34; and *Čadek and Others v The Czech Republic* App nos 31933/08, 60084/08, 6185/09, 46696/09, 52792/09, 53518/09, 10185/10, 42151/10, 3167/11 and 20939/11 (ECtHR, 22 November 2012, final 29 April 2013) para 94.

persons or groups of persons are distinguishable from one another. The ECtHR clarified that 'other status' must be widely understood.

On the one hand, the protection conferred extends to personal characteristics that are innate or inherent. The latter are traits closely linked to the identity or personality of an individual, such as one's religion or political beliefs. On the other hand, protection might also extend to features not sharing this association. The ECHR, for instance, has recognised that a person's military rank, 'length of a sentence', and 'place of residence' can fall under the 'other status' category.[70] Yet, its case law is not always as predictable. For example, the ECtHR found that differentiation grounds like 'the duration and nature of an employment contract' and 'having or not having acquired the right to a welfare benefit' cannot amount to discrimination.[71]

Through the flexible interpretation of the notion 'other status', Article 14 ECHR maintains some elasticity. Upon closer inspection, however, how these definitional boundaries map onto the AI environment remains unclear. What does it mean for a trait to be identifiable, objective, and personal in a digital society? Whereas identifiability could be achieved through increased transparency, the assessment is more challenging for the other components listed. AI-driven profiles often pertain to generalised rather than individualised information. Does this render their use non-personal?[72] Data-driven decisions are applied *to persons* and are usually derived from data *about or relating to persons*, but does this suffice? What about decisions based on non-tangible traits, such as a person's viewing behaviour or keystroke patterns? What about the requirement for information to be objective? Does it pertain to the empirical and intuitive connection between a measure's differentiating trait and purpose?[73] If so, how can this connection be established? The answer is currently far from clear.

Moreover, this assessment also necessitates a clear understanding of the risks AI systems threaten to impose. Yet, this requires proper insight into these systems' functioning. States might not provide such transparency. And even if openness is provided, this does not guarantee adequate understanding on the part of the judiciary. For example, in the case of Big Brother Watch, the ECtHR had to consider a United Kingdom law that enabled the interception of external electronic communications by intelligence services. Interceptions had to be referable to individuals in the British Islands to be legal. The ECtHR considered that using this criterion would not result in differential treatment based directly on nationality or national origin but rather on geographical location. The ECtHR argued that this difference

[70] *Clift v The United Kingdom* App no 7205/07 (ECtHR, 13 July 2010, final 22 November 2010) para 59.

[71] For an overview, see: Council of Europe, 'Guide on Article 14 of the European Convention on Human Rights and on Article 1 of Protocol No. 12 to the Convention: Prohibition of Discrimination', available at www.echr.coe.int/Documents/Guide_Art_14_Art_1_Protocol_12_ENG.pdf.

[72] See also L Naudts, 'Criminal Profiling and Non-Discrimination: On Firm Grounds for the Digital Era?' in A Vedder et al (eds), *Security and Law. Legal and Ethical Aspects of Public Security, Cyber Security and Critical Infrastructure Security* (Intersentia, 2019) 81.

[73] See on this requirement of empiricism also: Wachter (n 13).

could not be explained in terms of personal characteristics. In other words, it was not a relevant difference in treatment for Article 14 ECHR.[74] Yet, plenty of research has shown how geographic location often connects to socially significant markers of vulnerability and tends to place a disproportionate burden on historically disadvantaged groups, such as ethnic minorities or impoverished people.[75] Research into AI systems should inform future rulings to avoid the de facto acceptance of geography based on precedent case law.

2. *European Union*

In the EU, a different approach exists. The EU Equality Directives specify a series of treatments and behaviours designated as discriminatory. They pertain to disadvantageous treatment based on a selected number of protected grounds, namely those explicitly mentioned under Article 19 TFEU. These instruments are closed-circuit on a personal level: the grounds captured by their scope have been limited beforehand.

On multiple occasions, the CJEU was asked to consider whether those Directives, when interpreted in light of the Charter's open-ended equality and non-discrimination provisions, could be extended to cover additional grounds. As of writing, the CJEU answered this question negatively.[76] Article 19 TFEU exhaustively lists what traits can trigger legislative action and protection. Although specific grounds can be intrinsically linked to a protected attribute and consequently captured under that existing ground, no new characteristics can be added by analogy to the Equality Directives.[77] In the words of AG Geelhoed, the legislature had to make tragic choices. Moreover, introducing a general principle of non-discrimination on all forms of differentiation could breach the established boundary of EU fundamental rights law.[78]

The question has been raised whether, in areas not caught by the EU Equality Directives, Articles 20 and 21(1) CFR could allow the CJEU to follow a more expansive approach. Given the CJEU's general reluctance to expand the protective scope of equality to additional status-based grounds in areas identified as

[74] *Big Brother* (n 61) paras 516–518. In reference to: *Magee v the United Kingdom* App no 28135/95 (ECtHR, 20 June 2000) para 50.

[75] See on this point M Tzanou and S Karyda, 'Privacy International and Quadrature Du Net: One Step Forward Two Steps Back in the Data Retention Saga?' 28 *European Public Law* 123, 139–40.

[76] See for instance: Case C-13/05 *Sonia Chacon Navas v Eurest Colectividades SA* ECLI:EU:C:2006:456, [2006] ECR I-6467, paras 56–57; Case C-354/13 *Kaltoft v Municipality of Billund* ECLI:EU:C:2014:2463, [2015] 2 CMLR 19.

[77] ibid. Concerning the view that certain grounds are captured by existing ones, the CJEU has held that the right not to be discriminated against on grounds of sex 'cannot be confined simply to discrimination based on the fact that a person is of one or other sex'. It also applies to discrimination arising from the gender reassignment of the person concerned. Still, not every ground is as malleable as to enable such an extended interpretation. See for example Case C-13/94 *P v S and Cornwall County Council* ECLI:EU:C:1996:170, para 20.

[78] Opinion of Advocate General Jääskinen, Case C-354/13 *Kaltoft v Municipality of Billund* ECLI:EU:C:2014:2106, para 24.

socially significant, it is highly doubtful whether it would be willing to do so in other domains. For example, the aforementioned PNR Directive explicitly prohibits profiling based on a person's race or ethnic origin, political opinions, religion or philosophical beliefs, trade union membership, health, sexual life or sexual orientation. In the *Ligue des Droits Humains* case, AG Pitruzella argued that 'the general prohibition on discriminatory profiling must be understood as including all the grounds of discrimination referred to in Article 21 of the Charter, even where they are not referred to expressly'.[79] This reasoning would expand the profiling prohibition to include age and property. The CJEU, however, remained silent on this point. Instead, it concluded that the PNR Directive was compatible and consistent with Article 21 CFR. And this appears consistent with the CJEU's previous approach towards regulating discriminatory treatment: adding status-based grounds the EU legislator did not intend to govern could breach the established boundaries of the law.

That said, the CJEU did elaborate upon the discriminatory nature of certain data-driven criminal profiling practices, albeit without directly relying on the Charter's equality provisions. In the case of *GD v Commissioner of An Garda Siochana*, the CJEU questioned whether the differentiation criterion 'geographic location' could be discriminatory. The Court concluded it is not: 'areas marked by a high incidence of serious crime and areas particularly vulnerable to the commission of those acts [are not likely] to give rise to discrimination, as the criterion drawn from the average rate of serious crime is entirely unconnected with any potentially discriminatory factors'.[80] While this again betrays a lack of technical insight into the functioning of AI-driven techniques, the CJEU has nonetheless specified under what circumstances differentiating criteria might not be problematic: the data and models used should be reliable and topical and consider international research.[81]

B. Definitional Variations: Direct, Indirect and Intersectional Discrimination by Association and Assumption

Within their respective grounds-based systems, the two orders diverge in the conceptual limitations they place on discrimination. Their approaches also deviate, however, in their definition of discrimination in relation to those grounds. Areas of variation concern: (a) their reliance on the distinction between direct and indirect discrimination, (b) their recognition of intersectional harm, and

[79] Opinion of Advocate General Pitruzella (n 55) para 227.

[80] Case C-140/20 *G.D. v Commissioner of An Garda Siochana* ECLI:EU:C:2022:258, [2022] 3 CMLR 23, paras 79–80.

[81] Opinion 1/15 of the Court on the transfer of Passenger Name Record Data from the European Union to Canada, ECLI:EU:C:2017:592, [2018] 1 CMLR 36, para 172.

(c) the extension ratione personae of the law by association and assumption. Areas that could moreover affect the law's capacity to tackle AI-driven discrimination.

1. *Direct and Indirect Discrimination*

The distinction between direct and indirect discrimination is foundational to the EU's equality discourse. The CJEU introduced the distinction to increase the effectiveness of the EU non-discrimination law and subsequently it was incorporated as a cornerstone of the EU Equality Directives.[82] Direct discrimination occurs when one person is treated less favourably than another is, has been or would be treated in a comparable situation on aspects that include one's racial and ethnic origin, sex, sexual orientation, and age, among others.[83] Indirect discrimination occurs where an apparently neutral provision, criterion or practice would put persons having a particular ethnic origin, sex, sexual orientation, religion or belief, disability, or age at a particular disadvantage compared with other persons. Whereas direct discrimination targets the disadvantageous treatment faced by a person or group, indirect discrimination targets the disadvantageous impact faced by a group. In practice, a neutral rule is more likely to adversely impact non-dominant groups within society, such as historically disadvantaged or marginalised groups, due to the structural and systemic nature of the inequalities they face. Hence, legal protection against indirect discrimination is typically considered an exponent of substantive equality. In both instances, the protected traits are a symbolic shorthand whose use signals a violation of socially accepted norms. When a person or group either directly or indirectly experiences a disadvantage due to possessing these characteristics, this act is more likely to be morally reprehensible. At the same time, the protected traits

[82] The main elements of indirect discrimination are found in the disparate impact theory, first established by the Supreme Court of the United States. The concept was transplanted in the United Kingdom, later mobilised by the Court of Justice, and enshrined, with some singularities, in the Equality Directives in the EU as indirect discrimination. See among others *Griggs v Duke Power Co.*, 401 U.S. 424, 91 S. Ct. 849, 28 L. Ed. 2d 158 (1971). For the UK, see Race Relations Act of 1976. On the EU level: Case C-96/80 *JP Jenkins v Kingsgate* ECLI:EU:C:1981:80, [1981] ECR 911 and Case C-170/84 *Bilka – Kaufhaus GmbH v Karin Weber von Hartz* ECLI:EU:C:1986:204, [1986] ECR 1607. In EU Law: Directive 2000/43/EC of the Council implementing the principle of equal treatment between persons irrespective of racial or ethnic origin [2000] OJ L180/22 (Racial Equality Directive), Article 2(2)(b); Directive 2000/78/EC of the Council establishing a general framework for equal treatment in employment and occupation [2000] OJ L303/16 (Employment Equality Directive), Article 2(2)(b); Directive 2004/113/EC of the Council implementing the principle of equal treatment between men and women in the access to and supply of goods and services [2004] OJ L373/37 (Gender Goods and Services Directive), Article 2(1)(b). From an academic perspective, reference can be made to I Rorive, 'Lutter contre les Discriminations' in C Bricteux and B Frydman (eds), *Les Défis du Droit Global* (Bruylant, 2017) 49; C Tobler, 'Limits and Potential of the Concept of Indirect Discrimination' (2008) European Network of Legal Experts in the non-discrimination field.

[83] Racial Equality Directive, Article 2(2); Employment Equality Directive, Article 2(2)(a); Gender Goods and Services Directive, Article 2(a); Directive 2006/54/EC of the European Parliament and of the Council on the implementation of the principle of equal opportunities and equal treatment of men and women in matters of employment and occupation (recast) [2006] OJ L204/23 (Gender Equality Directive recast), Article 2(1)(a).

also symbolise the political efforts of civil society and historically suppressed groups to have their interests appropriately represented. As a specific set of exhaustively enumerated protected characteristics define the personal scope of EU law, it makes sense to maintain this distinction. Efforts to protect social norms and suppressed groups cannot be achieved by prohibiting direct discrimination alone. Hence indirect discrimination is a necessary complement.

Within the EU system, the indirect discrimination doctrine could be used to tackle the problem of algorithmic proxies. As most AI developers know or want to avoid their systems being discriminatory, AI-generated differentiation grounds will seldom take the form of a protected characteristic. Instead, they will take on a 'neutral' appearance. When AI systems are detrimental to historically disadvantaged groups, the differentiation ground in question can be reformulated as an indirectly discriminatory trait. Unfortunately, this definitional distinction plays an additional role during the justification process. Whereas the EU Equality Directives implement a principled prohibition (on most forms) of direct discrimination, indirectly discriminatory measures can be justified if they pursue a legitimate aim and are appropriate and necessary. Given the rational veneer of AI-driven analytics, scholars fear indirect discrimination will be easily justifiable.[84]

Because the ECtHR interprets Article 14 in a somewhat open-ended fashion, there was no immediate reason to introduce this distinction.[85] Yet, an open-ended clause brings along the same open-ended justification problem. Moreover, when the ECtHR eventually introduced the distinction, other challenges emerged. As aforementioned, the ECtHR identified its own variation of the protected characteristics paradigm. Certain traits, such as ethnicity, sex and intellectual and mental disability, trigger a heightened level of scrutiny by the ECtHR. According to established case law, very weighty reasons must be brought forward to justify differential treatment based on these criteria. According to Gerards: 'When it became clear that this test meant that such a justification could hardly ever be provided, it became attractive for applicants to show that a relatively 'neutral' case of unequal treatment disproportionately affected a group defined by 'suspect' characteristics'.[86] This observation might explain why the ECtHR was cautious to embrace the indirect discrimination doctrine. Indeed, it would extend the heightened level of protection to neutral measures having a disproportionate impact on protected groups. Instead, as the open discrimination clause still captured neutral actions, the latter could be evaluated on their own terms, rather than reformulated as relating to protected traits. In the landmark case of Biao, however, protection

[84] Moreover, the application of the indirect discrimination doctrine is not without problems itself. Difficulties may for example arise in the definition of the disadvantaged group, the disadvantage incurred by that group, and the demonstration of said disadvantage, including the means through which disadvantage can be demonstrated. For an exploration of these topics, in relation to algorithms, see: Gerards and Xenidis (n 4); Wachter, Mittelstadt and Russell (n 4).

[85] *Biao v Denmark* App no 38590/10 (ECtHR, 24 May 2016) para 103.

[86] Gerards, 'Non-Discrimination, the European Court of Justice and the European Court of Human Rights' (n 3) 141.

was ultimately maximised: the Grand Chamber mandated very weighty reasons to justify legislation that was found to be indirectly discriminatory based on ethnicity.[87] Applying this reasoning could potentially usher in a higher level of protection against indirect discrimination than the CJEU provides.

2. *Intersectional Discrimination*

Beyond models recognising the direct/indirect divide, a distinction can be made between single-axis and intersectional models. Single-axis discrimination models assess and evaluate the discriminatory impact of differentiation traits in an individualised and isolated manner. Intersectional discrimination, however, stems from an interlinkage of various identity traits: whereby, as Schiek remarks, 'either the specific contribution of any one of these grounds is indiscernible or the full extent of discrimination is only recognisable by acknowledging the combination of two or more grounds.'[88] Even though single-axis models can identify the additional harm each singular trait imposes on a person or group, they still fail to articulate the intersectional harm those multiply-burdened face. More specifically, intersectional harms are distinct, and the disadvantage cannot be measured as a sum of its parts. Thus far, this specificity has not yet been recognised by the Courts explicitly.

In the case of *BS v Spain*, the ECtHR was asked to review the racist behaviour of police authorities vis-à-vis an African woman working as a prostitute. The ECtHR observed how Spanish authorities failed to consider the particularly vulnerable position of the woman in question.[89] The open-ended nature of Article 14 ECHR allows the ECtHR to view a person's complex identity as one differentiating trait. Rather than explicitly invoking intersectionality, the ECtHR described the woman's position as one of increased vulnerability.[90] Still, as observed by Atrey, this ruling is ground-breaking for asserting that 'claims of intersectional theory should be investigated and redressed as such.'[91] Things are different in the

[87] *Biao v Denmark* (n 85) para 138.

[88] D Schiek, 'On Uses, Mis-Uses and Non-Uses of Intersectionality before the Court of Justice (EU)' (2018) 18 *International Journal of Discrimination and the Law* 82, 83. In reference to: T Makkonen, 'Multiple, Compound and Intersectional Discrimination: Bringing the Experiences of the Most Marginalized to the Fore.' (Åbo Akademi University Institute for Human Rights, 2002) 9–14; D Schiek, 'Multiple discrimination in EU Law – Opportunities for legal responses to intersectional gender discrimination? Executive summary' in S Burri and D Schiek (eds), *Multiple Discrimination in EU Law – Opportunities for Legal Responses to Intersectional Gender Discrimination?* (European Commission, 2009) 4–6. See www.researchgate.net/publication/46718012_Multiple_Discrimination_in_EU_Law_Opportunities_for_legal_responses_to_intersectional_gender_discrimination_European_Commission_Directorate_General_for_Employment_Social_Affaires_and_Equal_Opportunities. See also S Atrey, 'Beyond Universality: An Intersectional Justification of Human Rights' in S Atrey and P Dunne (eds), *Intersectionality and Human Rights Law* (Hart Publishing, 2020) 36, available at www.bloomsbury.com/uk/intersectionality-and-human-rights-law-9781509935314/.

[89] *B.S. v Spain* App no 47159/08 (ECtHR, 24 July 2012, final 24 October 2012) para 62.

[90] OM Arnardóttir, 'Vulnerability under Article 14 of the European Convention on Human Rights' (2017) 4 *Oslo Law Review* 150, 164.

[91] S Atrey, *Intersectional Discrimination* (Oxford University Press, 2019) 134, available at www.oxfordscholarship.com/view/10.1093/oso/9780198848950.001.0001/oso-9780198848950.

EU. In the infamous *Parris* case, the CJEU refused to recognise intersectionality as a specific harm: 'while discrimination may indeed be based on several […] grounds […], there is […] no new category of discrimination resulting from the combination of more than one of those grounds […] that may be found to exist where discrimination on the basis of those grounds taken in isolation has not been established'.[92]

This lack of recognition is unfortunate as AI-driven discrimination is often intersectional in nature.[93] For instance, Buolamwini and Gebru discovered that darker-skinned females were the most misclassified group in commercial gender classification systems.[94] The precarious situation of those affected must be explained in light of their complex identities (people of colour plus women in the case of gender classification systems). Likewise, data-driven differentiation grounds are often complex and contain multiple data points. The specific harm for those affected might only be fully explained when considering the totality of attributes used and their interlinkage.

3. *Discrimination by Assumption and Association*

Discrimination by association occurs when a person is discriminated against because they are associated with a person or group who belongs to a protected group. Discrimination by assumption (or perception) refers to situations where discrimination occurs because of one's assumed rather than actual membership of a protected group. Within a system built around the heightened protection of specific traits, recognising these doctrines would be beneficial in dealing with AI-driven discrimination. Indeed, when a generated profile serves as a proxy for a protected characteristic, protection would automatically extend to every person captured by the profile, even when they are not a member of a protected group or minority.[95] Whereas both Courts have progressed toward the recognition of (direct and indirect) discrimination by association,[96] the CJEU so far has yet to embrace the discrimination by assumption doctrine.[97]

[92] Case C-443/15 *David L Parris v Trinity College Dublin and Others* ECLI:EU:C:2016:897, [2016], para 80.

[93] See for instance also LM Weinberger, 'Kurt v. Austria: A Missed Chance to Tackle Intersectional Discrimination and Gender-Based Stereotyping in Domestic Violence Cases' (*Strasbourg Observers*, 8 August 2021), available at strasbourgobservers.com/2021/08/18/kurt-v-austria-a-missed-chance-to-tackle-intersectional-discrimination-and-gender-based-stereotyping-in-domestic-violence-cases/.

[94] J Buolamwini and T Gebru, 'Gender Shades: Intersectional Accuracy Disparities in Commercial Gender Classification', *Conference on Fairness, Accountability and Transparency* (PMLR, 2018) available at proceedings.mlr.press/v81/buolamwini18a.html.

[95] S Wachter, 'Affinity Profiling and Discrimination by Association in Online Behavioral Advertising' (2020) 35 *Berkeley Technology Law Journal* 367.

[96] See, for instance *Molla Sali v Greece* App no 20452/14 (ECtHR Grand Chamber, 19 December 2018); *Chez* (n 44); Case C-303/06 *S. Coleman v Attridge Law and Steve Law* ECLI:EU:C:2008:415, [2008] ECR I-5603.

[97] *Timishev v Russia* App nos 55762/00 and 55974/00 (ECtHR Second Section, 13 December 2005, final 13 March 2006).

VI. Conceptual Boundaries II: Justifying Discrimination

The ECtHR and CJEU depart from a similar procedural articulation of equality and non-discrimination: similar situations should be treated alike (or vice versa) unless an objective justification to do otherwise can be provided.[98] From this singular premise, a similar three-step review process follows: (1) a comparison of the parties affected by a differentiating measure, (2) an evaluation of the measure's legitimacy, and (3) an evaluation of the measure's proportionality. As part of the proportionality assessment, the Courts consider whether a measure is suitable or appropriate and necessary. For a measure to be appropriate, it must be reasonably likely to realise the objectives pursued. A measure is necessary when no less restrictive alternatives are available. However, even if a measure satisfies these conditions, the Courts may still engage in a fair balancing test (proportionality in a strict sense): considering the circumstances of the case, was a proper balance struck between the interests of the decision-maker and the parties affected?[99]

A. The Equality Review: A Difference in Evaluative Focal Point?

Despite their shared premise, the focal point of evaluation of the respective courts differs, partially explaining why similar cases are judged differently. According to Gerards, as the final arbiter of a measure, the ECtHR often positions a fair balancing of interests as the core component of its review. Depending on the case's context, the State's discretion to differentiate will be either broad or narrow. States are better positioned to decide upon the validity of a differentiating measure in matters that concern sensitive policy areas, such as welfare and security.[100] Conversely, their discretion will be narrower when differential treatment is contrary to democratic values, personal dignity and autonomy. The latter may be the case where a measure is motivated by stereotyped assumptions or targets vulnerable societal groups. In other words, the ECtHR will actively balance competing interests and consider the respective weight of each. While competing interests might be highlighted by the CJEU (or its Advocate Generals), the CJEU then primarily focuses on the

[98] See eg Case C-406/15 *Petya Milkova v Izpalnitelen direktor na Agentsiata za privatizatsia i sledprivatizatsionen control* ECLI:EU:C:2017:198, [2017] IRLR 566, para 55. On the CJEU's refusal to recognise assumed discrimination: L Waddington, 'Saying All the Right Things and Still Getting It Wrong: The Court of Justice's Definition of Disability and Non-Discrimination Law' (2015) 22 *Maastricht Journal of European and Comparative Law* 576.

[99] See for instance: Tridimas (n 35) 139; K Möller, 'Proportionality: Challenging the Critics' (2012) 10 *International Journal of Constitutional Law* 709.

[100] See for instance: *Stec and Others v the United Kingdom* App nos 65731/01 and 65900/01 (ECtHR Grand Chamber, 12 April 2006) para 52.

appropriateness and necessity of a given measure.[101] Even though the CJEU argues that the necessity condition must be analysed in light of a measure's context and adverse effects – which entails a fair balancing – under a preliminary review procedure, the latter is often for the referring judge to assess.[102]

Given the novel egalitarian challenges that AI systems risk imposing, a fair balancing approach can be valuable. Even if a measure is appropriate and necessary, the particular disadvantage this action generates might still be significant enough to reconsider its application. A financial institution might argue that AI systems are reasonable and essential to profile non-trustworthy customers. Yet, in the case of large-scale deployment, it also threatens the exclusion of whole groups of individuals from a particular socio-economic good. That is not to say that these systems cannot exist. For instance, as a contextual element of relevance, one can investigate whether measures have been implemented to prevent or compensate for any (arbitrary) disadvantage an excluded party might experience.[103] In the case of the CJEU, however, the national level will decide. Doing so, however, eliminates the fair balancing test as an area of convergence between the ECtHR and the CJEU. In addition, this approach has the potential to introduce disparity between EU Member States regarding the regulation of AI's (discriminatory) impact. Of course, as a result, the CJEU might avoid the criticisms of engaging in judicial activism or infringing on national sovereignty.[104] Still, it might undermine harmonisation, especially in light of upcoming AI legislation. That being said, in cases where national states have a wide margin of discretion, the ECtHR might approach the fair balancing test with leniency too. On several occasions, the ECtHR has considered the rightful use of broad categories within the law.[105] For example, in the case of *Burden v the UK*, the ECtHR observed that: 'Any system of taxation, to be workable, has to use broad categorisations to distinguish between different groups of tax payers [...]'. Moreover, the ECtHR accepted that 'The implementation of any such scheme must, inevitably, create marginal situations and individual cases of apparent hardship or injustice, and it is primarily for the State to decide how best to strike the balance between raising revenue and pursuing social objectives'.[106] Considering the deployment of AI systems, which often

[101] Gerards, 'Non-Discrimination, the European Court of Justice and the European Court of Human Rights' (n 3) 158.

[102] See eg *Chez* (n 44) para 124.

[103] See for instance Case C-270/16 *Carlos Enrique Ruiz Conejero v Ferroser Servicios Auxiliaires SA and Ministerio Fiscal* ECLI:EU:C:2018:17, [2018] 2 CMLR 27, para 55. In this case, the disadvantaged group were people with a disability.

[104] N Eder, 'Privacy, Non-Discrimination and Equal Treatment: Developing a Fundamental Rights Response to Behavioural Profiling' in M Ebers and M Cantero Gamito (eds), *Algorithmic Governance and Governance of Algorithms: Legal and Ethical Challenges* (Springer International Publishing, 2021), available at doi.org/10.1007/978-3-030-50559-2_2.

[105] *Bah v The United Kingdom* App no 56328/07 (ECtHR Fourth Section, 27 September 2011, final 27 December 2011) paras 44–47; *Burden and Burden v The United Kingdom* App no 13378/05 (ECtHR Fourth Section, 12 December 2006) para 60.

[106] *Burden* (n 105) para 60.

impose broad categorisations onto the population, a fair balancing test with a low level of scrutiny, might not be desirable either.

B. Fortifying Equality: Rationales Grounding Equality?

Several rationales have been identified to motivate the heightened protection of certain traits. These rationales play an essential role during the evaluation phase: they fortify a person or group's egalitarian claims against a decision-maker's competing interests.[107] Two broad motivations can be discerned. On the one hand, the wrongful nature of discrimination can be linked to the intrinsic nature of the trait. On the other hand, the wrongful nature of discrimination can be tied to the disadvantage associated with the attribute. In both cases, however, these rationales can be harnessed to protect the particular egalitarian, dignitarian or liberal interests discriminated persons have.[108]

1. Convergence in Rationales?

Trait-based rationales exemplify a procedural and formal approach towards equality because they do not consider the broader social context in which differentiation occurs.[109] One such rationale is the irrelevance argument. Differential treatment is less likely to find justification when the differentiating trait is considered irrelevant to the decision-making purpose. According to Cartibia, 'statements of non-discrimination entail comparisons of two persons by reference to some criteria that determine the relevant aspect in which those persons are alike or different'. In case there is no relevant difference, differential treatment must be justified.[110] Yet, in some instances, the law or judiciary may decide that such a review is unnecessary because the grounds in question are considered a priori irrelevant to the decision. For example, in the liberal colour-blind model of society, a person's ethnicity is considered irrelevant to hiring decisions.[111] Hence, in a hiring context, this specific trait should never play any considerable role. The irrelevance argument is a subset of the irrationality motivation. The rationality motivation

[107] See eg *Chapman v The United Kingdom* App no 27238/95 (ECtHR Grand Chamber, 18 January 2001) para 96.

[108] Wachter (n 13); Naudts (n 1).

[109] Fredman (n 22); Marc De Vos, 'The European Court of Justice and the March towards Substantive Equality in European Union Anti-Discrimination Law' (2020) 20 *International Journal of Discrimination and the Law* 62.

[110] M Cartabia, 'The European Court of Human Rights: Judging Nondiscrimination' (2011) 9 *International Journal of Constitutional Law* 808, 812.

[111] J Gerards, *Judicial Review in Equal Treatment Cases* (Brill Nijhoff, 2005) 131–32, available at brill.com/view/title/11318; J Gerards, 'Intensity of Judicial Review in Equal Treatment Cases' (2004) 51 *Netherlands International Law Review* 135. See for instance: Opinion of Advocate General Maduro, Case C-303/06 *S. Coleman v Attridge Law and Steve Law* ECLI:EU:C:2008:61, para 10, read in combination with para 14.

acts as a more general test that can be applied to any differentiating criterion. The criteria chosen must be consistently used, persuasive and acceptable.[112] Consistency is a procedural requirement. The other two standards pertain to the contextual reasonability and sensibility of the trait relied upon.[113] Still, the latter do not mandate an inquiry into the disadvantage linked to the trait's use. Instead, it is sufficient to establish an empirical connection between a differentiating criterion and the purpose for which it is used. A final rationale befitting this category is the immutability argument. Applying the equal treatment principle is politically legitimate when it guards people against discrimination based upon traits that are difficult to change or over which they have little or no control.[114]

When a trait is labelled immutable, irrational or irrelevant, one could wrongfully assume that these properties are intrinsic or absolute qualities of the attribute in question. These properties are static and do not require a comprehensive or holistic socio-economic contextual analysis. Consider the case of *Bah v United Kingdom*. In this case, the ECtHR argued that a person's status as an immigrant was a chosen trait. Yet, defining a characteristic as chosen implies that those who hold it are rational and are autonomous actors with complete control over their life's options. Yet, people often make choices pressured by social conditions over which they have little to no agency.[115] Would a person's immigrant status not fall under the latter category? A similar problem exists when a trait is irrevocably deemed irrational or irrelevant. For instance, ethnicity is rightfully considered irrelevant in most hiring decisions, but this quality should not carry over to situations where its use could be positively harnessed. Ethnicity might be a relevant criterion for implementing affirmative action measures to increase diversity in the workforce. Finally, the rationality of a given trait is seldom neutral but often socially conditioned. As observed by Young, supposedly rational criteria often internalise the values, social rules, and behaviour of a majority to the detriment of the minority.[116]

Formal-based rationales do not mandate an investigation into the intricate relationship between an attribute and the particular (socio-contextual) disadvantage connected to it. Consequently, they fail to articulate and capture the social dynamics that underlie social and economic inequality. Instead, formal rationales

[112] C McCrudden, 'The Concepts of Equality and Non-Discrimination in Europe: A Practical Approach' 12, available at papers.ssrn.com/sol3/papers.cfm?abstract_id=1762815.

[113] Creel and Hellman (n 15).

[114] I Solanke, *Discrimination as Stigma: A Theory of Anti-Discrimination Law* (Hart Publishing, 2017) 55. *Bah* (n 105) paras 45–47. Opinion of Advocate General Kokott, Case C-157/15 *Samira Achbita and Centrum voor Gelijkheid van Kansen en voor Racismebestrijding v G4S Secure Solutions NV*. ECLI:EU:C:2017:203, [2017] 3 CMLR 21, para 116.

[115] A Timmer and L Peroni, 'Bah v UK: On Immigration, Discrimination and Worrisome Reasoning' (Strasbourg Observers, 12 October 2011) strasbourgobservers.com/2011/10/12/bah-v-uk-on-immigration-discrimination-and-worrisome-reasoning/; Solanke (n 114) ch 2, Legal Protection from Discrimination.

[116] Young (n 11) 204.

befit the static and procedural conceptualisation of equality upon which European non-discrimination laws were built.[117]

Yet, over time, European non-discrimination law evolved, taking on the aspiration to counter these structural inequalities. As part of this transformation, lawmakers and the judiciary started to invoke more substantive rationales to ground equality protection. The protected grounds paradigm remained a central component of the law. The protected traits became symbolic indicators of social inequality. The (historical) prejudice, stereotypes and stigma experienced by social groups, and the vulnerable position the latter find themselves in, motivate heightened protection, not the inherent nature of the trait. For example, the CJEU and ECtHR have recognised how generalised assumptions or stereotypes can perpetuate social inequality and disadvantage by consolidating traditional power relationships and structures of oppression and domination.[118] Likewise, the notion of vulnerability gained significance in case law. In these cases, traits signify (political) powerlessness that might originate from negative social attitudes toward a particular group, such as negative prejudice, stigma, and stereotypes, but also from a group's (material) deprivation of resources vital for their meaningful socio-economic participation.[119]

2. *Traditional Equality Rationales and AI Produced Harm*

The normative rationales that ground current equality and non-discrimination discourse might be insufficiently robust to tackle the particular socio-relational and economic egalitarian disadvantage AI systems produce.

First, on a foundational level, formal rationales risk obfuscating social context, and in doing so, they limit the law's substantive and transformative potential. This conflict is particularly present when formal-based rationales are relied upon for the evaluation of socially driven inequalities. In the aforementioned case of *Bah v United Kingdom*, the ECtHR argued that: 'Given the element of choice involved in immigration status [...] the justification required will not be as weighty as in the case of a distinction based, for example, on nationality'.[120] Defining immigrant status as a chosen rather than a societally shaped indicator of political powerlessness provides decision-makers more leeway to lower the level of protection afforded to these groups.[121] Even in the case immigrants would be identified as more vulnerable, the immutability rationale renders people (wrongfully) co-responsible for being so. And as a consequence, decision-makers know that if they were to rely on this status for differentiation, their behaviour would be more easily justifiable.

[117] De Vos (n 109) 64.

[118] See for instance: *Konstantin Markin* (n 30) paras 142–43. See also: Case C-476/99 *H. Lommers v Minister van Landbouw, Natuurbeheer en Visserij* ECLI:EU:C:2022:183, [2022] ECR I-2891; *Chez* (n 44).

[119] L Peroni and A Timmer, 'Vulnerable Groups: The Promise of an Emerging Concept in European Human Rights Convention Law' (2013) 11 *International Journal of Constitutional Law* 1056, 1065. In reference to the work of Fraser.

[120] *Bah* (n 105) paras 45–47.

[121] Timmer and Peroni (n 115).

Second, both types of rationales may not provide the proper vocabulary to capture AI-driven egalitarian disadvantage.[122] Consider the formal-based rationales first. Regarding the application of the irrationality and irrelevance rationale, is it not the entire purpose of AI analytics to turn data into relevant points of distinction? The immutability criterion does not fare any better to make sense of AI discrimination. It is hard to determine whether a data-driven criterion actually reflects choice. Undoubtedly, many AI-driven decisions take into account attributes over which people had some degree of agency. But does this render their use appropriate? And what about complex profiles? Suppose a credit institution uncovers that a game enthusiast with a particular speech pattern is less likely to repay their loan. A person's hobbies may be chosen, but their speech is not. Does this profile then comprise a mutable or an immutable trait? In addition, decision-making systems are opaque. People often cannot foresee the consequences of their actions. Hence their agency over the conditions of their life is further reduced. The boundary between chosen and non-chosen, controlled and uncontrolled attributes has become increasingly blurred.

Substantive rationales capture the structural obstacles faced by (social) groups with a history of disadvantage. They substantiate why unjustified biases and prejudice within AI-based systems and data sets, which often have roots in pre-existing societal structures, institutions, practices, and attitudes, are problematic. Yet, their language cannot capture the egalitarian harms faced by groups defined by non-tangible and non-salient traits.[123] These groups might not have a known history of disadvantage. Yet, they too, can be unfairly disadvantaged and subjugated to representational and distributive egalitarian harm. For instance, when data-driven assumptions limit people's capacity to access socially prized (public) goods.

As an alternative, though not the only way forward, reference can be made to a ruling issued by the Finnish anti-discrimination body regarding the rightful use of algorithmic statistical models for credit scoring. The Finnish authorities argued that sole reliance on data-driven generalisations constitutes discrimination as it (among others) fails to recognise individualised information: disregarding the personal condition of creditors in favour of generalised assumptions was deemed disproportionate and in violation of discrimination law.[124] In doing so, the Finnish

[122] See on the next points also Wachter (n 13) 165–181.

[123] See Wachter (n 13); Naudts (n 1).

[124] Though the specific model also relied upon prohibited characteristics, such as gender and age, the Finnish equality tribunal noted the following: 'at the same time, the company ignored the information regarding A's own credit behaviour and creditworthiness even though these factors would have favoured extending credit to A. Disregarding such information about A by using formal and abstract statistical credit data based on the credit behaviour of others, without performing an individual assessment of A's financial standing, was disproportionate and therefore not acceptable as intended by section 11 of the Non-Discrimination Act'. National Non-Discrimination and Equality Tribunal of Finland (21 March 2018, 216/2017), translation available at www.yvtltk.fi/material/attachments/ytaltk/tapausselosteet/45LI2c6dD/YVTltk-tapausseloste-_21.3.2018-luotto-moniperusteinen_syrjinta-S-en_2.pdf.

authorities did not need to sacrifice the higher level of protection offered to specific groups. Instead, its argumentation complimented the law's traditional scope of protection by recognising how the wrongful nature of discrimination could also be situated in a particular practice or disadvantage, bypassing the need to connect the wrongful nature of discrimination to a specific trait or social group.

VII. Concluding Remarks

Data- and Artificial Intelligence-driven technologies have become firmly embedded into our social (eg, social media recommender systems), institutional (eg, predictive policing and the automation of the welfare state), and economic (eg, credit scoring and recruitment algorithms) structures.[125] AI has given decision-makers the capacity to derive and apply complex data-driven knowledge at a large scale. The choices made during the development and deployment of these systems significantly impact how society is and will be structured, including the inequality that may arise therein. Research has shown how data-driven technologies replicate and reinforce the historical and structural injustice faced by historically disadvantaged social groups. At the same time, those choices might introduce inequality alongside less tangible social dimensions. AI systems classify and categorise (groups of) individuals for various purposes in various societal contexts. How (groups of) people are treated within and as part of these technological processes can significantly impact their social (eg, wrongful generalisations, stereotypes, and stigma) and economic (e.g., exclusion from the employment market) position. Although historically disadvantaged groups are particularly vulnerable, AI-generated inequality is nonetheless a threat shared by all.

Within the law, the legal principles of equality and non-discrimination govern the conditions under which differential treatment can be justifiably imposed. This chapter examined the evolution and interpretation of these principles in the CoE and EU. The purpose was twofold: to investigate the discrepancies between both orders' understanding of equality and non-discrimination while simultaneously mapping their ability to challenge AI-generated egalitarian and discriminatory harm. This exploration gives rise to two related but distinct questions. First, should the CoE and EU develop a concerted approach to AI governance? Second, should the AI risks identified be handled by these principles and the laws that express them, or should these harms be regulated elsewhere? These are tough questions the current chapter did not, nor intended to, fully address.

Within the CoE and EU, the general principle of equality and non-discrimination transitioned from a procedural and institutional benchmark to an aspirational ideal aimed toward social and cultural inclusivity, diversity, and tolerance. Both

[125] I Gabriel, 'Towards a Theory of Justice for Artificial Intelligence' (2022) 151 *Daedalus* 12; Naudts (n 1).

notions nonetheless remain subject to different institutional and interpretative dynamics. They, therefore, differ in terms of the egalitarian and discriminatory harms they can capture. Moreover, the ECtHR and CJEU will be confronted with novel AI-related questions at different points in time. Yet, divergence need not be problematic per se. First, as suggested by Gerards, national actors should be particularly mindful of the underlying dynamics that explain potential disparity and, where need be, make use of their capacity to request further guidance from the ECtHR and CJEU.[126] Second, the principle of equality and non-discrimination should be adaptive to societal and cultural change. Such changes might be triggered by technological progress. Given the novelty of the risks involved however, both Courts might err in their assessment or anticipation of a given practice or behaviour. In these instances, the principle of equality and non-discrimination should maintain its flexibility to facilitate its reinterpretation. For example, new knowledge might emerge concerning the specific societal risk AI technologies pose. Through trial and error, as well as judicial dialogue, both orders could gradually evolve towards further alignment in their confrontation with novel questions. Each Court could leverage its knowledge regarding its respective area of expertise – the civil and political for the ECtHR and the socio-economic for the CJEU – to arrive at a more holistic, consistent, and complementary approach to equality and non-discrimination. Third, even if both orders fundamentally disagree on how a particular instance of AI-driven discrimination should be resolved, this disagreement might be justifiable. Moreover, unless we expect both Courts to take an identical approach to equality, consistency and legal certainty might never be attained. Above all then, the legal rules and procedures through which equality and non-discrimination are given shape should be applied in a clear, coherent and consistent manner. Courts should clearly articulate the normative underpinnings that ground their approach to equality. They should also carefully explain why people's right to equality and non-discrimination was outweighed by other interests. Likewise, if the current approach to equality should be reinterpreted, the motivations and reasons for doing so should be visible. Such clarity might also benefit the guiding function of equality, and its subsequent operationalisation, throughout the AI value chain.

Not all AI-related challenges will be solved through judicial dialogue and clarity alone. This chapter identified two such challenges. First, given the law's distributive underpinnings, current legal frameworks insufficiently recognise how inequality manifests from the socio-relational dynamics within and as part of AI-driven systems. Second, the law's focus on specific protected grounds might limit the law's personal scope of protection. Though the CoE's model of equality appears more flexible than that of the EU, both approaches tend to classify as particularly harmful acts of differentiation based upon objective, identifiable or personal grounds

[126] Gerards, 'Systeemverklaringen voor verschillen tussen de gelijkebehandelingsrechtspraak van het HvJ EU en het EHRM' (n 3) 581.

that are likely to be recognised by society as having a certain degree of social significance or social saliency. Likewise, the core rationales that motivate the heightened level of scrutiny in case these characteristics are relied on, make sense in a system built around the protection of social groups. Yet, in so doing, they fail to articulate and capture the harms non-tangible AI-generated groups might face.[127] These two challenges, however, mandate a reflection regarding the structural and conceptual foundations of European non-discrimination law.

In conclusion, European equality and non-discrimination laws find themselves at a crossroads regarding the future regulation of AI systems. Should these laws harmoniously alter their grammar and vocabulary to accommodate the indiscriminate threat AI systems pose to people's socio-relational and distributive egalitarian interests? This question remains open for now. Still, the dual exercise performed in this chapter can guide future research to those areas relevant to finding the response thereto.

[127] See also Wachter (n 13).

3

Faced with the Non-Harmonisation of Data Protection Law, the Two European Courts Carve Out a Shared Path[1]

BART VAN DER SLOOT

I. Introduction

The European Convention on Human Rights (ECHR) drafted in 1950 by the Council of Europe (CoE) contains a right to privacy, but no right to data protection. The Charter of Fundamental Rights of the European Union 2000 (CFREU) contains both a right to privacy and a right to data protection. The relationship between these rights has never been made clear by the European Union and its attempts to harmonise data protection legislation throughout Europe have not been a resounding success. Against this backdrop, the European Court of Human Rights (ECtHR) and the Court of Justice (CJEU) have taken it upon themselves to ensure consistency and harmony between the two legal doctrines, the first taking the lead in the interpretation of the right to privacy and the latter in the interpretation of the right to data protection. The ECtHR has in particular tried to incorporate as many principles developed under the EU data protection legislation as possible in its jurisprudence. Put bluntly, the CoE cleans up the mess of the EU's sloppy lawmaking; the EU is accustomed to regulate markets, not to ensure the protection of fundamental rights.

This chapter will focus on ten points, which serve as illustrations of how the two courts, to the extent that such is within their discretion, strive towards a

[1] Bits and pieces of this chapter have been elaborated on in previous publications, such as, but not limited to: B van der Sloot, 'Legal consistency after the General Data Protection Regulation and the Police Directive' (2018) 9 *European Journal of Law and Technology* 1; B van der Sloot, 'Wij zijn twee vriendjes, jij en ik: de innige tango van de twee Europese hoven op het gebied van privacy en gegevensbescherming' (2021) 12 *Sociaal-economische wetgeving SEW* 582; and several editorials for the European Data Protection Law Review (EDPL).

harmonious interpretation of the rights to privacy and data protection and the respective CoE and EU legal instruments in this field. Both courts have chosen to elevate 'their' right to a 'super right' underlying other human rights (Section II), which has led them to extend both the material scope (Section III) and the personal scope (Section IV) of the rights and to reinterpret the limitations that apply to data processing in the private sphere (Section V). Mutual learning experiences can also be discerned with regard to privacy in the public sphere (Section VI), rules on the waiver and abuse of right (Section VII), the assessment of the activities of intelligence agencies (Section VIII) and of private parties (Section IX). Both courts have become increasingly keen on ensuring that the high levels of protection that apply within Europe are upheld abroad when data are transferred (Section X). Finally, the two courts no longer exclusively assess complaints from individuals regarding actions by the executive or judicial branch, but are also willing to pass judgement on legal regimes as such and even prescribe what such regimes should look like (Section XI).

Finally, the analysis will show how the EU has failed to harmonise the one fundamental right that it has introduced itself, the right to data protection, and how it left it up to the courts to interpret this right and to ensure consistency in the interpretation of the rights to privacy and data protection throughout Europe. There is legal consistency between the approaches taken by the ECtHR and the CJEU and as a consequence, both the rights to privacy and data protection have, more or less, a clearly demarcated scope. Internal legal consistency between the EU's data frameworks and their implementation by Member States, however, is very rare (Section XII).

II. Super Rights

The right to privacy is arguably the oldest legal doctrine there is, pertaining to the separation of the public and private sphere and the limitation of government power as such. The protection of the home and bodily integrity were part and parcel of the earliest known legal systems. Yet, privacy was not contained in the first human rights declarations such as the Magna Carta,[2] the Bill of Rights,[3] the Virginia Declaration of Rights[4] and the Déclaration des Droits de l'Homme et du Citoyen.[5] Even under the ECHR, the right to privacy has a particular genesis. The right was not initially included in the list of human rights to be protected when the Convention was drafted and was inserted in the final text only later in the legislative process. In addition, there was a lively debate about whether privacy rights

[2] www.legislation.gov.uk/aep/Edw1cc1929/25/9/contents.
[3] www.legislation.gov.uk/aep/WillandMarSess2/1/2#commentary-c2144673.
[4] www.archives.gov/founding-docs/virginia-declaration-of-rights.
[5] www.legifrance.gouv.fr/contenu/menu/droit-national-en-vigueur/constitution/declaration-des-droits-de-l-homme-et-du-citoyen-de-1789.

should be contained in one provision, or several, and whether privacy should not essentially be seen as a sub-right of other human rights.[6]

What did the right to protect private communications have to do with the protection of family life? Shouldn't there be a separate provision combining in one doctrine the 'family rights', such as the protection of family life, the right to marry and found a family (Article 12 ECHR) and the right to education (Article 2 1st Protocol)? Should not the protection of home be subsumed under the protection of property (Article 1 1st Protocol)? And should the protection of a person's honour and reputation (Article 10 § 2 ECHR) also be included in the privacy provision or should this aspect be left out as its reputational harm is usually inflicted by private parties, not public authorities? The privacy provision was eventually adopted as a kind of umbrella right, incorporating a number of more or less related aspects, but was not seen as the strongest or most essential of the provisions under the Convention.

The legal recognition of the right to data protection is of an even more recent genesis. Initially, when the first legal instruments in this field were adopted by the Council of Europe in the 1970s,[7] the right was seen as a sub-right to the right to privacy, as was the case when the CoE adopted the 1981 Convention, which is still in force in modified form.[8] In this regard, the ECtHR only evaluates data protection issues to the extent they are covered by the right to privacy (Article 8 ECHR). When the EU entered the field of data protection regulation from the 1990s onwards, the right to data protection was gradually separated from the right to privacy and was eventually included in the EU Charter of Fundamental Rights as an independent fundamental right (Article 8 CFREU), separate from the right to privacy (Article 7 CFREU).[9] The Treaty on the Functioning of the European Union (TFEU) even contains an explicit mandate for the Union to regulate this right,[10] which it did through the most far-reaching type of secondary legislation, namely a Regulation: the 2016 General Data Protection Regulation (GDPR).[11]

Interestingly, given their genesis, academics and experts have questioned whether each of the rights should actually be seen as a human right. In the case of privacy, it

[6] Council of Europe, '*Collected edition of the "Travaux préparatoires" of the European Convention on Human Rights*' (Martinus Nijhoff, 1975–1985, 8 vols).

[7] Council Of Europe – Committee Of Ministers, Resolution (73)22 On The Protection Of The Privacy Of Individuals Vis-A-Vis Electronic Data Banks In The Private Sector (26 September 1973, 224th Meeting Of The Ministers' Deputies); Council Of Europe – Committee Of Ministers Resolution (74)29 On The Protection Of The Privacy Of Individuals Vis-A-Vis Electronic Data Banks In The Public Sector (20 September 1974, 236th Meeting Of The Ministers' Deputies).

[8] Council of Europe, Convention for the Protection of Individuals with regard to Automatic Processing of Personal Data [1981] ETS 108; Council of Europe, Convention 108+ – Convention for the protection of individuals with regard to the processing of personal data [2018].

[9] Charter of Fundamental Rights of the European Union [2012] OJ C 326/391 (CFREU), Article 8.

[10] Consolidated Versions of the Treaty on European Union and the Treaty on the Functioning of the European Union [2012] C 326/47, Article 16.

[11] Regulation (EU) 2016/679 of the European Parliament and of the Council on the protection of natural persons with regard to the processing of personal data and on the free movement of such data, and repealing Directive 95/46/EC (General Data Protection Regulation) [2016] OJ L119/1.

has often been argued that the right is 'redundant', that is, that it can be subsumed under one of the other human rights, such as the right to property,[12] the right to freedom of expression or one of the other freedoms.[13] In the case of data protection, it has been questioned whether every processing of personal data (eg someone blogging 'Boris Johnson has blue eyes') should be seen as an interference with a human right (legitimate or not). In addition, the GDPR is best seen primarily as a market regulation instrument and the Data Protection Authority (DPA) as a market regulator. This market-oriented approach to data protection is unsurprising given the EU's background primarily in internal market integration, but it has raised the question to what extent data protection actually is a right on par with 'real' human rights as contained in the ECHR.[14] Moreover, it has been argued that data protection issues can be brought back to a number of other fundamental rights, such as the right to privacy, the prohibition of discrimination (eg when it comes to automated decision-making), freedom of expression (eg when it comes to access to information) and freedom of religion (eg when it comes to processing sensitive data).[15]

Interestingly, it is precisely the relative vagueness and fluidity of the two rights that has allowed the two courts to transform the right to privacy and the right to data protection into 'super rights'. According to the ECtHR, the right to privacy provides protection to the core values underlying the ECHR, such as human dignity, individual autonomy and personal development, and is thus used by the Court to bring cases under its jurisdiction when that does not follow directly from the Convention, such as in issues revolving around air, water and noise pollution, limitations on euthanasia and other medical-ethical issues, minority rights and several economic rights.[16] Alluding to the unique status of freedom of expression under the American constitution, the right to privacy has been coined 'the first amendment of Europe'.[17]

The CJEU has followed more or less the same path with respect to the right to data protection. On the one hand, it has significantly widened the scope of the concept of 'personal data' and decided that all processing of personal data,[18]

[12] P Samuelson, 'Privacy as intellectual property?' (2000) 52 *Stanford Law Review* 1125; RA Posner, 'Privacy, Secrecy, and Reputation' (1979) 28 *Buffalo Law Review* 1, 11–17.

[13] R Gavison, 'Privacy and the Limits of Law' (1980) 89 *The Yale Law Journal* 421.

[14] B Van der Sloot, 'Legal fundamentalism: is data protection really a fundamental right?' in R Leenes, S Gutwirth, P De Hert and R van Brakel (eds), *Data Protection and Privacy: (In)visibilities and Infrastructure* (Springer, 2017).

[15] In the beginning of the ECtHR's approach to data protection issues, such was actually the case: P de Hert, 'Mensenrechten en bescherming van persoonsgegevens. Overzicht en synthese van de Europese rechtspraak 1955–1997' in *Jaarboek 1996/97 van het Interuniversitair Centrum Mensenrechten* (Maklu, 1998).

[16] B Van der Sloot, 'Privacy as personality right: why the ECtHR's focus on ulterior interests might prove indispensable in the age of Big Data' (2015) 31 *Utrecht Journal of International and European Law* 25.

[17] B Petkova, 'Privacy as Europe's first Amendment' (2019) 25 *European Law Journal* 140.

[18] B Van der Sloot, S Van Schendel and CAF López, 'The influence of (technical) developments on the concept of personal data in relation to the GDPR' (2022), repository.wodc.nl/bitstream/handle/20.500.12832/3229/3224-influence-of-technical-developments-on-concept-personal-data-full-text.pdf?sequence=1.

no matter how insignificant the data and how small the number of data, should be seen as affecting a fundamental right. Since in the current day and age, almost all operations within companies, public organisations and households are data-driven, data protection law plays a role in more and more legal cases. For example, discrimination cases increasingly deal with discriminatory computer systems and algorithms, fair trial issues increasingly have a data element, partly due to the rise of online dispute resolution mechanisms, and matters on the freedom of expression often concern digital expressions, blogs by amateur journalists and the liability of internet providers. This is a trend which is only likely to continue over the coming years.[19]

III. Ratione Materiae

Although both rights have turned out to be super rights of sorts, the right to privacy and the right to data protection both continue to have a distinct scope of application. The right to privacy covers matters not related to data processing, such as the protection of private life, family life and the home. There are also important differences between the two rights in the area of data processing. The right to privacy essentially covers two aspects: the processing of data that reveal something about an individual's private life and data obtained through the interception of private communications. The former aspect generally does not cover mundane and everyday information about a person (eg her name); the latter involves any data, as long as they were communicated through private channels. If A calls B to talk about the lovely weather and that telephone conversation is wire tapped, this counts as an interference with the right to privacy.[20]

Data protection law involves the processing of all data, public or private, sensitive or insensitive, big or small, as long as they relate to a private individual. Even if a person publishes a blogpost stating 'Emanuel Macron has blue eyes', such a post will fall under the material scope of data protection law. Under data protection law, the only relevant question is whether the data that are processed relate to an identifiable person. To the contrary, such data processing will usually not fall under the material scope of the right to privacy, because it does not pertain to privately communicated data and the data are not particularly sensitive nor do they reveal essential aspects of a person's private life.

The ECtHR initially adhered to this strict separation between both rights and only assessed data processing operations insofar as they directly affected one of the four concepts contained in Article 8 ECHR (private life, family life, home and correspondence). Gradually, however, it has adopted an interpretation that comes

[19] M Brkan, 'The Unstoppable Expansion of the EU Fundamental Right to Data Protection: Little Shop of Horrors?' (2016) 23 *Maastricht Journal of European and Comparative Law* 812.

[20] Van der Sloot (n 16).

close to the material scope attributed to the right to data protection under the EU legal acquis. Although it does not adopt the CJEU's broad interpretation of the scope of the concept of 'personal data', the ECtHR has held that the protection of private life covers, inter alia, the processing of dynamic IP addresses,[21] audio recordings,[22] image recordings in universities,[23] bodily material,[24] GPS signals[25] and meta data,[26] which covers information about where, when and with whom a person has communicated, but not the content of the communication itself.

In doing so, the ECtHR applies the standard that applies under data protection law, namely the question of identifiability of a person through the processing of data: '[T]he Court is not persuaded that the acquisition of related communications data is necessarily less intrusive than the acquisition of content. For example, the content of an electronic communication might be encrypted and, even if it were decrypted, might not reveal anything of note about the sender or recipient. The related communications data, on the other hand, could reveal the identities and geographic location of the sender and recipient and the equipment through which the communication was transmitted. In bulk, the degree of intrusion is magnified, since the patterns that will emerge could be capable of painting an intimate picture of a person through the mapping of social networks, location tracking, Internet browsing tracking, mapping of communication patterns, and insight into who a person interacted with.'[27]

IV. Ratione Personae

Besides the *ratione materiae*, the material scope, the *ratione personae*, the personal scope, is relevant. The standard interpretation of this doctrine under the ECHR is that for a complaint to be declared admissible, it must have been brought by a person who has an interest in the case.[28] This means, among other things, that this person must be able to demonstrate an individualisable interest; in addition, minimal harm will not be considered to be interference by the ECHR.[29] This was later enshrined in the so-called *de minimis* principle, from which it follows that a complaint will be dismissed if 'the applicant has not suffered a significant disadvantage.'[30]

[21] *Benedik v Slovenia* App no 62357/14 (ECtHR, 24 April 2018).
[22] *P.G. and J.H. v United Kingdom* App no 44787/98 (ECtHR, 25 September 2001).
[23] *Antovic and Mirkovic v Montenegro* App no 70838/13 (ECtHR, 28 November 2017).
[24] *S. and Marper v United Kingdom* App nos 30562/04 and 30566/04 (ECtHR, 4 December 2008).
[25] *Uzun v Germany* App no 35623/05 (ECtHR, 2 September 2010).
[26] *Big Brother Watch and others v United Kingdom* App nos 58170/13, 62322/14 and 24960/15 (ECtHR Grand Chamber, 25 May 2021).
[27] *Big Brother Watch and Others v United Kingdom* App nos 58170/13, 62322/14 and 24960/15 (ECtHR First Section, 13 September 2018) para 356.
[28] www.echr.coe.int/documents/d/echr/admissibility_guide_eng.
[29] See eg *Campion v France* App no 25547/94 (ECtHR, 6 September 1995).
[30] European Convention for the Protection of Human Rights and Fundamental Freedoms, as amended by Protocols Nos 11 and 14 [1950] ETS 5 (ECHR), Article 35(3) sub 2.

Under data protection law, the *ratione materiae* and *ratione personae* have been merged. If personal data are processed, both requirements are met; there is no *de minimis* rule. Moreover, data protection is not just a subjective human right; the GDPR provides objective legal rules that parties processing personal data must comply with independent data subjects invoking their subjective rights. This means that not only data subjects can take a case to court, but also civil society organisations and the DPAs.[31]

Again, the ECtHR, although leaving intact its dominant approach, has decided to follow this path in certain data protection-related cases in order to harmonise the interpretation of the right to privacy under the ECHR and the right to data protection under the EU legal acquis. An additional motive for this move was that a problem it faced is that people often do not know whether their data are part of a data processing operation and have difficulty finding out, either because the data controllers themselves do not know who the data they process refer to, such as with bulk data collections, because data processing is ubiquitous, such as with smart cities, or because parties will not share that information, such as with intelligence agencies. Inter alia, the ECtHR has recently decided to declare admissible so-called *in abstracto* complaints, which do not revolve around alleged individual harm, but address the quality of laws and legal regimes that legitimise data processing as such. Doing so, it let go of the requirement of personal harm by way of exception with the following justification:

> In such circumstances the threat of surveillance can be claimed in itself to restrict free communication through the postal and telecommunication services, thereby constituting for all users, or potential users, a direct interference with the right guaranteed by Article 8. There is therefore a greater need for scrutiny by the Court, and an exception to the rule denying individuals the right to challenge a law in abstracto is justified. In such cases the individual does not need to demonstrate the existence of any risk that secret surveillance measures were applied to him. By contrast, if the national system provides for effective remedies, a widespread suspicion of abuse is more difficult to justify. In such cases, the individual may claim to be a victim of a violation occasioned by the mere existence of secret measures or of legislation permitting secret measures only if he is able to show that, due to his personal situation, he is potentially at risk of being subjected to such measures.[32]

V. Private Sphere

In the case of the right to privacy, if someone enters a person's private sphere and if the *de minimis* rule is met, such constitutes an interference with Article 8 ECHR.

[31] ECHR, Article 58(5).
[32] *Roman Zakharov v Russia* App no 47143/06 (ECtHR, 4 December 2015).

For example, if someone enters a person's house without permission or legal basis, this is almost by definition a breach of privacy. The same applies to the processing of data; if data is collected in the private sphere, it is almost by definition an interference of the right to privacy.[33]

By contrast, under data protection law, the focus is not on the sphere in which the victim was located; instead the household exemption places emphasis on the sphere in which the data controller was located when processing personal data of others, or put more precisely, the nature of the activities for which personal data were processed. The GDPR does not apply to data processing 'by a natural person in the course of a purely personal or household activity'.[34] As stated in recital 18: 'This Regulation does not apply to the processing of personal data by a natural person in the course of a purely personal or household activity and thus with no connection to a professional or commercial activity. Personal or household activities could include correspondence and the holding of addresses, or social networking and online activity undertaken within the context of such activities. However, this Regulation applies to controllers or processors which provide the means for processing personal data for such personal or household activities.'

The CJEU has handed down two important cases with respect to the household exemption.[35]

In *Bodil Lindqvist*, a women kept a personal blog, on which she shared information about acquaintances and colleagues, including that one of them had broken a leg. The question that led to a legal dispute was whether the household exemption applied, as the purpose for which the data were processed was primarily personal and the internet page was intended for a small circle of friends and colleagues. The CJEU held to the negative: 'That exception must therefore be interpreted as relating only to activities which are carried out in the course of private or family life of individuals, which is clearly not the case with the processing of personal data consisting in publication on the internet so that those data are made accessible to an indefinite number of people.'[36]

In *Ryneš*, a person had installed a camera on his house for security purposes. The question that was raised was whether the recordings fell under the household exemption, as the purpose of the processing of personal data (in this case of people illegally seeking access to the house and the private property) was primarily of a personal nature and the data were not intended to be made public. Yet the CJEU ruled negative again. 'To the extent that video surveillance such as that at issue in the main proceedings covers, even partially, a public space and is accordingly

[33] It is conceivable that when a person accidentally navigates a drone over the neighbour's backyard and deletes the non-sensitive recordings immediately afterwards, such will not be seen as an interference with Article 8 ECHR, but such is the exception that confirms the rule. www.echr.coe.int/documents/d/echr/Guide_Data_protection_ENG.

[34] GDPR, Article 2(2)(c).

[35] See B Van der Sloot, 'Home is where the heart is: the household exemption in the 21st century' (2023) 14 *Journal of intellectual property, information technology and electronic commerce law* 34.

[36] Case C-101/01 *Bodil Lindqvist* ECLI:EU:C:2003:596, [2003] ECR I-12971, para 47.

directed outwards from the private setting of the person processing the data in that manner, it cannot be regarded as an activity which is a purely "personal or household" activity'.[37]

It follows from *Bodil Lindqvist* that the intention of the data controller is not decisive for the Court when determining whether the household exemption applies; instead, it looked to the sphere in which the data were disseminated. In *Rynes*, the Court did not look to the intention of the data controller or the purpose of the data processing operation, but to the sphere from which the data were collected. Herewith, the CJEU seemingly diverges from the text of the GDPR and significantly narrows the role of the household exemption. It still is unclear whether data collected from the private sphere – for example, A visits B in her home and B registers the visit through a hidden camera in the smoke detector, or B navigates a minidrone through A's bathroom window and films there – will fall under the household exemption, if B uses the collected data only for personal activities. The Court has not given an explicit opinion on this point, but it seems plausible that because it finds that data collection from the public sphere does not fall within the scope of the exception, this will certainly not be the case for the collection of personal data from the private sphere of others nor for the secret surveillance of visitors to a person's home. Consequently, the CJEU has interpreted the household exemption in such a strict fashion that the discrepancy between the right to privacy and the right to data protection on the point of processing data in the private sphere has been significantly reduced.

VI. Public Sphere

The right to privacy traditionally does not apply, or only to a limited extent, in the public sphere. For example, in a case from 1998, the Commission noted that 'the photographic systems of which the applicant complains are likely to be used in public places or in premises lawfully occupied by the users of such systems in order to monitor those premises for security purposes. Given that nothing is recorded, it is difficult to see how the visual data obtained could be made available to the general public or used for purposes other than to keep a watch on places. The Commission also notes that the data available to a person looking at monitors is identical to that which he or she could have obtained by being on the spot in person. Therefore all that can be observed is essentially, public behaviour. The applicant has also failed plausibly to demonstrate that private actions occurring in public could have been monitored in any way. Applying the above criteria, the Commission has reached the conclusion that there is, in the present case, no appearance of an interference with the first applicants, private life.'[38]

[37] Case C-212/13 *Rynes* ECLI:EU:C:2014:2428, [2015] 1 WLR 2607, para 33.

[38] *Herbecq and Association des droits des homme v Belgium* App nos 32200/96 and 32201/96 (Commission Decision, 14 January 1998).

The starting point for the right to privacy is that what is public and what takes place in the public sphere, is not private and therefore does not, or only to a limited extent, fall within the scope of Article 8 ECHR. In principle, this also applies to technical infrastructure through which activities in the public sphere can be recorded, such as cameras, as long as the data are not stored for long periods of time.[39] This is different for the right to data protection. Data gathered from public sources and from the public sphere fall under the data protection regime.

Step by step, the ECtHR has decided to bring the public sphere within the scope of Article 8 ECHR, inter alia by using its own interpretation of the 'reasonable expectation of privacy' doctrine from the United States.[40] While in the US, this doctrine entails that in principle, people cannot reasonably expect that their privacy will be respected in the public sphere,[41] the ECtHR, by contrast, uses the same phrase or the 'legitimate expectation of privacy' to find exactly the opposite, namely that people in public spaces can invoke Article 8 ECHR and that this even applies to public figures and celebrities. The first time it ruled along this line was in the Von Hannover case, in which Caroline Von Hannover, Princess of Monaco, argued that all her activities in public, whether it concerned taking her children to school or running errands, were closely followed by paparazzi and gossip journalists. The Court ruled that even public figures should be able to enjoy a 'legitimate expectation' of privacy in the public sphere:

> Increased vigilance in protecting private life, it stressed, is necessary to contend with new communication technologies which make it possible to store and reproduce personal data, adding that 'the distinction drawn between figures of contemporary society '*par excellence*' and 'relatively' public figures has to be clear and obvious so that, in a State governed by the rule of law, the individual has precise indications as to the behaviour he or she should adopt. Above all, they need to know exactly when and where they are in a protected sphere or, on the contrary, in a sphere in which they must expect interference from others, especially the tabloid press.[42]

People's private life, the ECtHR has increasingly emphasised, takes place not only in the private sphere, but in all spheres of life. This means, among other things, that people's dismissal from their work and their opportunities to enter into social and professional relationships are also covered by the right to privacy, according to the Court.[43]

[39] See for a deep analysis of the public space: M Galič, 'Surveillance and privacy in smart cities and living labs: Conceptualising privacy for public space' (2019) pure.uvt.nl/ws/portalfiles/portal/31748824/Galic_Surveillance_19_11_2019.pdf.

[40] See further B Van der Sloot, 'Expectations of Privacy: The Three Tests Deployed by the European Court of Human Rights' in D Hallinan, R Leenes and P De Hert (eds), *Data Protection and Privacy, Volume 14: Enforcing Rights in a Changing World* (Hart Publishing, 2021) 67.

[41] *Katz v United States*, 389 U.S. 347 (1967).

[42] *Von Hannover v Germany* App no 59320/00 (ECtHR, 24 June 2004) para 69.

[43] See for the first time *X. v Iceland* App no 6825/74 (ECRM, 18 May 1976).

VII. Abuse of Waiver of Right

Under data protection law, in principle, it is prohibited to process sensitive personal data – that is, data relating to a person's racial or ethnic origin, political opinions, religious or philosophical beliefs, trade union membership, genetic data, biometric data, health data or data relating to a person's sexual behaviour or sexual orientation – unless an exception applies. Of the exceptions contained in the GDPR, one is the situation in which 'processing relates to personal data which are manifestly made public by the data subject.'[44] In a sense, the data subject has waived their right to protection by making their data available to the public.

The ECtHR has adopted a similar approach to the right to privacy. For example, if a father does not contact his children for years, the consequence may be that he can no longer successfully rely on his right to family life. However, the Court has made an exception with respect to the processing of personal information. An example is the case of *Pay v UK* in which a man was employed by the probation service, where he treated sex offenders. He also was the director of Roissy, an organisation that advertised its services on the internet as a builder and supplier of BDSM products and as an organiser of BDSM events and performances. Pictures in which Pay was displayed with two half-naked women were shown on a website which promoted male dominance over women. The probation service noticed Pay's activities and discharged him because of the incompatibility of such activities with effective treatment of sex offenders. When the case was brought before the ECtHR, the UK stressed that the right to privacy did not apply in this case because Pay himself had posted the sexually explicit information online. However, the ECtHR found that even though the man's publications 'could give rise to doubts as to whether the applicant's activities may be said to fall with the scope of private life and, if so, whether [] there has been a waiver or forfeiture of the rights guaranteed by Article 8. The Court notes, however, that the applicant's performances took place in a nightclub which was likely to be frequented only by a self-selecting group of like-minded people and that the photographs of his act which were published on the internet were anonymised'.[45] Therefore, the ECtHR was not ready to immediately reject Pay's claim, but moved to a substantive evaluation of the case.

Seemingly following this line of interpretation, the CJEU has decided to restrictively interpret the rule concerning the disclosure of sensitive data wherewith a data subject is held to have waived their right to data protection. It was already clear that manifestly making public sensitive data does not include a person wearing a headscarf, therewith disclosing their religious beliefs, nor a person wearing an arm sling, therewith disclosing medical information. Manifestly making public sensitive data

[44] GDPR, Article 9(2)(e).
[45] *Pay v United Kingdom* App no 32792/05 (ECtHR, 16 September 2008).

is restricted to examples such as a politician voluntarily announcing they are gay.[46] In addition, the CJEU has made clear that even in the case of manifest disclosure, data subjects may still subsequently request others to stop processing that data, although there are instances in which they do not need to abide by such a request.[47]

Under the right to data protection, there is no doctrine concerning the abuse of right; though there is the general prohibition of abuse of right in the CFREU, which is based on Article 17 ECHR, this provision is not applied regularly, if at all, to the data protection context.[48] Article 17 ECHR provides: 'Nothing in this Convention may be interpreted as implying for any State, group or person any right to engage in any activity or perform any act aimed at the destruction of any of the rights and freedoms set forth herein or at their limitation to a greater extent than is provided for in the Convention.' This provision relates to all subjective rights under the Convention, such as the right to privacy, the freedom of religion, the right to a fair trial and the right to marry and found a family. Yet, the ECtHR has decided to apply Article 17 ECHR only to a small number of rights, in particular the freedom of expression and the freedom of assembly.[49] For example, a person has no right to found a political party which has the objective to overthrow democracy and the rule of law. However, the ECtHR has decided not to apply Article 17 ECHR to most rights under the Convention, such as the right to privacy.

For example, in a case regarding a person who had downloaded and distributed child pornography, the Court emphasised that the person in question expected his activities to remain private and that his identity would not be disclosed. While the ECtHR accepted that he did not hide his dynamic IP address, and thus had at least not reduced the likelihood that his actions would be discovered, it also underlined that this could not be decisive in assessing whether his expectation of privacy was reasonable from an objective point of view. On that point, the Court reiterated that anonymity on the Internet is an important aspect of the right to privacy, that a dynamic IP address, even if visible to other users of the network, cannot be traced to the specific computer without verification from the ISP, and concluded that it was sufficient 'to note that Article 37 of the Constitution guaranteed the privacy of correspondence and of communications and required that any interference with this right be based on a court order. Therefore, also from the standpoint of the legislation in force at the relevant time, the applicant's expectation of privacy with respect to his online

[46] See for a good overview of the various WP29 and EDPS guidelines and other relevant sources: ES Dove and J Chen, 'What does it mean for a data subject to make their personal data "manifestly public"? An analysis of GDPR Article 9(2)(e)' (2021) 11 *International Data Privacy Law* 107.

[47] Case C-136/17 *GC and Others* ECLI:EU:C:2019:773, [2020] 1 CMLR 26.

[48] CFREU, Article 54.

[49] PE de Morree, *Rights and Wrongs under the ECHR: The prohibition of abuse of rights in Article 17 of the European Convention on Human Rights* (Intersentia, 2016) www.echr.coe.int/documents/d/echr/Guide_Art_17_ENG.

activity could not be said to be unwarranted or unreasonable.'[50] The Court therefore held that even a person who abuses his internet connection to distribute child pornography can still invoke the right to privacy.

VIII. Intelligence Services

Initially, the European Union had limited competence over matters concerning national law enforcement, such as data processing by law enforcement authorities. Although this competence has been broadened when the EU pillar structure was abandoned, while general data protection matters are covered by a Regulation, data processing by law enforcement authorities is still covered by a Directive.[51] In addition, the EU has no competence to regulate matters regarding national security, such as bulk data collections by intelligence agencies. The GDPR provides: 'This Regulation does not apply to the processing of personal data [...] in the course of an activity which falls outside the scope of Union law.'[52] This means that for a long time, the ECtHR was the leading authority when it came to assessing the powers of intelligence agencies.[53]

However, the CJEU has found creative ways to attribute to itself competence over data processing operations by intelligence agencies.[54] First, it has decided that a provision in the *lex specialis* of the GDPR, the e-Privacy Directive,[55] which holds that Member States can collect data in the context of state security in a manner that meets the conditions of necessity, proportionality and subsidiarity, gives the Court a say in how Member States approach this matter.[56] Because this Directive must

[50] *Benedik* (n 21). Judge Yudkivska, together with Bosnjak, even emphasised in a concurring opinion that the majority was not clear enough on this point: 'there should be no doubt that his expectations of privacy were perfectly legitimate, notwithstanding the abhorrently illegal character of his activity [].' Judge Vehabovic, however, wrote a dissenting opinion: 'In nearly all cases, criminals would not wish their activities to be known to others. This kind of expectation of privacy would not be reasonable when based on an unlawful, or in this case a criminal, incentive. An expectation to hide criminal activity should not be considered as reasonable. On a second issue concerning the reasonable expectation of privacy, the applicant exchanged files including child pornography through a public network account which was visible to others. The applicant therefore knew, or ought to have known, that his actions were not anonymous. The applicant did not intend to conceal his activity at the time of commission of the offence.'

[51] Directive (EU) 2016/680 of the European Parliament and of the Council on the protection of natural persons with regard to the processing of personal data by competent authorities for the purposes of the prevention, investigation, detection or prosecution of criminal offences or the execution of criminal penalties, and on the free movement of such data, and repealing Council Framework Decision 2008/977/JHA [2016] OJ L 119/89.

[52] GDPR, Article 2(2).

[53] www.echr.coe.int/documents/fs_mass_surveillance_eng.pdf.

[54] Joined Cases C-293/12 and C-594/12 *Digital Rights Ireland* ECLI:EU:C:2014:238, [2014] 3 CMLR 44; Joined Cases C-203/15 and C-698/15 *Tele2 Sverige* ECLI:EU:C:2016:970, [2017] 2 CMLR 30.

[55] Directive 2002/58/EC of the European Parliament and of the Council concerning the processing of personal data and the protection of privacy in the electronic communications sector (Directive on privacy and electronic communications [2002] OJ L201/37, Article 15.

[56] Case C-623/17 *Privacy International* ECLI:EU:C:2020:790, [2021] 1 CMLR 30.

be seen in light of the GDPR and the Charter, the Court grants itself full jurisdiction to assess the necessity, proportionality and subsidiarity of bulk data regimes by intelligence agencies. Second, under the GDPR, personal data may in principle not be transferred outside the EU unless an equivalent level of protection applies there.[57] The CJEU has found that this means that it may judge whether the legal regimes of non-EU countries and the agreements that the European Commission concludes with these countries are in harmony with the Charter, to which end it will also assess the rules and regulations applicable to the intelligence agencies of that non-EU country, eg their right to access EU-citizens' data.[58]

IX. Private Sector, Public Sector

The earliest data protection instruments in Europe were adopted by the Council of Europe in the 1970s; it adopted one resolution for the private sector and another for the public sector.[59] Later, with the 1981 Convention, the Council adopted one instrument that regulated both sectors, a path that was followed by the EU in the 1995 Data Protection Directive and the GDPR. Still, especially under the EU legal acquis, many exceptions to the data protection principles and obligations apply for public sector bodies. Not only do intelligence agencies fall outside the scope of the GDPR and the activities of law enforcement authorities are regulated through the less stringent Law Enforcement Directive, the activities of the EU itself do not fall within the scope of the Regulation.[60] In addition, Member States may adopt exemptions to the GDPR with respect to data processing in light of numerous public interests, such as government activities in the context of security and public order, the protection of judicial independence, the prevention, investigation, detection and prosecution of breaches of ethics for regulated professions and the enforcement of civil law claims.[61]

The replacement of the 1995 Data Protection Directive with the 2016 General Data Protection Regulation was mainly motivated by the desire to better regulate tech companies, in particular those based outside the EU.[62] To a large extent,

[57] GDPR, Article 44 and further.

[58] See inter alia: Case C-362/14 *Schrems* ECLI:EU:C:2015:650, [2016] 2 CMLR 2; C-311/18 *Facebook Ireland and Schrems* ECLI:EU:C:2020:559, [2021] 1 CMLR 14.

[59] Council Of Europe – Committee Of Ministers, Resolution (73)22 On The Protection Of The Privacy Of Individuals Vis-A-Vis Electronic Data Banks In The Private Sector (26 September 1973, 224th Meeting Of The Ministers' Deputies); Council Of Europe – Committee Of Ministers Resolution (74)29 On The Protection Of The Privacy Of Individuals Vis-A-Vis Electronic Data Banks In The Public Sector (20 September 1974, 236th Meeting Of The Ministers' Deputies).

[60] Regulation (EC) 45/2001 of the European Parliament and of the Council on the protection of individuals with regard to the processing of personal data by the Community institutions and bodies and on the free movement of such data [2001] OJ L8/1.

[61] GDPR, Article 23.

[62] L Downes, 'GDPR and the End of the Internet's Grand Bargain' (*Harvard Business Review*, 9 April 2018) hbr.org/2018/04/gdpr-and-the-end-of-the-internets-grand-bargain.

the data protection framework was tailored to the private sector. Yet, changes are visible. As explained, the CJEU has gradually decided to oversee relevant aspects of data processing by intelligence agencies and while the EU has not adopted a Regulation for the law enforcement sector, it did adopt a Directive in 2016, while prior to 2016 that had been a Framework Decision.[63] In addition, the GDPR lays down additional duties of care for governmental organisations.[64]

The opposite trend can be witnessed under the ECHR. The European Convention on Human Rights was adopted in the wake of World War II and was intended to set limits on the use of governmental power. Thus, it contained negative obligations for states – not to abuse their power – and negative rights for citizens – to be free from governmental interference, inter alia in the enjoyment of their private life. That is why paragraph 2 of Article 8 ECHR, among other doctrines, sets limits that are relevant to public sector organisations: 'There shall be no interference by a public authority with the exercise of this right except such as is in accordance with the law and is necessary in a democratic society in the interests of national security, public safety or the economic well-being of the country, for the prevention of disorder or crime, for the protection of health or morals, or for the protection of the rights and freedoms of others.'

Yet this picture is gradually tilting, partly due to the more general trends of horizontalisation of fundamental rights[65] and the ECtHR laying down both positive rights for citizens and positive duties for states.[66] Inter alia, this means that when private organisations or individuals violate the human rights of a citizen, the Member State is under a legal obligation to stop that violation and take action. The Court also imposes increasingly many obligations on Member States to prevent interferences with human rights by private parties.[67] In addition, the ECtHR will assess how governmental organisations and the judiciary have arrived at their decision in national procedures, meaning that when two private parties go to court over a privacy violation, they cannot submit that claim to the ECtHR as such, as a citizen can only complain about the action or inaction of a governmental organisation, but they can submit a case to the ECtHR in which they complain about the decision of the judge (the judiciary being a branch of government). The same applies when a citizen's right to privacy is violated by a company; she cannot go to the ECtHR over this matter directly, but can submit a claim under the Convention mechanism stressing that the government failed in protecting her against human rights violations by private parties. This means that in reality, the fact that citizens

[63] Council Framework Decision 2008/977/JHA on the protection of personal data processed in the framework of police and judicial cooperation in criminal matters [2008] OJ L350/60.

[64] See eg GDPR, Article 37(1)(a).

[65] C Mak, *Fundamental rights in European contract law (Vol. 12)* (Kluwer Law International BV, 2008).

[66] D Xenos, *The positive obligations of the state under the European Convention of Human Rights* (Routledge, 2012).

[67] *Hatton and others v the United Kingdom* App no 36022/97 (EctHR, 8 July 2003); *Fadeyeva v Russia* App no 55723/00 (EctHR, 9 July 2005); *Ledyayeva, Dobrokhotova, Zolotareva and Romashina v Russia* App nos 53157/99, 53247/99, 53695/00 and 56850/00 (EctHR, 26 October 2006).

cannot bring claims against private parties under the ECHR has become less and less important, to the point of being redundant.

X. Transfer of Data

Both courts also take a more proactive stance vis-à-vis the CoE, the EU and the national legislator, in particular when it comes to cross-border data transfer (discussed in this section) and the assessment of legal regimes facilitating the processing of personal data (discussed in the next section). The GDPR is essentially a market regulation instrument. Like similar instruments, it lays down a level playing field for organisations operating within the EU. It allows for agreements between the EU and other countries and for bilateral agreements between EU based and non-EU based organisations with respect to cross-border data transfer. Essential to such agreements is that the non-EU country or organisation commits to the EU data protection regime. In order to harmonise cross-border data trade and ensure that non-EU based organisations do not have competitive advantages, they must adhere to an essentially equivalent level of protection.[68] Likewise, if non-EU based organisations want to do business within the EU, they must fully comply with the GDPR.[69] As a result, a large proportion of internationally operating organisations have to comply with EU data protection rules either because they do business in the EU, share data with EU-based partners or gather data about EU-citizens.[70]

The ECHR contains no provision on the transfer of data from Europe to non-European countries or vice versa. Nevertheless, the ECtHR has imposed increasingly strict obligations on this point. For instance, it is not always clear what foreign intelligence agencies do with the data they receive from their European counterparts. There are suspicions that regimes (ab)use these data to locate and incarcerate (or worse) dissidents and opposition leaders. The Court is aware of this problem and notes that 'the mentioned lack of specification in the provisions regulating the communication of personal data to other states and international organisations gives some cause for concern with respect to the possible abuse of the rights of individuals.'[71]

The Court speaks out even more clearly with regard to the receipt of data by European intelligence services from their non-European counterparts, because it is not always clear how those data have been collected and whether they have been gathered in a way that would have been legal in Europe. This creates the risk of circumventing legal restrictions. For example, if US intelligence agencies are bound by fewer rules than their European counterparts, the former could simply

[68] GDPR, Article 44 and further.
[69] GDPR, Article 3.
[70] A Bradford, 'The Brussels effect' (2012) 107 *Northwestern University Law Review* 1.
[71] *Centrum för Rätttvisa v Sweden* App no 35252/08 (EctHR, 19 June 2018).

collect the data that the latter want and then pass them on to them. 'Indeed, as the Venice Commission noted, as States could use intelligence sharing to circumvent stronger domestic surveillance procedures and/or any legal limits which their agencies might be subject to as regards domestic intelligence operations, a suitable safeguard would be to provide that the bulk material transferred could only be searched if all the material requirements of a national search were fulfilled and this was duly authorised in the same way as a search of bulk material obtained by the signals intelligence agency using its own techniques.'[72] Thus, both on data transfer from Europe to non-European countries and vice versa, the ECtHR has set restrictions.

XI. Legal Regimes

Both courts have changed their stance when it comes to their discretion to not only assess the activities of the judicial and the executive branch, but also of the legislative branch. Initially, both courts (and in particular the ECtHR) were very reticent on this point and focussed primarily on individual cases, balancing the specific interests of a citizen against the public interests served by limiting her rights. They generally did not, however, go beyond the particularities of the case and refused to assess legal regimes giving rise to structural data violations as such, as this was deemed to fall under the democratic prerogative of the legislative branch. Gradually, both courts have decided to leave this stance and evaluate as such legislative regimes that create a legal basis for data processing operations that affect thousands or millions of citizens.

The general background for this move is that both within the European Union and the Council of Europe, it is becoming increasingly clear that certain organisations and countries simply do not or only marginally care about the rulings of both courts. They simply pay the damages imposed on them in an individual case when a violation is established, but leave in place the legal regime or policy that gave rise to the breach. As a result, there are sometimes many thousands of cases brought before them on the same point (eg, resulting from a law which allows prison authorities to monitor all prisoners' communication without reason). To this end, the CoE has introduced so-called pilot judgments,[73] and the EU is looking at ways to legally address countries like Poland and Hungary for their blatant disregard for the rule of law.[74]

The specific reason for this move within the fields of privacy and data protection law is that modern data processing operations are often not so much targeted at specific individuals or small groups, but rather, affect large groups or simply every

[72] *Big Brother Watch* (n 27).
[73] www.echr.coe.int/documents/pilot_judgment_procedure_eng.pdf.
[74] ec.europa.eu/commission/presscorner/detail/en/ip_21_1524.

citizen. This means, on the one hand, that granting individual rights to specific citizens may be misplaced in such a constellation, because the problem is not that a specific individual has been affected by the data collection (the data collection is not even targeted at the individual) and, on the other hand, that the issue with large scale data processing operations is more about abstract questions of legality and rule of law than about the protection of individual interests. In addition, as previously, individuals often do not know whether they have been affected by such data processing operations, and in modern society, their data are processed by thousands of parties, which makes reliance on subjective rights practically infeasible. Therefore, both courts have increasingly chosen to focus their attention on an assessment of the legal regime as such.

The European Court of Human Rights goes furthest in this regard and has formulated nine minimum conditions that regulatory regimes that provide the legal basis for processing personal data must meet: (1) the law must be accessible, and it must lay down (2) the scope of application of the measures, (3) the duration of the measures, (4) the procedures for processing the data, (5) authorisation procedures, (6) ex post supervision of the implementation of the measures, (7) the conditions for communicating data to and receiving data from counterparts, (8) the moment parties affected will be notified of the processing of their data and (9) the available remedies for those affected. Anyone can complain about a potential violation of these minimum requirements, not only those that can prove they were affected by the data processing operations.[75]

The CJEU follows the ECtHR down this path. Becoming increasingly activist over the years, it is willing to assess legal regimes as such and draw far-reaching conclusions about them. It does so particularly when it comes to the transfer of data to non-EU countries. The *Schrems* cases, for example, had the effect that data transfers from the EU to the US, which is the largest data flow to and from the EU, were in principle unlawful.[76] In doing so, it went against the decision of the European Commission, which had adopted a somewhat peculiar regime to ensure that data could be transferred to the United States without much in the way of legal safeguards.[77] Also, the CJEU gives detailed advice on what international

[75] B van der Sloot, 'The quality of law: How the European Court of Human Rights gradually became a European Constitutional Court for privacy cases' (2020) 11 *Journal of Intellectual Property, Information Technology and E-Commerce Law* 160; G Malgieri and P de Hert, 'One European legal framework for surveillance: The EctHR's expanded legality testing copied by the CJEU' in V Mitsilegas and N Vavoula (eds), *Surveillance and privacy in the digital age: European, transatlantic and global perspectives* (Bloomsbury Publishing, 2021) 255.

[76] *Facebook Ireland and Schrems* (n 58).

[77] Commission Decision 2000/520/EC pursuant to Directive 95/46/EC of the European Parliament and of the Council on the adequacy of the protection provided by the safe harbour privacy principles and related frequently asked questions issued by the US Department of Commerce [2000] OJ L215/7; Council Decision (EU) 2016/920 on the signing, on behalf of the European Union, of the Agreement between the United States of America and the European Union on the protection of personal information relating to the prevention, investigation, detection, and prosecution of criminal offences [2016] OJ L154/1.

agreements on data transfers should look like in order to be compliant with the European Union's Charter of Fundamental Rights.[78] In doing so, it sometimes seems to go so far as to take the seat of the EU regulator.

XII. Analysis

Because of the discrepancy between the legal acquis of the CoE and the EU, it matters for the outcome of a legal dispute whether it is treated under EU law or the ECHR, and whether it is judged by the CJEU or the ECtHR. This means that one party may favour going to the CJEU, while the other might prefer the ECtHR, which entails not only the danger of forum shopping but also of explicit inconsistencies between the judgments of both courts on the same case. This is no less true for the rights to privacy and data protection. But amid this legislative quagmire created by the EU, the two courts have taken it upon themselves to ensure, as far as possible and within their competence and jurisdiction, consistency and clarity regarding the relationship between the rights to privacy and data protection and the interpretation of both rights in concrete cases and contexts. This chapter has discussed several points on which the courts have either chosen to take the same path or follow each other's lead. These can be briefly summarised as follows:

Figure 1 How the two Courts have harmonised in their interpretation of the right to privacy and data protection

	ECtHR	CJEU
Right to privacy	ECtHR takes the lead, has an elaborate body of jurisprudence.	CJEU follows/has virtually no jurisprudence on this right, separate from the right to data protection.
Right to data protection	Not in the ECHR; ECtHR follows EU legal acquis as far as possible.	CJEU takes the lead and has penned several revolutionary rulings.
Super right	ECtHR has turned Article 8 ECHR into a super right, protecting values that underlie the ECHR, eg human dignity, individual autonomy and personal development.	The scope of the concept of personal data has been widened significantly over time, so that in more and more legal cases, the right to data protection plays an essential role.

(continued)

[78] Opinion 1/15 of the Court on the transfer of Passenger Name Record Data from the European Union to Canada, ECLI:EU:C:2017:592.

Figure 1 ***(Continued)***

	ECtHR	CJEU
Material scope	ECtHR largely brought processing of personal data within the scope of Article 8 ECHR, adopting the standard of identifiability.	Almost all data are or can be considered 'personal data'.
Personal scope	ECtHR has chosen, under certain circumstances, to drop the requirement of personal harm.	Under the right to data protection, the *ratione materiae* and *ratione persona* principles are merged.
Private sphere	Article 8 ECHR protects the private sphere of the rights bearer.	The CJEU has interpreted the household exemption restrictively.
Public sphere	ECtHR has found that the right to privacy also applies in the public sphere, even for public figures.	Personal data gathered from the public sphere or from public sources fall under the right to data protection.
Waiver of right	ECtHR has ruled that the disclosure of data by a person does not mean she has waived her right to privacy.	CJEU has limited the processing of sensitive data having been made manifestly public by the data subject.
Abuse of right	Article 17 ECHR is not applied to Article 8 ECHR, not even when distributing child pornography.	There is no abuse of right doctrine applicable to the right to data protection in the EU.
Intelligence services	ECtHR takes the lead in overseeing intelligence agencies.	CJEU attributed itself competence over intelligence agencies.
Private sector	Disputes between private parties are covered by the ECtHR, through positive obligations or by reviewing the national court cases.	The GDPR should be mainly seen as a market regulation instrument, intended to set rules in particular for large technology companies.
Public sector	ECHR was written in order to set limits to governmental organisations' use of power.	Though there are exceptions, the EU and CJEU have limited the special position for public authorities.
Data transfers	ECtHR imposes limits on the transfer of data from Europe to outside Europe and vice versa.	GDPR essentially regulates cross-border data transfers, creating a level playing field for all parties.
Legal regimes	ECtHR has laid down nine minimum conditions for legal regimes; it also indicates how legal regimes should be changed.	CJEU assesses regulatory regimes, especially on the transfer of data to non-EU countries; it feels free to issue far-reaching legislative advice.

Given the EU's imperfect approach to lawmaking, the endeavour by the two Courts, and in particular the ECtHR, is laudable. It ensures legal consistency between the frameworks of the CoE and the EU. This, however, was of course the EU's task in the first place. The fact that the EU is negligent in ensuring legal consistency in the data protection realm is visible in domains where the ECtHR cannot come to the rescue.

This is all the more painful because the EU's reason for getting involved in the data protection domain was precisely to guarantee legal consistency. The Data Protection Directive was adopted because the various EU countries had adopted different rules for the processing and transfer of personal data. This meant that if a company operated in both France, Germany and Italy, it had to abide by three different sets of rules, which were sometimes incompatible. Also, it meant that the transfer of data between different private or public sector organisations that were based in different countries was difficult and sometimes impossible. This hampered economic growth in the EU and crippled organisations in effectuating their policies. By laying down one regime for all EU countries, the hope was that the rights of citizens would be respected while at the same time allowing organisations to transfer data across European borders without further restrictions.

This goal, however, was only marginally achieved. Among others, being a Directive, countries had a large discretion as to how to implement the rules in their national legal order and consequently, did so in a wide variety of ways. This meant that although the differences were not so stark as before the introduction of the 1995 Directive, organisations still needed to abide by a different set of rules when sharing personal data or operating in different jurisdictions. In addition, it was clear that some countries had a rather minimal implementation of the data protection rules in their legal order, while others invested in a high level of protection for citizens. Not surprisingly, many companies based their headquarters in those countries with the lowest regulatory burden. These countries often also had invested minimally in staffing their DPA. This was another element that was left to the Member States. Ireland, where many of the silicon valley tech companies had based their European headquarters, famously had 1.5 FTE available for the DPA, which had a tiny office in a storefront.

The GDPR, adopted in 2016 and coming into effect in 2018, aimed at tackling the lack of harmonisation yet again. Though much attention has been paid to supposed new GDPR rights and obligations, virtually all those were included in the 1995 Directive already or developed in the jurisprudence of the CJEU. Three things were novel. First, being a Regulation, there is less room for countries to adopt their interpretation of the rules in their national legal order. The rules in the GDPR have direct effect. Second, there is much more possibility for DPAs to collaborate or to take over investigations if one fails to adequately perform its duties. Also, the body in which the national DPAs are united, the European Data Protection Board, has gained a number of powers to set rules and intervene when necessary. Third, previously, organisations could ignore the data protection rules because the consequences were mild. Under the GDPR, their operations can be stopped permanently or a fine of up to 20 million euros or 4 per cent of the total worldwide annual turnover can be imposed.[79]

Although there were high hopes that these changes would finally lead to the harmonisation first sought in 1995, the GDPR has not lived up to its promise. There are several reasons.

First, although it is formally a Regulation, the GDPR contains many provisions which national legislators need to interpret and implement. The GDPR has been called a 'regulation light', a hybrid between a Directive and a Regulation and a RINO: Regulation in Name Only. Thus, the countries may and even should give further clarity regarding the exact interpretation of the GDPR principles in their laws. Generally, however, they have not done so. Although all EU countries have adopted a GDPR implementation law, they have only provided the most marginal concretisation of the EU rules. For example, an evaluation of the Dutch implementation law suggested: 'This evaluation makes it clear that the GDPR implementation law only has a limited meaning. It is clear that the law does not provide any further interpretation of the GDPR standards. This is probably due to the genesis of the GDPR implementation law, the limited time available for its creation and the choice for a 'policy-neutral' conversion of the existing standards. The consequence is that the added value of the implementation law is limited. This is problematic because for many parties have difficulty understanding how to effectuate the GDPR in practice.'[80]

Second, the EU has adopted many, and has proposed even more, legal instruments in the field of information, technology and digital infrastructure. Besides the GDPR, there is the Law Enforcement Directive,[81] the Open Data Directive[82] and the Regulation on the free flow of non-personal data,[83] just to name a few. In addition, the Data Governance Act,[84] the AI Act,[85] the e-Privacy Regulation,[86]

[79] See GDPR, Articles 51–84.

[80] H Winter et al., 'Bescherming gegeven?, WODC Rapport 3249' (2022) repository.wodc.nl/handle/20.500.12832/3193. Quote translated by the author of this chapter.

[81] Directive (EU) 2016/680 of the European Parliament and of the Council on the protection of natural persons with regard to the processing of personal data by competent authorities for the purposes of the prevention, investigation, detection or prosecution of criminal offences or the execution of criminal penalties, and on the free movement of such data, and repealing Council Framework Decision 2008/977/JHA [2016] OJ L 119/89.

[82] Directive 2019/1024 of the European Parliament and of the Council on open data and the re-use of public sector information (recast) [2019] OJ L172/56.

[83] Regulation 2018/1807 of the European Parliament and of the Council on a framework for the free flow of non-personal data in the European Union [2018] OJ L303/59.

[84] Regulation (EU) 2022/868 of the European Parliament and of the Council on European data governance and amending Regulation (EU) 2018/1724 (Data Governance Act) [2022] OJ L152/1.

[85] Proposal of the Commission for a Regulation of the European Parliament and of the Council laying down harmonised rules on Artificial Intelligence (Artificial Intelligence Act) and amending certain Union Legislative Acts, COM(2021) 206 final (Proposed AI Act).

[86] Proposal of the Commission for a Regulation of the European Parliament and of the Council concerning the respect for private life and the protection of personal data in electronic communications and repealing Directive 2002/58/EC (Regulation on Privacy and Electronic Communications), COM(2017) 10 final.

the Digital Services Act[87] and the Digital Markets Act[88] are under discussion. Then there are various policy initiatives, such as the European Strategy for Data,[89] the European Health Data Space,[90] the White Paper on AI,[91] the EU Open Data initiative[92] and the EU Smart Cities Market Place.[93] How these legal instruments relate to each other, however, is mostly left open, even when it is clear that various instruments contain conflicting rules. An example is the relationship between the GDPR and the Open Data Directive, the latter stressing that the GDPR must be respected when making data publicly available, without making clear what that entails. This tension has been left open by the EU ever since 2003,[94] ignoring several calls to make clear how the two legal regimes can be reconciled. It is only in recent years that the Court of Justice has provided scant clarity on this point.[95]

Third, the same occurs on Member State level. Most countries have simply implemented the GDPR in their national legal system without making clear what that means for the other national legal instruments. It should be noted here that the concept of 'personal data' has been extended considerably, so that almost all other laws in some way or another are affected by the GDPR. It is clear that it will be almost impossible to check every legal instrument on Member State level that requires or regulates the processing of personal data on the question of whether they are in conformity with the GDPR, the Law Enforcement Directive or Article 8 CFREU. This means that it is left to data controllers to assess how various legal instruments and conflicting legal requirements must be reconciled, which they have done in a wide variety of ways.[96]

Fourth, the core problem of the data protection regime in light of harmonisation is that in fact, it provides little clarity on its own. Though it is true that different from most other human rights, the right to data protection is regulated in detail, first in 34 Articles under the Data Protection Directive and now in 99 Articles under the General Data Protection Regulation, these rules often provide little more than the obvious or are elaborations of the general principles of

[87] Regulation (EU) 2022/2065 of the European Parliament and of the Council on a Single Market For Digital Services and amending Directive 2000/31/EC (Digital Services Act) [2002]OJ L277/1.

[88] Regulation (EU) 2022/1925 of the European Parliament and of the Council on contestable and fair markets in the digital sector and amending Directives (EU) 2019/1937 and (EU) 2020/1828 (Digital Markets Act) [2022] OJ L265/1.

[89] Communication from the Commission to the European Parliament, the Council, the European Economic and Social Committee and the Committee of the Regions – A European Strategy for Data, COM(2020) 66 final.

[90] Proposal of the Commission for a Regulation of the European Parliament and of the Council on the European Health Data Space, COM(2022) 197 final.

[91] Commission, White Paper on Artificial Intelligence – a European approach to excellence and trust, COM(2020) 65 final.

[92] See data.europa.eu/data/datasets?locale=en.

[93] See smart-cities-marketplace.ec.europa.eu/.

[94] Directive 2003/98/EC of the European Parliament and of the Council on the re-use of public sector information [2003] OJ L345/90.

[95] Case C-439/19 *Latvijas Republikas Saeima* ECLI:EU:C:2021:504, [2022] 1 CMLR 9.

[96] Van der Sloot, 'Legal consistency after the General Data Protection Regulation and the Police Directive' (n 1).

necessity, proportionality and subsidiarity. Formulate a clear goal before processing personal data, process no more data than necessary for that goal, delete the data when no longer necessary for that goal, store data safely and securely, etc. In practice, parties processing data struggle with what those general principles mean for their specific situation: when is a goal specific enough and when is a subsequently goal exactly 'incompatible' with the original purpose for processing data; against which standards should the data quality principle be tested; can multiparty computation be considered to result in data anonymisation, and if so, under which conditions; etc.? While the other human rights benefit from an elaborate system of case law by the European Court of Human Rights, in which it specifies in detail what the general principles of necessity, proportionality and subsidiarity mean in specific contexts, this does not hold true for the right to data protection, which is left with a small number of judgments by the CJEU.

Fifth, from the beginning (in contrast to the American sectoral approach), the EU has opted for an omnibus approach to data protection, which means that the same set of principles applies to all types of data processing by all types of parties (with small deviations for law enforcement authorities). Although this approach has worked well for a long time, it is challenged by technical and societal developments. A general regime with a set of fairly broadly defined rules worked well in the 1990s, when only a small number of parties had access to large databases and the processing techniques needed to analyse those data. This is different in contemporary society. Data and data processing techniques have been democratised and are consequently used for increasingly diverse purposes. Nudging citizens in smart cities is incomparable to sick leave registration by employers, the sharing of customer data by banks with the tax authorities is fundamentally different from the use of patient data for total genome analysis, making drone images for a birthday party video has a different nature than a smart toilet that meticulously analyses the user's stool. Yet the same general regime applies to all of these processes.

Sixth, this means that a very general set of open norms applies to virtually all situations in which personal data is processed; neither the European Union nor the Member States have taken it upon themselves to provide more clarity about what these general rules actually mean or how they should be interpreted in practice. Neither has the European Data Protection Board nor the national Data Protection Authorities, give or take a handful of guidelines. There was the hope that sectors would develop codes of conduct themselves in which they would detail what the general principles would mean for their specific sectors, for example a code of conduct by the universities of a Member State, a code of conduct on the use of personal data for total genome analysis or a code of conduct on the processing of personal data by financial institutions. So far, however, only six codes of conduct have been approved EU wide.[97]

[97] edpb.europa.eu/our-work-tools/accountability-tools/register-codes-conduct-amendments-and-extensions-art-4011_en.

Figure 2 Lack of harmonisation in the field of data protection

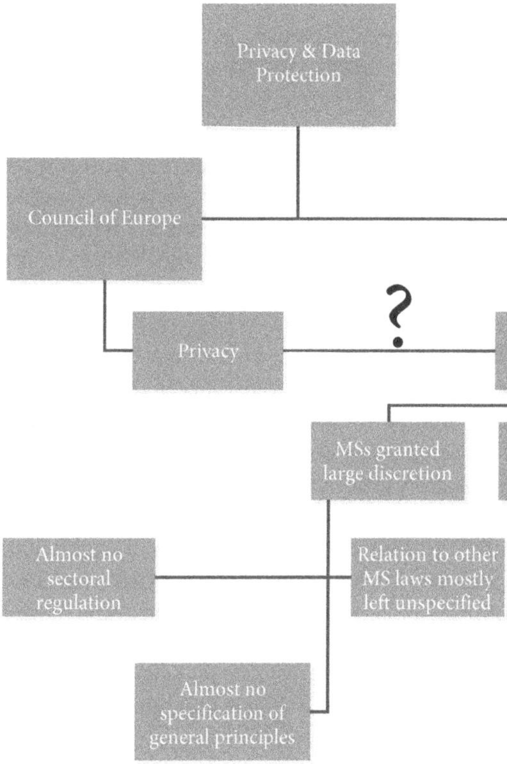

Seventh, although the EU has formally separated the right to data protection from the right to privacy, it has never made clear how the two rights relate to and differ from each other. This has resulted in a large number of academic papers on this matter, with widely varying positions and interpretations.[98] Yet there is no official guidance on this point by the EU legislator, nor has it ever been precisely clear what led the authors of the Charter to separate those two rights and whether, when doing so, they fully understood the consequences of their decision. More generally, the EU has never explained how its move to enter the domain of fundamental rights should be seen and how its regulation on this point should be understood

[98] See eg R Gellert and S Gutwirth, 'The legal construction of privacy and data protection' (2013) 29 *Computer Law & Security Review* 522; P De Hert and S Gutwirth, 'Privacy, data protection and law enforcement. Opacity of the individual and transparency of power' (2006) *Privacy and the criminal law* 61; LA Bygrave, 'Privacy and data protection in an international perspective' (2010) 56 *Scandinavian studies in law* 165; J Kokott and C Sobotta, 'The distinction between privacy and data protection in the jurisprudence of the CJEU and the ECtHR' (2013) 3 *International Data Privacy Law* 222; A Forde, 'The Conceptual Relationship Between Privacy and Data Protection' (2016) 1 *Cambridge Law Review* 135.

vis-à-vis the legislative acquis of the Council of Europe and the jurisprudence of the European Court of Human Rights.

Eighth, it is clear that there are significant discrepancies in how the EU and the CoE, CJEU and the ECtHR, approach fundamental rights matters. For example, there are stark differences between the prevention of discrimination under Article 14 ECHR and the EU laws on specific forms of discrimination, such as on grounds of race and ethnic origin (Directive 2000/43/EC), discrimination at work on grounds of religion or belief, disability, age or sexual orientation (Directive 2000/78/EC), equal treatment for men and women in matters of employment and occupation (Directive 2006/54/EC), equal treatment for men and women in the access to and supply of goods and services (Directive 2004/113/EC) and discrimination based on age, disability, sexual orientation and religion or belief beyond the workplace (Directive Proposal (COM 2008/462). To provide another example, there are stark differences between the EU's approach to liability of internet intermediaries, focusing on safe harbours and notice and take action regimes, and the ECtHR's focus on the freedom of expression and obligations for publishers.[99]

In conclusion, the EU seems to care little about legal consistency. To the extent that there is legal consistency, this is mostly thanks to the efforts of the two European Courts, and in particular the European Court of Human Rights. On points where the ECtHR has no competence, however, legal uncertainty remains, such as with respect to the relationship between the GDPR and other data related EU frameworks, the exact meaning of the general principles contained in the GDPR and the relationship and difference between the EU fundamental rights to privacy and data protection. Given the high number of data regulations that have recently been adopted or proposed, this may pose a real and significant danger in the future. Although the EU wants to be the world's data and AI regulator, through what is known as the Brussels effect,[100] pride goes before a fall.

[99] B van der Sloot, 'Welcome to the Jungle: the liability of internet intermediaries for privacy violations in Europe' (2015) 6 *Journal of Intellectual Property, Information Technology and E-Commerce Law* 211.

[100] A Bradford, *The Brussels effect: How the European Union rules the world* (Oxford University Press, 2020).

PART III

Legal Consistency between the Various EU Frameworks

4

Regulatory Siblings: The Unfair Commercial Practices Directive Roots of the AI Act

CATALINA GOANTA

I. Introduction

During the past two years, the European Commission has been issuing one regulatory proposal after another in the field of technology regulation. One of the proposed instruments is the Artificial Intelligence Act (AI Act),[1] which is expected to shape the future of technology innovation on the internal market, while proposing stringent normative boundaries for the development of artificial intelligence (AI) in the European Union space.

A quick read of the lengthy AI Act proposal reveals a highly complex and cumbersome piece of regulation, which might further complicate harms arising out of the deployment of AI products, rather than clarify the regulatory boundaries of its use. Particularly for the consumer protection reader, Article 5 is reminiscent of an earlier, principle-based regulatory instrument, namely the Unfair Commercial Practices Directive (UCPD).[2] In a very similar fashion, Article 5 of the AI Act sets forth a prohibition of certain artificial intelligence practices, just as Article 5 of the UCPD establishes a prohibition of unfair commercial practices and certain categories thereof. Yet the UCPD, for all its benefits, has also led to pitfalls, particularly in the harmonisation of its interpretation and enforcement.

As it currently stands, the UCPD's broad range also includes commercial practices arising out of the use of technology. In 2018, after the revelations of undisclosed data sharing with third parties by Facebook, the Italian Competition Authority fined Facebook on the ground of the company having used misleading

[1] Proposal for a Regulation of the European Parliament and of the Council Laying Down Harmonised Rules on Artificial Intelligence (Artificial Intelligence Act) and Amending Certain Union Legislative Acts, COM/2021/206 final. This contribution will focus on the text of the proposal.

[2] Directive 2005/29/EC of the European Parliament and of the Council concerning unfair business-to-consumer commercial practices in the internal market [2005] OJ L-149/22 (UCPD).

and aggressive practices.[3] The initial investigation[4] leading to this fine subsequently resulted in a second investigation which attracted, in 2021, another fine for Facebook's lack of compliance with the earlier warnings.[5] While this move was not followed by the rest of the authorities in Member States with powers to enforce the UCPD, it proved that not just data protection, but also the manipulation of consumer behaviour in commercial transactions, can be sanctionable activities on the digital internal market. This is all the more important since the General Data Protection Regulation (GDPR)[6] has played a central role in remedying harms arising in the data economy.[7] So much so, that the attention paid to data protection enforcement as a *sui generis* Internet legal framework undermined enforcement in other regulation sectors, such as the UCPD.[8]

Given the UCPD's structure, combining a list of prohibited practices, special tests for misleading and aggressive practices, as well as a general unfairness test, it could be argued that it already possesses all the necessary future-proof features for a regulatory instrument that has the flexibility to be applied to a very wide range of technological practices, while also not specifically defining them. Yet the proposal of a separate regulation aimed at governing technologies defined as 'artificial intelligence' will give rise to certain tensions with existing regimes. This chapter will explore the tensions arising out of the similarities and potential overlaps of the manipulation tests in the AI Act and the UCPD. This comparison is followed by the introduction of the concept of 'regulatory siblings' in the European Union landscape: similar or identical legal rules used across different legal instruments, which may sound the same but have very different interpretations and thereby create risks for legal consistency.

To better understand regulatory siblings in the context of principled-based regulation, this chapter proposes a comparative analysis of Article 5 of the UCPD and Article 5 of the AI Act proposal, aimed at fleshing out the similarities between the AI Act and the UCPD relating to terminology and concepts. In doing so, the chapter first describes both texts and further extracts their common characteristics. It additionally offers insights for the interpretation of these characteristics

[3] 'AGCM – Autorita' Garante Della Concorrenza e Del Mercato', en.agcm.it/en/media/press-releases/2018/12/Facebook-fined-10-million-Euros-by-the-ICA-for-unfair-commercial-practices-for-using-its-subscribers%E2%80%99-data-for-commercial-purposes.

[4] 'AGCM – Autorita' Garante Della Concorrenza e Del Mercato', en.agcm.it/en/media/detail?id=a275df5f-079b-4772-9870-3148c9ca558c.

[5] 'Facebook's Dodgy Defaults Face More Scrutiny in Europe' (*TechCrunch*, 2020) techcrunch.com/2020/01/24/facebooks-dodgy-defaults-face-more-scrutiny-in-europe/.

[6] Regulation (EU) 2016/679 of the European Parliament and of the Council of 27 April 2016 on the protection of natural persons with regard to the processing of personal data and on the free movement of such data, and repealing Directive 95/46/EC (General Data Protection Regulation) [2016] OJ L-119/1 (GDPR).

[7] 'Meta Hit with ~$275M GDPR Penalty for Facebook Data-Scraping Breach' (*TechCrunch*, 2022) techcrunch.com/2022/11/28/facebook-gdpr-penalty/.

[8] F Zuiderveen Borgesius, N Helberger and A Reyna, 'The perfect match?a closer look at the relationship between eu consumer law and data protection law' (2017) 54 (5) *Common Market Law Review* 1427–65.

on the basis of UCPD case law from the Court of Justice of the European Union (CJEU). Lastly, the chapter critically addresses some problematic concepts embedded in the Article 5 AI Act proposal in the light of the legal uncertainty raised by the prior application of the general test in Article 5 UCPD.

II. The UCPD as a Technology Regulation Instrument

A. A Crash Introduction to the UCPD

In order to understand the similarities and differences between Articles 5 of the UCPD and the AI Act proposal, it is first necessary to understand their contexts. The UCPD was adopted in 2005, with the goal of improving consumer confidence and cross-border trade. In doing so, the European regulator looked at commercial practices occurring before, during and after a business-to-consumer transaction.[9] The UCPD reflects the field of unfair competition, also known as unfair trade law, which has a dual purpose: on the one hand, to protect consumers from manipulative practices which would negatively impact their decision-making processes; on the other hand, as a result, to protect competitors from dishonest businesses practices that can harm the market at the same time.[10] Its rules include requirements for businesses to provide clear and accurate information to consumers, to be transparent about the nature of their products and services, and to refrain from using aggressive or misleading tactics in their advertising.

The UCPD Preamble further clarifies its scope. According to Recital 7, the UCPD 'addresses commercial practices directly related to influencing consumers' transactional decisions in relation to products', and excludes other forms of commercial communication, such as that targeting investors. Furthermore, Recital 15 clarifies that it includes commercial communication, advertising and marketing targeting consumers. Moreover, Article 2(d) defines business-to-consumer commercial practices as 'any act, omission, course of conduct or representation, commercial communication including advertising and marketing, by a trader, directly connected with the promotion, sale or supply of a product to consumers'. This also includes services, in addition to products.[11] While this definition

[9] Article 3(1) UCPD.

[10] H Collins (ed), *The Forthcoming EC Directive on Unfair Commercial Practices* (Kluwer Law International, 2004); M Durovic, *European Law on Unfair Commercial Practices and Contract Law* (Hart Publishing, 2016); N van Eijk, C J Hoofnagle and E Kannekens, 'Unfair Commercial Practices' (2017) 3 *European Data Protection Law Review* 325; OK Osuji, 'Business-to-Consumer Harassment, Unfair Commercial Practices Directive and the UK – A Distorted Picture of Uniform Harmonization?' (2011) 34 *Journal of Consumer Policy* 437.

[11] European Commission, Guidance on the interpretation and application of Directive 2005/29/EC (C/2021/9320) [2021] OJ C-526/1. See also Case C-388/13, *Nemzeti Fogyasztóvédelmi Hatóság v UPC Magyarország kft.* ECLI:EU:C:2015:225, [2015] 3 CMLR 25, para 35; C-304/08, *Zentrale zur Bekämpfung unlauteren Wettbewerbs eV v Plus Warenhandelsgesellschaft mbH* ECLI:EU:C:2010:12, [2010] ECR I-217, para 39.

is very broad when it comes to the commercial implications of the relationship between businesses and consumers, it does not reflect the full spectrum of practices in which businesses may engage, such as practices which involve businesses and citizens (instead of consumers), with the prime example being that of political advertising.[12] This restriction can be understood to have been implemented in an attempt to not overlap with other policy sectors, in this case more geared towards fundamental rights. However, in more recent times the interplay between the market of political advertising and commercial practices has raised new questions relating to the potential inspiration, if not harmonisation, which different policy fields could benefit from when dealing with considerable similarities.[13]

Still, even with these sectoral limitations, it is noteworthy that when it comes to the practices of technology companies, they will often make statements about the accuracy, parameters or terms for the use of their technologies. To the extent these technologies are consumer-facing, the UCPD applies. This was the case in the aftermath of the Cambridge Analytica scandal, where Facebook was found to have deceived its users in relation to its data sharing practices. While telling consumers a more concise and less concerning version of what it was doing with their data, Facebook was funnelling data at an industrial level through its Graph Application Programming Interface to a wide volume of third parties, without having obtained specific consent for this distribution.[14] Data sharing practices such as in the Cambridge Analytica public scandal showed the legal and regulatory community the potential of the UCPD to address harms arising out of data collection and profiling through machine learning.

In 2019, the UCPD was updated through the Modernisation Directive,[15] which added a number of novel provisions,[16] and overall made the UCPD more fit to deal with business practices in the digital economy.[17] The UCPD is one of the Directives in the consumer acquis currently undergoing a fairness check led by the European Commission, to explore additional ways in which it can be consolidated even further to meet the needs of a fast-moving digital market.[18]

[12] For instance, political advertising practices, albeit facilitated by business activity, are generally not covered by the UCPD. See G De Gregorio and C Goanta, 'The Influencer Republic: Monetizing Political Speech on Social Media' (2022) 23 *German Law Journal* 204; N Helberger, T Dobber and C de Vreese, 'Towards Unfair Political Practices Law: Learning Lessons from the Regulation of Unfair Commercial Practices for Online Political Advertising' (2021) 12 *JIPITEC.*

[13] Helberger, Dobber and de Vreese (n 12).

[14] C Goanta and S Mulders, '"Move Fast and Break Things": Unfair Commercial Practices and Consent on Social Media' (2019) 8(4) *Journal of European Consumer and Market Law* 136–46.

[15] Directive (EU) 2019/2161 of the European Parliament and of the Council of 27 November 2019 amending Council Directive 93/13/EEC and Directives 98/6/EC, 2005/29/EC and 2011/83/EU of the European Parliament and of the Council as regards the better enforcement and modernisation of Union consumer protection rules [2019] OJ L 328 (Modernisation Directive).

[16] Including the formalisation of case law on the scope of the UCPD with respect to both services and products, see Article 3 Modernisation Directive.

[17] B Duivenvoorde, 'The Liability of Online Marketplaces under the Unfair Commercial Practices Directive, the E-commerce Directive and the Digital Services Act' (2022) 11(2) *Journal of European Consumer and Market Law* 43–52.

[18] European Commission, 'Digital Fairness Check', ec.europa.eu/info/law/better-regulation/have-your-say/initiatives/13413-Digital-fairness-fitness-check-on-EU-consumer-law_en..

B. Article 5 UCPD

The tiered structure of the UCPD reflects three parts which guide how the Directive is supposed to be applied. First, the UCPD straight out bans practices listed in its Annex 1. For instance, dishonestly claiming to be a signatory of a code of conduct is a practice which is in all circumstances considered to be a misleading commercial practice.[19] Similarly, falsely limiting the availability of products and services is also considered unfair, and in particular a misleading commercial practice.[20] Examples of aggressive practices are also covered by the Annex. For instance, ads including direct exhortations targeting children, to buy products or to persuade parents to buy products, is considered to be not merely a misleading practice, as much as an actually aggressive practice.[21] Second, the UCPD operates with specific tests in Articles 6–9. These are tests for misleading actions, misleading omissions and aggressive practices. The tests introduce specific contextual details that may be taken into account to determine the unlawful nature of commercial practices. Last, if practices are difficult to define under the Annex or the special tests, the UCPD also provides for a general test in Article 5.

According to Article 5(1), unfair practices are prohibited. To test the unfairness of a commercial practice, subparagraph 2 introduced two conditions:

(i) That a commercial practice is contrary to the requirements of professional diligence; and
(ii) That it 'it materially distorts or is likely to materially distort the economic behaviour with regard to the product of the average consumer whom it reaches or to whom it is addressed, or of the average member of the group when a commercial practice is directed to a particular group of consumers.'

The two conditions are cumulative. On the one hand, the test reflects professional diligence, defined in Article 2(h) as 'the standard of special skill and care which a trader may reasonably be expected to exercise towards consumers, commensurate with honest market practice and/or the general principle of good faith in the trader's field of activity'. In other words, this echoes the expectation that businesses should not engage with consumers to the detriment of their interests, namely in an attempt to negatively manipulate them, but rather initiate transactions in good faith.[22] On the other hand, the test makes reference to specific concepts such as 'material distortion', 'economic behaviour' and 'average consumer' as an implied standard for the average targeted consumer. The average consumer qualification has been a subject of intense debate in European private law literature,[23] particularly

[19] Point 1 of Annex I UCPD.
[20] Point 7 of Annex I UCPD.
[21] Point 28 of Annex I UCPD.
[22] Good faith is however not defined in the Directive.
[23] R Incardona and C Poncibò, 'The Average Consumer, the Unfair Commercial Practices Directive, and the Cognitive Revolution' (2007) 30 *Journal of Consumer Policy* 21; B Duivenvoorde, *The Consumer Benchmarks in the Unfair Commercial Practices Directive* (Springer, 2015).

due to the fact that the UCPD does not see it as a statistical or economic concept. The average consumer is rather a doctrinal benchmark reflecting a reasonably well-informed and reasonably observant and circumspect consumer, when taking into account social, cultural and linguistic factors.[24] In other words, '[t]he average consumer test is not a statistical test. National courts and authorities will have to exercise their own faculty of judgement, having regard to the case-law of the Court of Justice, to determine the typical reaction of the average consumer in a given case'.[25]

In addition, Article 5(3) also makes reference to a special average consumer, namely the vulnerable consumer, as part of a 'clearly identifiable group of consumers who are particularly vulnerable to the practice or the underlying product because of their mental or physical infirmity, age or credulity in a way which the trader could reasonably be expected to foresee'.

III. The AI Act: Another Layer of Regulation

The proposal on the AI Act, dating from 2021, aims to 'improve the functioning of the internal market by laying down a uniform legal framework in particular for the development, marketing and use of artificial intelligence in conformity with Union values'.[26] In doing so, the European Union hopes to set a global example in the governance of new technologies, as it is said to have achieved in the context of the GDPR.[27] The AI Act is part of the European AI Strategy, which pursues two goals. First, the Strategy aims to create an innovative Digital Single Market, in an attempt to be competitive on the international technology playing field. Second, it aims to promote European Union values, such as those reflected by the European Charter of Fundamental Rights, at the heart of new technologies, all while supporting legal certainty.[28]

It is outside the scope of this chapter to give a comprehensive overview of the AI Act. This chapter will focus on Article 5, and in particular on the prohibitions enshrined therein. Article 5 enumerates and prohibits a list of so-called 'artificial intelligence practices', namely:

(i) The commercialisation and use of AI systems that 'deploy[..] subliminal techniques beyond a person's consciousness in order to materially distort a person's behaviour in a manner that causes or is likely to cause that person or another person physical or psychological harm';

[24] Recital 18 of UCPD Preamble.
[25] ibid.
[26] Recital 1 of AI Act preamble.
[27] N Helberger and N Diakopoulos, 'The European AI Act and How It Matters for Research into AI in Media and Journalism' (2022) 0 *Digital Journalism* 1.
[28] ibid.

(ii) The commercialisation and use of AI systems aimed at exploiting vulnerable persons 'due to their age, physical or mental disability, in order to materially distort the behaviour of a person pertaining to that group in a manner that causes or is likely to cause that person or another person physical or psychological harm';

(iii) The commercialisation and use of AI systems by or on behalf of public authorities aimed at evaluating or classifying 'the trustworthiness of natural persons over a certain period of time based on their social behaviour or known or predicted personal or personality characteristics', with rankings ('social scores') leading to any of the following two options (or both):

   a. Discriminatory treatment for natural persons or groups in situations unrelated to the contexts in which the original data generation or collection took place;
   b. Discriminatory treatment of natural persons or groups which is considered unjustified or disproportionate;

(iv) Real-time remote biometric identification for purposes of law enforcement, unless this is strictly necessary for one of the following goals:

   a. Targeting the search for specific potential crime victims;
   b. Preventing terrorist acts or other public safety dangers;
   c. Finding criminals.

Sub-paragraphs 2, 3 and 4 continue to address more details relating to biometric identification.

The four practices identified in Article 5 fall into two main categories. A first category of commercial practices (*private practices*) entails 'the placing on the market, putting into service or use of an AI system' and includes Articles 5(1)(a) and (b). This category seems to govern business practices on consumer markets, even though the terminology of 'person' is used instead of 'consumer'. The second category of practices (*public practices*) reflects the same terminology, namely 'the placing on the market, putting into service or use of an AI system', but this time it also involves a public administration component. Article 5(1)(c) refers to 'public authorities' or practices 'on behalf of public authorities', and Article 5(1)(d) refers to 'publicly accessible spaces' and 'law enforcement'. For the purposes of a comparison with a consumer law instrument such as the UCPD, this chapter will only address the first category, namely private practices.

IV. Comparing the Two Articles 5

A. Mapping Similarities

So far, Sections II and III were focused on providing the basic characteristics of two articles from two separate legal instruments which bear considerable similarities – and even the same numbering. Earlier literature on the AI Act has already noted the similarities between the two Articles 5 discussed in this chapter. According to Veale and Zuiderveen Borgesius, the AI Act adds little to existing EU law, because, among others, the two prohibited practices regulating manipulation (referred to as private practices above), and which the authors call 'manipulative systems', resemble the UCPD.[29] In what follows, this resemblance will be explored in more depth, to reflect upon whether such resemblance is desirable to start with. While the AI Act is still merely a proposal, the UCPD has been applied to a considerable number of industries and commercial practices. The purpose of the comparison is to determine what interpretational pitfalls have been identified in the text of Article 5 UCPD, and consider whether these pitfalls may be risks for the consistent interpretation of Article 5 AI Act.

On the basis of the analyses in Sections II and III, it can be noted that the overlap between the two articles only takes into account the first category of practices under the AI Act (private practices), as the UCPD does not address practices undertaken by public authorities.[30] Using a rather classical comparative approach in analysing the text of the two articles, Table 1 below makes an overview of the terminological similarities identified therein.

Table 1 includes highlighted terms which are common (whether in that order or another) across the two different articles. The table reveals two types of similarities:

(i) The setting of a clear prohibition of unfair commercial practices and of particular artificial intelligence practices; and
(ii) The common terminology in Articles 5(2) and (3) UCPD and 5(1)(a) and (b) AI Act.

Looking more closely at these similarities, we can notice a few specific concepts across the two instruments, namely: the material distortion of behaviour (which is economic behaviour in the UCPD and general behaviour in the AI Act); and a clearly identifiable group (UCPD) or specific group (AI Act) of vulnerable consumers (UCPD) or individuals (AI Act) on the basis of mental or physical infirmity and age (UCPD) or age and physical or mental disability (UCPD).

[29] M Veale and F Zuiderveen Borgesius, 'Demystifying the Draft EU Artificial Intelligence Act – Analysing the Good, the Bad, and the Unclear Elements of the Proposed Approach' (2021) 22 *Computer Law Review International* 97.

[30] This perspective can be in itself a source of criticism, since academic literature across multiple disciplines has identified that the identity of consumers and that of citizens often overlap. See for instance J Davies, *The European Consumer Citizen in Law and Policy* (Palgrave Macmillan, 2011); A Mol, 'Good Taste: The Embodied Normativity of the Consumer-Citizen' (2009) 2 *Journal of Cultural Economy* 269; E Porter, *The Consumer Citizen* (Oxford University Press, 2021); CH de Vreese, 'Digital Renaissance: Young Consumer and Citizen?' (2007) 611(1) *The Annals of the American Academy of Political and Social Science* 207–16.

Table 1 Selected provisions from Article 5 UCPD and Article 5 AI Act

UCPD		AI Act	
Article 5(1)	'[u]nfair commercial practices shall be prohibited.'	Article 5(1)	'[t]he following artificial intelligence practices shall be prohibited'
Article 5(2)(b)	'[…] it **materially distorts or is likely to** materially distort the economic **behaviour** with regard to the product of the average consumer whom it reaches or to whom it is addressed, or of the average member of the group when a commercial practice is directed to a particular group of consumers.'	Article 5(1)(a)	'the placing on the market, putting into service or use of an AI system that deploys subliminal techniques beyond a person's consciousness in order to **materially distort** a person's **behaviour** in a manner that causes **or is likely to** cause that person or another person physical or psychological harm'
Article 5(4)	'[i]n particular, commercial practices shall be unfair which: (a) are misleading as set out in Articles 6 and 7, or (b) are aggressive as set out in Articles 8 and 9.'		
Article 5(3)	'commercial practices which **are likely to materially distort** the economic **behaviour** only of a **clearly identifiable group** of consumers who are particularly **vulnerable** to the practice or the underlying product because of their **mental or physical infirmity**, **age** or credulity in a way which the trader could reasonably be expected to foresee, shall be assessed from the perspective of the average member of that group. This is without prejudice to the common and legitimate advertising practice of making exaggerated statements or statements which are not meant to be taken literally.'	Article 5(1)(b)	'the placing on the market, putting into service or use of an AI system that exploits any of the **vulnerabilities** of a **specific group** of persons due to their **age, physical or mental disability**, in order to **materially distort** the **behaviour** of a person pertaining to that group in a manner that causes or **is likely to** cause that person or another person physical or psychological harm'

So how should we interpret the similarities between these articles, and what do they mean?

B. A General versus a Specific Prohibition

Article 5(1) UCPD sets out a general prohibition to use unfair commercial practices, and it outlines a general test to determine what may amount to an unfair commercial practice. Furthermore, according to Article 5(4), certain types of practices (misleading and aggressive) are mentioned as a particular category of prohibited practices. Similarly, Article 5(1) AI Act lists a number of particular artificial intelligence practices which are prohibited.[31] This reveals the similarity in approach between the two legal instruments, namely to create categories of prohibited practices, loosely defined, and with their own self-standing tests. The difference is that while in the AI Act these tests are contained within one article, in the UCPD, the practices are further elaborated upon in subsequent articles.

As can be observed, a general prohibition is missing from the AI Act, as artificial intelligence practices are not by themselves a harmful category; it is only manipulative practices that are considered to be problematic. By contrast, even though the UCPD also does not prohibit all commercial practices, it does single out and define an entire category of unwanted practices under the umbrella of unfairness, loosely characterised by the existence of deceit that may result in consumer manipulation.

C. Manipulation and Causality

The first cluster of terminological similarities revolve around Articles 5(2) UCPD and 5(1)(a) AI Act, where the concepts of material distortion and behaviour can be discussed. Although it must be noted that the similar concepts are built slightly differently in the causal mechanisms referred to across the two articles, they actually seem to offer protection against similar types of harms.

According to the Commission's 2021 UCPD Guidelines, the determination of whether a commercial practice materially distorts or is likely to materially distort the economic behaviour of the consumer is the test of whether the practice causes or is likely to cause a different transactional decision than the consumer would have taken in the absence of that commercial practice.[32] The Guidelines also note that the definition of 'transactional decision' is very broad, as also emphasised by the CJEU in the *Trento Sviluppo srl* case, where it was held that the definition 'covers not only the decision whether or not to purchase

[31] See Section IV(A) above.

[32] European Commission, Guidance on the interpretation and application of Directive 2005/29/EC (C/2021/9320) [2021] OJ C-526/1.

a product, but also the decision directly related to that decision, in particular the decision to enter the shop'.[33] The Commission notes that this broad concept 'allows for the UCPD to apply to a variety of cases where a trader's unfair behaviour is not limited to causing the consumer to enter into a sales or service contract'.[34] As a consequence, the causal link or the likely causal link need not be solely considered with respect to a commercial practice and a purchase decision, but also additional aspects of consumer behaviour such as entering a shop, spending more time on an Internet booking process, deciding to continue using the services of the business engaging in unfair commercial practices, clicking on links or ads on the Internet, or even continuing to use Internet services through browsing or scrolling.[35] What is more, it is not only the actual distortion of economic behaviour that is covered by Article 5(2)(b) UCPD, but also the likelihood that this behaviour has been distorted.[36] Put differently, the assessment regards the potential impact a commercial practice may have on the average or the targeted consumer.[37]

By contrast, although Article 5(1)(a) AI Act operates along similar concepts, the causal or likely causal link is part of a more convoluted test. First of all, the article includes a number of specific practices deemed as 'artificial intelligence practices', which are all defined in Article 3. According to the latter, 'placing on the market' entails 'the first making available of an AI system on the Union market';[38] 'making available on the market' entails 'any supply of an AI system for distribution or use on the Union market in the course of a commercial activity, whether in return for payment or free of charge';[39] and 'putting into service' entails the 'supply of an AI system for first use directly to the user or for own use on the Union market for its intended purpose'.[40] The causal or likely causal link bridges the aforementioned AI practices with the following additional conditions. These practices need to have a 'a significant potential to manipulate persons through subliminal techniques beyond their consciousness or exploit vulnerabilities of specific vulnerable groups such as children or persons with disabilities in order to materially distort their behaviour in a manner that is likely to cause them or another person psychological or physical harm'.[41] Recital 16 of the AI Act further clarifies that AI systems deploy 'subliminal components

[33] Case C-281/12, *Trento Sviluppo srl and Centrale Adriatica Soc. coop. arl v Autorità Garante della Concorrenza e del Mercato* ECLI:EU:C:2013:859, [2014] 1 WLR 890, para 36.

[34] European Commission, Guidance on the interpretation and application of Directive 2005/29/EC (C/2021/9320) [2021] OJ C-526/1.

[35] ibid.

[36] GB Abbamonte, 'The Unfair Commercial Practices Directive: An Example of the New European Consumer Protection Approach' (2006) 12 *Columbia Journal of European Law* 695.

[37] F Gomez, 'The Unfair Commercial Practices Directive: A Law and Economics Perspective' (2006) 2(1) *European Review of Contract Law* 4–34.

[38] Article 3(9) AI Act.

[39] Article 3(10) AI Act.

[40] Article 3(11) AI Act.

[41] AI Act, Explanatory Memorandum, §5.2.2.

individuals cannot perceive', and which are intended to materially distort a person's behaviour in a way that causes or is likely to cause that person (or someone else) physical or psychological harm.[42]

There is a lot to unpack in this test, to the extent that the article itself is very difficult to follow. In the UCPD, the concept of economic behaviour is central, and even though very specifically defined (eg in terms of transactional decisions), it still benefits from a wide interpretation, and it represents the manipulation benchmark: to the extent the behaviour is affected, there is manipulation. The AI Act speaks about the material distortion of individual behaviour not as an outcome in itself, but as a means to inflict physical or psychological harm, not only upon the person whose behaviour is materially distorted, but also upon others. Thus in other words, the subliminal techniques that lead to the material distortion of individual behaviour are supposed to cause or be likely to cause physical or psychological harm. Manipulation is not the outcome of the test; rather harm is the outcome, and manipulation is the way in which harm has been achieved. Furthermore, it has been pointed out that in this test, the AI Act also requires the element of intent, as 'the manipulator wants to intentionally but covertly make use of another's decision-making to further their own ends through exploiting some vulnerability'.[43]

Although this can be seen as a difference between the two articles, it is important to consider how the UCPD deals with consumer harms. The implicit general harm embedded in Article 5 UCPD is limiting consumer choice, and in the process, affecting consumer choice architecture.[44] Consumer harm is thus implied in the manipulation of economic behaviour. In this case, consumer harm can be a direct pecuniary loss given a purchasing decision which the consumer would not have taken in the absence of manipulation. However, a subcategory of unfair practices is that of aggressive practices, where the harm paradigm slightly changes, and where physical and psychological harm can also be considered. Although the UCPD is an unfair trade instrument which did not aim to harmonise any contractual matters at national level, its roots in the classical contractual concept of defects of consent are undeniable. As a matter of fact, in Article 9, where dealing with the context of aggressive commercial practices, the UCPD makes reference to 'harassment, coercion, including the use of physical force, or undue influence', which all have equivalents in national contract systems in concepts such as threat, undue influence or abuse of circumstances. Here, even if the underlying goal of an unfair commercial practice is to engage the consumer in a transactional decision, the psychological distress associated with threats, as well as the physical force which may result in physical harm, very much echo the types of harm and the causal discussions embedded in the AI Act.

[42] L Edwards, 'Regulating AI in Europe: four problems and four solutions' (Ada Lovelace Institute, March 2022), www.adalovelaceinstitute.org/wp-content/uploads/2022/03/Expert-opinion-Lilian-Edwards-Regulating-AI-in-Europe.pdf.

[43] Veale and Borgesius (n 29).

[44] J Trzaskowski, 'Lawful Distortion of Consumers' Economic Behaviour – Collateral Damage Under the Unfair Commercial Practices Directive' (2016) 27(1) *European Business Law Review* 25–49.

D. The Concept of Vulnerability

Moving on to the next cluster of terminological similarities identified, vulnerability is a concept that both frameworks use. Here too it can be argued that vulnerability is defined in similar ways across the UCPD and the AI Act's Articles 5.

According to the Commission, vulnerability is not merely limited to the characteristics described in UPCD Article 5(3), namely by relating to mental or physical infirmity or age. Rather, 'multi-dimensional forms of vulnerability are particularly acute in the digital environment, which is increasingly characterised by data collection on socio-demographic characteristics but also personal or psychological characteristics, such as interests, preferences, psychological profile and mood'.[45] The UCPD Guidelines further recognise the need to refer to commercial practices from the perspective of various age ranges, including, but not limited to, children, teenagers or elderly people.[46] Moreover, consumer vulnerability is linked to the condition that traders are supposed to reasonably be expected to foresee the existence of this vulnerability and its impact on the economic behaviour of vulnerable consumers. Particularly as a result of policy interest in the phenomenon of dark patterns, namely manipulative user interfaces, the Commission has taken the approach that 'the concept of vulnerability in the UCPD is dynamic and situational, meaning, for instance, that a consumer can be vulnerable in one situation but not in others'. The example offered by the Commission reflects a hypothetical situation in which some consumers may be more susceptible to manipulation through personalised digital practices, while not so much so when dealing with offline environments.[47] This is a modern interpretation of vulnerability, which at least in the European consumer *acquis* has until recently entailed a more traditional enumeration of demographic characteristics which could be detrimental to some individuals.

The AI Act does not define vulnerability, nor does it refer to the factors to be taken into account when contextualising vulnerability, as is the case with the UCPD. The only references to vulnerability in the Explanatory Memorandum revolve around the concept of exploiting vulnerabilities, and giving examples such as age (eg children as a vulnerable group) or disability (both physical and mental).[48] These examples are equally found in the UCPD, so from a terminological perspective it can be argued that the initial UCPD vulnerability framework can be read in the AI Act. What was, however, not borrowed was the recently emerged concern of the European Commission, particularly in relation to the UCPD and its implication in the regulation of dark patterns, that defining vulnerability ought to take into account a more situational context. As a result, vulnerability ought to be freed from traditional legal classifications such as those used in the wording

[45] European Commission, Guidance on the interpretation and application of Directive 2005/29/EC (C/2021/9320) [2021] OJ C-526/1.
[46] ibid.
[47] ibid.
[48] AI Act, Explanatory Memorandum, §5.2.2.

of the AI Act, to reflect a digital reality where any individual, of any age and in any circumstance can be vulnerable against a commercial surveillance system.

V. Regulatory Siblings: If it Looks Like a Duck …

The preceding section aimed to compare two legal provisions in the AI Act and the UCPD which present considerable similarities. The paragraphs selected from Article 5 UCPD and Article 5 AI Act show that the two provisions are not only terminologically, but also conceptually similar. This section critically reflects on these similarities by introducing the notion of 'regulatory siblings', namely legal rules which bear a striking terminological resemblance, if not sometimes an identical form. Comparative law literature often refers to the borrowing of specific legal rules from one system of laws to another as a 'legal transplant'.[49] As a concept with a very rich connotation, the notion of legal transplants has been increasingly used to illustrate more systematic processes of legislative borrowing,[50] all in the context of legal reforms across different jurisdictions. Regulatory siblings are different in two ways. First, because they are rooted within one legal system, across different instruments pertaining to European law, as opposed to across different legal systems. European law has an inherent goal of legal harmonisation, that brings with it important questions of consistency across the European *acquis*. Second, because legal transplants are rarely (if at all) so granular as to only envisage specific provisions, but are rather discussed in a more systematic context, whereas the regulatory siblings discussed in this chapter are examples of specific (albeit central) provisions included in different European legal instruments adopted or proposed in different industry sectors and drafted by different Directorates-General.

Regulatory siblings can be identified across many laws. In the consumer *acquis*, we can see regulatory siblings particularly in the definitions that cross-pollinated the different instruments belonging to this sector of regulation. As early as 1993, the Unfair Contract Terms Directive[51] would define the notion of consumer, yet additional consumer protection instruments added self-standing, often identical definitions of the same concept (see Table 2 below), which have even been adopted beyond consumer protection, in regulatory sectors where consumers were an important stakeholder to consider, such as platform liability.

[49] A Watson, 'Legal transplants and law reform' (1996) 92 *Law Quarterly Review* 79. See also R Michaels, 'Make or buy – a new look at legal transplants' in H Eidenmüller (ed), *Regulatory Competition in Contract Law and Dispute Resolution* (Beck, 2013).

[50] M Siems, 'Malicious Legal Transplants' (2018) 38 *Legal Studies* 103.

[51] Council Directive 93/13/EEC of 5 April 1993 on unfair terms in consumer contracts [1993] OJ L 95 (UCTD).

Table 2 The evolution of the concept of 'consumer' as a regulatory sibling

Year	Directive	Article	Definition
2005			
1993	Unfair Contract Terms Directive (consumer protection)	Article 2(b)	'consumer' means any natural person who, in contracts covered by this Directive, is acting for purposes which are outside his trade, business or profession
2011	Consumer Rights Directive[52] (consumer protection)	Article 2(1)	'consumer' means any natural person who, in contracts covered by this Directive, is acting for purposes which are outside his trade, business, craft or profession
2019	Digital Content Directive[53] (consumer protection)	Article 2(6)	'consumer' means any natural person who, in relation to contracts covered by this Directive, is acting for purposes which are outside that person's trade, business, craft, or profession
2005	UCPD (consumer protection)	Article 2(a)	'consumer' means any natural person who, in commercial practices covered by this Directive, is acting for purposes which are outside his trade, business, craft or profession
2000	E-Commerce Directive[54] (intermediary liability)	Article 2(e)	'consumer' means any natural person who is acting for purposes which are outside his or her trade, business or profession
2022	Digital Services Act[55] (intermediary liability)	Article 3(c)	'consumer' means any natural person who is acting for purposes which are outside his or her trade, business, craft, or profession

[52] Directive 2011/83/EU of the European Parliament and of the Council of 25 October 2011 on consumer rights, amending Council Directive 93/13/EEC and Directive 1999/44/EC of the European Parliament and of the Council and repealing Council Directive 85/577/EEC and Directive 97/7/EC of the European Parliament and of the Council [2011] OJ L 304 (CRD).

[53] Directive (EU) 2019/770 of the European Parliament and of the Council of 20 May 2019 on certain aspects concerning contracts for the supply of digital content and digital services [2019] OJ L 136 (Digital Content Directive).

[54] Directive 2000/31/EC of the European Parliament and of the Council of 8 June 2000 on certain legal aspects of information society services, in particular electronic commerce, in the Internal Market [2000] OJ L 178 (ECD).

[55] Regulation (EU) 2022/2065 of the European Parliament and of the Council of 19 October 2022 on a Single Market For Digital Services and amending Directive 2000/31/EC [2022] OJ L 277 (DSA).

As an alternative to regulatory siblings, legal instruments can also cross-reference other, earlier or special instruments for concepts they ought to use. For instance, in its Article 2(5), the Copyright Directive[56] makes reference to the Information Society Services Directive[57] to define 'information society services', just as the DSA in Article 3(a). This is an anchoring mechanism aiming to preserve the conceptual consistency of European law by expressly linking instruments where this is desirable from a policy perspective. Regulatory siblings have a more implicit anchoring effect. If the regulator decides to duplicate an earlier concept and introduce it independently in a new regulatory instrument, it will become self-standing. Indeed, it is always possible – particularly in judicial proceedings – to find the rationale of specific sector regulation and extend it across multiple instruments and similar concepts. However, this is less cohesive than cross-referencing the same concept from earlier instruments. Thus it can be argued that while the use of regulatory siblings does contribute to the improvement of legal consistency across laws (see Table 2 above)), there might be better ways to enhance this consistency.

Definitions are of course different than manipulation tests. They are more basic, and generally, the repetition of definitions does not create any interpretational issues, provided that they do not conflict. The manipulation tests exemplified in the two Articles 5 are more complex than that, and they depict an example of when regulatory siblings, which otherwise might lead to some coherence in fragmentation, are too much of a good thing. Two specific dangers can be highlighted here, namely overlaps that may result in the cannibalisation of the instruments' scope of application; and their specific content in this case, namely the use of a general test which is future-proof to the detriment of legal certainty.

With respect to the first danger, in illustrating the type of situations it considers as falling under the private practices cluster of Article 5 AI Act, the European Commission referred to what Veale and Borgesius rightfully identified as examples that 'border on the fantastical': '[a]n inaudible sound [played] in truck drivers' cabins to push them to drive longer than healthy and safe [where] AI is used to find the frequency maximising this effect on drivers'; and '[a] doll with integrated voice assistant [which] encourages a minor to engage in progressively dangerous behavior or challenges in the guise of a fun or cool game'.[58] The first example reflects an employment situation where the behaviour of an employee would be surveilled and influenced. While this regards a private relationship between an employer and an employee, no commercial element is involved here.[59] However, the second

[56] Directive (EU) 2019/790 of the European Parliament and of the Council of 17 April 2019 on copyright and related rights in the Digital Single Market and amending Directives 96/9/EC and 2001/29/EC [2019] OJ L 130 (Copyright Directive).

[57] Directive (EU) 2015/1535 of the European Parliament and of the Council of 9 September 2015 laying down a procedure for the provision of information in the field of technical regulations and of rules on Information Society services [2015] OJ L 241.

[58] Veale and Borgesius (n 29) 99.

[59] There is of course a commercial element in the relationship between the employer and the seller/provider of the AI system. This point should also be investigated further, particularly as an additional scope similarity between the UCPD and the AI Act, namely the coverage of parties in the supply chain around the prohibited practices.

example refers to a product, which makes the situation likely to also fall under the ambit of the UCPD.[60] The Commission acknowledges in the Explanatory Memorandum that 'other manipulative or exploitative practices affecting adults that might be facilitated by AI systems could be covered by the existing data protection, consumer protection and digital service legislation that guarantee that natural persons are properly informed and have free choice not to be subject to profiling or other practices that might affect their behaviour'.[61] However, it does not acknowledge how exactly these additional sectors of regulation can and should interact with the AI Act, and what should guide a cross-sectoral interpretation. Would judges, in applying the AI Act, have to look into the case law and doctrinal debates around the UCPD to look for complementarity? Will enforcement authorities end up informally dividing their areas of expertise and deferring activities to one another based on unclear policy objectives, as has happened with data protection and consumer authorities in the aftermath of Cambridge Analytica? The only way in which these questions can be currently answered is through speculation. This remains a rather complex issue, since the AI Act and the UCPD will most likely have a considerable overlap. It could take strenuous and long-lasting interpretation cycles to delineate this overlap even if courts take terminological similarities as a starting point. Yet if they do not, and the AI Act manipulation test to be considered is completely different from the UCPD's similar test in technical legal arguments, this may pose even worse legal certainty issues.

Turning to the similarities between the general tests in terms of regulatory techniques, regulatory siblings that overlap across sectors of legislation, particularly when the content of the overlap reflects vague rules, risk disrupting the systematisation and consistency of European law as attributes of legal certainty. In the case at hand, basing a general behaviour test for manipulative AI practices on some of the structural and conceptual elements of the UCPD may be in some ways welcomed. Although the UCPD was updated in 2019, its general unfairness test is generally considered to be future-proof: a test that enumerates a set of conditions applicable to atemporal practices and technologies. Yet what is clear from less than two decades of UCPD, is that a general unfairness test is useless without further interpretation, in the form of guidelines, case law and commentaries, aimed at clarifying the scope of the test and its conditions. It is true that this is how the law works. Subsequently, it will be the job of companies, regulators and judges to interpret such legal tests. However, harmonisation techniques that leave too much discretion in the hands of complex national and supranational actors seldom lead to legal consistency. This is currently the case of the consumer law debate around dark patterns, where the general test can theoretically fit a very wide array of interface design options that may negatively impact the consumer's choice architecture, yet drawing a clear line to determine what is an unlawful dark pattern remains highly debatable. In this context, the result has been that the general test

[60] It is worth noting that product liability legislation would also likely apply.
[61] AI Act, Explanatory Memorandum.

has been too easily applied to design options, to the extent that any manipulation may be considered a dark pattern. The same can happen with the specific tests in the AI Act. Given their wide scope, and lack of clear definitions for what 'subliminal techniques' beyond 'a person's consciousness' may be, as well as what threshold is desirable for physical or psychological harm, these tests may end up covering a considerably broader category of practices than initially considered. The resulting effect can be the trivialisation of harm, just as in the case of dark patterns: if everything is harmful, then nothing is really harmful. To reduce this risk, it is important to have a clear understanding of what legal values and conduct can be expected to be protected with the adoption of the AI Act. The adoption process of the AI Act will most certainly not remedy this; so we must look to the Commission for further initial guidelines, and hope that case law will soon be available to define some of the more convoluted concepts.

VI. Conclusion

This chapter dealt with the terminological and conceptual similarities between selected provisions of Article 5 UCPD and Article 5 AI Act. The general similarity between these provisions was noted in earlier literature, but so far no in-depth comparisons were made between the two. This chapter fills this gap. In particular, it explored similarities linked to general tests versus specific tests for prohibited practices, causal links between conditions of the tests, and individual vulnerability. The analysis resulted in the conclusion that the articles, in spite of some differences in scope and terminology, share a considerable amount of characteristics: so much so, that they can could even be labelled as regulatory siblings – a novel concept introduced in this chapter to depict similar or identical legal rules used across regulatory instruments. Regulatory siblings can bring coherence in fragmented and complex legal systems, but they can also become too much of a good thing, and pose issues related to the overlap of policy scope, leading to cannibalisation between legal instruments. In addition, these particular legal siblings, based on general tests otherwise considered future-proof, may also lead to the reduction of legal certainty due to their unpredictable application. On a conceptual level, regulatory siblings should be further investigated, particularly in the field of technology legislation.

Regulatory siblings are starting to emerge as inspiration links between existing and upcoming instruments. Acknowledging these links and using them in judicial interpretation or regulatory clarifications such as guidelines can help sharpen the intention of the European legislator. If Article 5 AI Act has elements which are visibly common to Article 5 UCPD, this source of inspiration should be clarified. This can help not only with the interpretation and delineation of legal concepts, but also promote legal consistency in the current overly complex context of European regulation.

5

Open Public Data Policies and Data Protection Law: Foes or Allies?

MARIA LILLÀ MONTAGNANI AND LAURA ZOBOLI*

I. Introduction

Increasing the openness of public data is at the heart of the EU data strategy and can be identified as the frontrunner among the initiatives to ameliorate access to and re-use of data in the European internal market.[1]

In this context, public data has been the focus of a succession of regulatory provisions at EU level, which culminated in the current set-up consisting of the Open Data Directive 2019/1024/EU (ODD)[2] and the Data Governance Act (DGA).[3] In particular, the latter seeks to expand the public data available for re-use by setting conditions for re-use of those categories of public data that are subject to existing protections, such as commercial confidentiality, intellectual property rights or data protection regulation.

This chapter intends to focus precisely on the complex relationship between open data policies and data protection at EU level as personal data protection has always represented an obstacle to the full openness of public data, considering that the fundamental rights of Articles 7 and 8 of the Charter of Fundamental of the European Union prevail over private interests of re-users.[4] In the aftermath of the adoption of the DGA, one may argue that currently its combination with the ODD

* The authors acknowledge the support of the National Science Center, Poland (UMO-2018/31/B/HSS/01192).

[1] Communication from the Commission to the European Parliament, the Council, the European Economic and Social Committee and the Committee of the Regions, *A European strategy for data*, COM/2020/66 final. In particular, at p 7, opening up government-held information is defined as a 'long-standing EU policy'.

[2] Directive (EU) 2019/1024 of the European Parliament and of the Council of 20 June 2019 on open data and the re-use of public sector information (recast) PE/28/2019/REV/1, OJ L 172 [2019] 56/83.

[3] Regulation (EU) 2022/868 of the European Parliament and of the Council of 30 May 2022 on European data governance and amending Regulation (EU) 2018/1724 (Data Governance Act) PE/85/2021/REV/1, OJ L 152 [2022] 1/44.

[4] Namely by the respect for private and family life (Article 7) and the protection of personal data (Article 8). With regard to the *constitutionalisation* of the right to the protection of personal data, see inter alia F Rossi dal Pozzo and L Zoboli, 'To protect or (not) to protect: definitional complexities concerning personal (and non-personal) data within the EU' (2021) 1 *Eurojus* 315, 316.

contributes to enlarge the availability of public data by building a bridge between open data policies and the protection of personal rights, in line with the principle that data should be as open as possible, as closed as necessary.[5]

However, on closer scrutiny, this bridge is rather slippery. Several commentators have already highlighted that the ODD and DGA – while sharing common objectives – present various inconsistencies that are the result of a pre-existing tension between data protection rules prohibiting by default the processing of personal data, and European policies aiming to stimulate as much as possible the opening of data.[6]

Against this background, the chapter investigates the relationship between the EU legislation governing the openness of public data and the need to protect personal data held by public sector bodies (PSBs). In particular, it analyses how the provisions regulating access and re-use of public data evolve in addressing personal data protection, from the initial public sector information (PSI) Directives to the DGA, passing by the ODD. Moreover, this chapter takes a position on the congruence of the legal framework resulting from ODD, DGA and the General Data Protection Regulation (GDPR).[7] It maintains that while, in principle, the DGA enables a broader opening of public data of a personal nature – in compliance with the GDPR – its application may in practice be more arduous that it seems.

To do so, Section II starts by retracing the development of open data policies in the EU and the evolution of their relationship with the GDPR. Section III discusses the criticism that the interplay between the ODD and DGA raises. Section IV concludes by depicting a viable interpretation of such interplay, including its shortcomings, and suggesting possible technical simplification tools based on the privacy by design and privacy by default models. The underlying assumption is that technology itself may provide the means to widen the scope of reusability of public information containing personal data, making them as open as possible and as closed as (actually) necessary.[8]

II. Open Data Policies: From the 2003 PSI Directive to the DGA

Public data is the first category of data for which the European legislator has set up a framework for wider sharing. Consequently, it is the area that has opened

[5] A Landi et al, 'The "A" of FAIR – as open as possible, as closed as necessary' (2020) 2 *Data Intelligence* 47.

[6] C Wendehorst, 'Of Elephants in the Room and Paper Tigers: How to Reconcile Data Protection and the Data Economy' in S Lohsse, R Schulze and D Staudenmayer (eds), *Trading Data in the Digital Economy: Legal concepts and Tools* (Münster Co, Nomos/Hart Publishing, 2017).

[7] Regulation (EU) 2016/679 of the European Parliament and of the Council of 27 April 2016 on the protection of natural persons with regard to the processing of personal data and on the free movement of such data, and repealing Directive 95/46/EC (General Data Protection Regulation), OJ L 119 [2016] 1/88.

[8] See G Bruzzone and K Debackere, 'As Open as Possible, as Closed as Needed: Challenges of the EU Strategy for Data' (2021) 56 *les Nouvelles-Journal of the Licensing Executives Society* 41.

the discourse on the potential that could result from the re-use of public data.[9] However, it can be argued that, to date, the existing regulatory framework is far from conducive to open public data as much as possible. In order to properly discuss this assertion, this section will quickly frame the open data policies adopted at the EU level over the last 20 years and discuss how they intersect with the protection of personal data, which still represents one of the main barriers to PSI re-use.

From a chronological point of view, the first Directive on the re-use of public sector information (the PSI Directive) was adopted in 2003,[10] revised in 2013,[11] and it has been replaced by the ODD in 2019.[12] The ODD has been recently complemented by the mentioned DGA.

Directive (EC) 2003/98 was the first piece of legislation establishing a regulatory framework for the re-use of public data by introducing minimum requirements for EU Member States regarding making PSI available for re-use.[13] It attempted to remove (some of) the barriers that were hindering the re-use of PSI throughout the Union by introducing the possibility – not (yet) the obligation – for PSBs to make the data they held available for re-use. As far as it is of specific interest for the purposes of this chapter, the 2003 PSI Directive already contained a reference to the protection of personal data and, in defining its scope, stipulated that it would in no way affect the level of protection of individuals with regard to the processing of personal data.[14]

In line with the idea of enlarging the quantity of public data available for re-use, every following amendment to the PSI legislative framework aimed at widening the notion of public data as well as providing increasingly more articulated mechanisms to share them. Amongst these, the 2013 revision introduced a fundamental innovation by *mandating* PSBs to make information in their possession available for re-use – as long as such re-use did not undermine the provisions of the applicable data protection legislation and did not violate any third parties' rights.[15]

[9] European Commission, Directorate-General for the Information Society and Media, W Carrara, S Fischer, E Steenbergen et al, 'Creating value through open data: study on the impact of re-use of public data resources' (2020) *Publications Office*, data.europa.eu/doi/10.2759/328101.

[10] Directive 2003/98/EC of the European Parliament and of the Council of 17 November 2003 on the re-use of public sector information [2003] OJ L 345/90.

[11] Directive 2013/37/EU of the European Parliament and of the Council of 26 June 2013 amending Directive 2003/98/EC on the re-use of public sector information [2013] OJ L 175/1.

[12] Directive (EU) 2019/1024 of the European Parliament and of the Council of 20 June 2019 on open data and the re-use of public sector information [2019] OJ L 172/56.

[13] See G Aichholzer and H Burkert (eds), *Public Sector Information in the Digital Age* (Edward Elgar, 2004); K Janssen, *The Availability of Spatial and Environmental Data in the European Union* (Wolters Kluwer, 2010); J Drexl, 'The Competition Dimension of the European Regulation of Public Sector Information and the Concept of an Undertaking' in J Drexl and V Bagnoli (eds), *State-Initiated Restraints of Competition* (Edward Elgar, 2015) 64, 77; B Lundqvist, 'Turning Government Data Into Gold: The Interface Between EU Competition Law and the Public Sector Information Directive' (2013) 44 *IIC* 79.

[14] Article 1(4), Directive 2003/98/EC.

[15] Article 3, Directive 2013/37/EU. On this profile, see also Article 29 Data Protection Working Party, 'Opinion 06/2013 on open data and public sector information ('PSI') reuse', Adopted on 5 June 2013, 1021/00/EN WP207 3, 2; M Alovisio, 'Criticità Privacy nel riuso dei dati pubblici' (2011) 1–2 *Informatica e Diritto* 46.

The 2013 Directive was subject to a recast in 2019 with the main goal of adapting its provisions to technological developments by further reducing remaining barriers to developing PSI data markets.[16] The ultimate goal of the 2019 ODD is to make the 'open by default' paradigm a general rule applicable in all Member States and to prohibit cross-border discrimination, thereby enabling third parties to develop products and services based on data that are available within the internal market.[17] More specifically, the ODD further expands the scope of the re-use obligation of public data by including public undertakings within its scope[18] and, even more so, by enlarging the category of PSI to data generated by utilities and transport sectors, regardless of their public or private nature, insofar as they are fully or partially funded by public money. The same criterion applies to research data that results from public funding which, even when in the hands of private organisations, are subject to the obligation of access and re-use entailed in the Directive.[19] In addition, the ODD allows real-time access to data and reduces the costs for re-use by requiring the access and re-use of data through the uptake of application programme interfaces (APIs).[20] This means that third parties could build the offer of their services – for example an application on public transport – by linking them to the data held by public transport bodies in a dynamic way.

As far as the interplay with data protection is concerned, the ODD confirms its application without prejudice to Union and national laws on personal data protection and the exclusion of those documents to which access is not permitted or is restricted for reasons of personal data protection.[21] It also makes steps in the direction of a better harmonisation by incorporating, albeit partially, what was stated in the opinion of the Article 29 Working Party ('Art 29WP') on PSI and data protection[22] and in the opinions expressed by the European Data Protection Supervisor in 2012[23]

[16] See the 'Impact Assessment Accompanying the document Proposal for a Directive of the European Parliament and of the Council on the re-use of public sector information' SWD(2018)127 32.

[17] On this aspect, see S Gobbato, 'Open Science and the reuse of publicly funded research data in the new Directive (EU) 2019/1024' (2020) 2(2) *Journal of Ethics and Legal Technologies* 145.

[18] H Richter, 'Exposing the Public Interest Dimension of the Digital Single Market: Public Undertakings as a Model for Regulating Data Sharing' (2020) *Max Planck Institute for Innovation and Competition Research Paper No. 20-03* 7.

[19] Member States are required to develop policies for open access to publicly funded research data, while harmonised rules on re-use will apply to all publicly funded research data made accessible through repositories. Article 10 Directive 2019/1024/EU.

[20] More specifically, public sector bodies are no longer allowed to charge more than the marginal cost for re-using their data, except in very limited cases. On this aspect, see Article 6 Directive 2019/1024/EU.

[21] Article 1(2)h Directive (EU) 2019/1024. As well as to parts of documents that are accessible but contain personal data whose re-use has been defined by law as incompatible with data protection law.

[22] Article 29 Data Protection Working Party, 'Opinion 06/2013 on open data and public sector information ('PSI') reuse', Adopted on 5 June 2013, 1021/00/EN WP207 3, 19–20.

[23] European Data Protection Supervisor, 'Opinion on the "Open-Data Package" of the European Commission including a Proposal for a Directive amending Directive 2003/98/EC on re-use of public sector information (PSI), a Communication on Open Data and Commission Decision 2011/833/EU on the reuse of Commission documents' (2012) edps.europa.eu/sites/default/files/publication/12-04-18_open_data_en.pdf.

and 2018.[24] In this sense, the preamble of the ODD better clarifies what falls under the protection of individuals in relation to the processing of personal data, including, among other things, the permissibility of the re-use of personal data only when the principle of purpose limitation set forth in Articles 5(1)(b) and 6 of the GDPR is respected.[25] In addition, the Directive specifies that where decisions are to be made on the scope and conditions of the re-use of public sector documents containing personal data, the obligation to conduct a data protection impact assessment may be imposed in accordance with Article 35 GDPR.[26] These two references, while provided for at preamble level – and while already resulting from the text of the GDPR alone – for all intents and purposes indicate the effort to increase the coordination between the Directive and data protection rules.

In this direction, the ODD also offers a better guidance on PSI anonymisation.[27] For example, public personal data on household energy consumption, once anonymised, can be made available for re-use. Once again, anonymisation is a means to reconcile the protection of personal data with their re-use. In this regard, the Directive establishes that the costs of anonymising personal data should be included in the so-called eligible cost that can be charged for re-use.[28] While the re-use of public documents should generally be free of charge,[29] nevertheless, the recovery of marginal costs incurred by the public administration for the anonymisation of personal data may be allowed.[30]

As to its interplay with the data protection framework, the ODD does not exclude personal data from its scope altogether, but only does not apply to those documents, access to which is excluded or restricted by virtue of the access regimes on grounds of protection of personal data.[31] In fact, Article 3(1) ODD clarifies that personal data not falling under this exception – and therefore being freely accessible and re-usable without undermining personal data protection – can be made available for re-use in accordance with the conditions set out in the ODD and in compliance with the requirements of the GDPR.

Following the modernisation of the PSI framework in the ODD,[32] the DGA – which entered into force in June 2022 – aims to further enlarge the re-use of public data by focusing on those categories of data that are subject to third parties' rights,

[24] European Data Protection Supervisor, 'Opinion on the proposal for a recast of the Public Sector Information (PSI) re-use Directive' (2018) edps.europa.eu/sites/default/files/publication/18-07-11_psi_directive_opinion_en.pdf.

[25] Paragraph 52 of the preamble, Directive (EU) 2019/1024.

[26] Paragraph 53 of the preamble, Directive (EU) 2019/1024.

[27] Article 2(7) Directive (EU) 2019/1024.

[28] Paragraphs 36 and 38 of the preamble, Directive (EU) 2019/1024.

[29] Article 2 Directive (EU) 2019/1024.

[30] Article 6 Directive (EU) 2019/1024.

[31] Article 1(2)h Directive (EU) 2019/1024.

[32] A better interplay between data protection and public open data and an enlargement of the (personal) data available for re-use was crucial to unlock the potential of public sector information; see Groupement Français de l'Industrie de l'Information, Paris, 'Position Paper, Key Issues for Successful PSI Policies in Europe: Improve the Articulation with GDPR and Enhance Data Quality' (2018).

such as commercial confidentiality, intellectual property, or data protection.[33] In particular, the DGA envisages the introduction of a legal regime complementary to the ODD which finds application toward PSI that is excluded from the ODD,[34] as if public data of a personal nature were divided into two categories: one falling within the scope of the ODD and the other one falling within the scope of the DGA.

In concrete terms, the DGA is embodied in a series of obligations imposed on both PSBs and PSI re-users. As to the PSBs, Article 5(1) mandates them to ensure personal data protection is granted through anonymisation. Moreover, when data are accessed and re-used remotely this should take place within a secure processing environment that is provided or controlled by the PSB itself. When the data are accessed and re-used within the physical premises, PSBs shall ensure that the secure processing environment is located in accordance with high security standards.

Besides offering a set of harmonised basic conditions under which the re-use of data might be permitted, the DGA also assigns specific duties to PSBs. Namely, according to Article 5(4) DGA, when re-use is allowed, the PSBs must impose 'conditions aimed at preserving the integrity of the functioning of the technical systems of the secure processing environment used'. Moreover, PSBs have the right – and the duty – to verify the process, the means and any results of processing of data undertaken by re-users, so to protect the integrity of personal data and prohibit those re-uses jeopardising the rights and interests of third parties. However, when a prohibition to re-use PSI is adopted, PSBs are required to explain it in a comprehensible and transparent manner.

As an alternative, if a PSB cannot grant access for re-use to certain data it holds, according to Article 5(6) it should make best efforts to assist the potential re-user in either seeking the individual's consent to re-use their personal data or the permission of the data holder whose rights or interests may be affected by the re-use, where this is feasible without forming a disproportionate burden for the PSB.

Moving on to the obligations imposed on re-users, pursuant to Article 5(5), they are prohibited from re-identifying any data subject to whom the data relate, must take technical and operational measures to prevent re-identification, and should notify any data breaches resulting in the re-identification of the data subjects concerned with the PSB.

The DGA itself clarifies that it does not prejudice data protection rules even when the personal and non-personal data in a dataset are inextricably linked, and that it does not create any new legal basis for the processing of personal data, nor does it change the information obligations under the GDPR.[35] Moreover, all

[33] The DGA also prohibits public entities from granting exclusive rights on data. Furthermore, if a public body grants or refuses access for data re-use, it must ensure that the terms of such access (or refusal) are non-discriminatory, proportionate, and objectively justified, and it must make those terms available to the public.

[34] Article 3(1)(d) DGA.

[35] Paragraph 4 of the preamble, DGA.

obligations and mechanisms introduced by the DGA represent an expression of the principles established by the GDPR, oriented towards the activity of PSBs and the need for a wider re-use of public personal data. At the same time, by establishing the aforementioned framework of rules, the DGA also seems to attribute a much more proactive role to PSBs.

III. The Interplay between the Open Data Directive and the Data Governance Act

Although the DGA is welcome as a piece of legislation that unlocks the potential of personal data held by PSBs, several commentators claim that it translates into a set of provisions that lack coordination with the European open data policies and that collide with the GDPR. The current criticism of the DGA is manifold and can be systematised in two clusters of concerns dealing with, on the one hand, the lack of legal certainty and clarity of the resulting open data regulatory framework, and, on the other hand, the clash with established principles of data protection.

As to the former, in the first place, there appears to be uncertainty concerning the normative value of the DGA's obligations to access and re-use that PSBs have to fulfil. The DGA introduces a 'cascade' of 'may' or 'shall' obligations, which PSBs may struggle with.[36] In more detail, there is not a provision mandating PSBs to provide re-use of data beyond the ODD. Rather, several provisions clarify the conditions that PSBs should follow when they decide to enable re-use of the personal data that they hold. However, as mentioned, Article 5(6) DGA provides for a (presumably mandatory) obligation on PSBs that – when unable to grant re-use of data – are required to adopt best efforts in supporting re-users to seek the consent of the data subjects or the permission from the legal entities whose rights and interests may be affected by such re-use, as long as this is feasible without placing a disproportionate burden on the PSB. The mandatory nature of the last obligation appears to be in contrast with the optional nature of the regime under which PSBs *may* (not shall) decide to open public data of personal nature.[37]

On closer inspection such a 'cascade' of 'may' and 'shall' obligations might be more effective than it seems and generate an incentive for PSBs to open up public data of a personal nature at first hand – considering that in the opposite scenario they still have to assist re-users in acquiring the conditions for re-use. This interpretation is also in line with the role that PSBs perform under the DGA, namely that of proactive players in fostering open data to the extent of becoming data intermediaries themselves.[38]

[36] J Baloup, E Bayamlıoğlu, A Benmayor, C Ducuing, L Dutkiewicz, T Lalova-Spinks, Y Miadzvetskaya and B Peeters, 'White paper on the data governance act' (2021) CiTiP Working Paper, 15.

[37] Baloup et al (n 36) 16.

[38] Baloup et al (n 36) 20.

In the second place, regardless of the nature of the DGA's obligations, the same commentators also raise the point that the relationship between the ODD and DGA may not be as clear as it appears. It remains to be established whether and how the DGA obligations complement those already adopted in the ODD.[39] The starting point of the critique is that the DGA is based on a 'black or white' perspective, where public data would be either *in* the scope of the ODD (and can be opened up without affecting the rights of third parties) *or* outside it (when subject to the rights of third parties and therefore within the scope of the DGA).[40] Assuming that this is the case,[41] the DGA would lack the ability to consider the grey areas in between, for example those 'documents' (according to the wording of the ODD) encompassing personal data that PSBs *adapt* so that they can be accessed and re-used according to the ODD – and without infringing third parties' rights. This is to say that even before the adoption of the DGA, any adaptation should have occurred in compliance with the GDPR, meaning that PSBs would have to delete, anonymise or aggregate personal data.[42] The question that herein arises concerns the set of obligations on PSBs in relation to such adapted documents (and data).[43] In other words, in case a PSB has already made available for re-use a dataset encompassing personal data in compliance with the GDPR – following the indications suggested by Art 29WP or required by national law or according to the best practices of the sector – would these data fall within the scope of the ODD or the DGA? The answer to this question is endowed with considerable practical relevance since, depending on the answer, different sets of obligations apply.

Although the disorientation of PSBs could be an issue, this should not be overstated. Indeed, PSBs' conduct in opening up personal data is to be in any case aligned with the data protection principles and rules that are mirrored in both the ODD and the DGA. Moreover, once the DGA is applicable, it is likely that it will become the standard for re-use of public data of personal nature, no matter when the 'opening' took place. If a double regime is envisaged, thus, this concerns the public data, on the one hand, and the public data that are subject to third parties' rights, on the other.

As to the clash with data protection, the ODD and the DGA do not seem to converge on the *purpose* for which third parties can re-use public data of personal nature.[44] The driving force behind the concept of 'open data' is that information

[39] Baloup et al (n 36) 15. See also, for the interplay between DGA, GDPR and the AI Act, M Grafenstein, 'Reconciling conflicting interests in data through data governance. An analytical framework (and a brief discussion of the data governance act draft, the data act draft, the AI regulation draft, as well as the GDPR)' (2022) *HIIG Discussion Paper Series* 33.

[40] Baloup et al (n 36) 15–16.

[41] According to the EDPB-EDPS, 'Joint Opinion 03/2021 on the Proposal for a regulation of the European Parliament and of the Council on European data governance (Data Governance Act)' (2021), paras 68–71, this is not the case as the ODD directive already applies also to personal data as long as they are made available in compliance with the GDPR.

[42] Article 29 Data Protection Working Party, 'Opinion 06/2013' (n 22).

[43] Baloup et al (n 36) 17.

[44] Baloup et al (n 36) 15–16.

should be available for re-use for innovative products and services – purposes that cannot be clearly foreseen.[45] The common point of the ODD and DGA in this respect is that consideration is given to the principle of purpose limitation as far as personal data are concerned. The ODD, however, defers to the GDPR principle of purpose limitation,[46] in line with what had already been clarified by Art 29WP's opinion on open data and PSI re-use.[47] In particular, Art 29WP points out that, in the case of re-use of personal data that are publicly available, purpose limitation remains a key element of protection. Thereby, the mere fact that personal data are publicly available for a specific purpose – such as, for example, transparency reasons – does not mean that such personal data are re-usable for *any* purpose.[48] Moreover, the opinion also stresses that when PSBs select the licensing regime to which opened data are made available for re-use to third parties, they can also decide that only 'specific purposes' are allowed, so to prevent a generic re-use.[49]

The DGA, instead, is deemed to go beyond the principle of purpose limitation to adopt a 'purpose re-use approach'.[50] Such an approach would emerge from the obligations to which PSBs are now subject under the DGA. In the first place, the obligation to support re-users in seeking consent of data subjects and permission from legal entities whose rights and interests may be affected by such re-use implies that a PSB identifies the purpose for which the re-use is sought. In the second place, the right – and duty – to verify the results of the data processing undertaken by the re-user and eventually to prohibit the use of results that contain information jeopardising the rights and interests of third parties requires that PSBs enter into the merits of each re-use, for example that they understand what is used and for what purpose.

That said, even the significance of the 'purpose re-use approach' should not be excessively emphasised, being, once again, perfectly consistent with the more proactive role that PSBs will perform pursuant to the DGA.

Finally, a more systemic weakness of the DGA arises from the underlying distinction between personal data and non-personal data.[51] Gellert and Graef

[45] For a depiction of the 'openness by default concept' see M Bargmann, G Pfeifer, and B Piwinger, 'A Citizen's Perspective on Public Sector Information' (2004) Public sector information in the digital age: between markets, public management and citizens' rights 255, 256, eprints.rclis.org/6563/1/citizens-perspective-endversion.pdf.

[46] Paragraph 52 of the preamble, Directive (EU) 2019/1024. For the application of the purpose limitation to PSBs see Grafenstein (n 39) 27–28.

[47] Article 29 Data Protection Working Party, 'Opinion 06/2013' (n 22) 19–20.

[48] As a matter of fact, PSBs process two categories of personal data: (i) personal data that they have to make public as required by the law, as, for example, in the case of electoral lists or land registries; and (ii) personal data that they accumulate but are not required to make public. These latter may be – but not necessarily are – encompassed in public information documents.

[49] Article 29 Data Protection Working Party, Opinion 06/2013 (n 22) 11–12, where it addresses the question as to when a re-use is compatible with the purposes specified by the public sector body. This would be the case, eg, if the re-use of tax payment information by financial institutions for credit reporting purposes could be relevant as they are still potential re-users.

[50] Baloup et al (n 36) 18–19.

[51] I Graef and R Gellert, 'The European Commission's proposed Data Governance Act: some initial reflections on the increasingly complex EU regulatory puzzle of stimulating data sharing' (2021)

note that – by formulating specific rules for personal data, eg Articles 5(3), 7(4)(b) and 9(2), and for non-personal data, eg Articles 5(9)–(14) and 31 – the DGA confirms the assumption that data have a specific personal or non-personal nature and that a neat line can be drawn between these two categories. Similar to most legislative instruments targeting data, the DGA appears to ignore that the majority of databases are of a mixed nature,[52] and introduces a regime that requires PSBs to be able to make the distinction and act accordingly. The impossibility of dividing data according to their nature is further highlighted by the ambiguous nature of personal data themselves and the uncertainties surrounding anonymisation processes. On the one hand, the notion of personal data is dynamic and 'contextual', eg, what can be deemed non-personal today could become personal in the future.[53] On the other hand, anonymised data can be de-anonymised through updated techniques, which make vain if not useless the effort of PSBs to open up the personal data that they hold in a data protection-compliant manner.[54]

In line with the existing regulation for data, whenever the distinction becomes impracticable due to the inextricability between personal and non-personal data, the preamble of the DGA (paragraph 4) gives way to data protection, and the GDPR applies to the entire dataset.[55] However, although the distinction between personal and non-personal data is burdensome for PSBs, one can claim that the DGA was not the appropriate framework to address such a problem which is rooted in the entire European data regulation system.

IV. Building a Bridge between Data Protection and Open Data

Despite the criticism that the DGA raises, its adoption should be welcomed. It tackles a specific category of data, those subject to third parties' rights – and in so doing it provides guidance to PSBs and fosters the opening up of data. When considering the targeted subcategory of personal data, we should therefore read

TILEC Discussion Paper No. DP2021-006, ssrn.com/abstract=3814721. Also L Vardanyan and H Kocharyan, 'The GDPR and the DGA Proposal: are They in Controversial Relationship?' (2022) *European Studies* 91, 102.

[52] Graef and Gellert (n 51) 5–6.

[53] N Purtova, 'The Law of Everything. Broad Concept of Personal Data and Future of EU Data Protection Law' (2018) 10 *Law, Innovation and Technology* 40; and I Graef, R Gellert and M Husovec, 'Towards a Holistic Regulatory Approach for the European Data Economy: Why the Illusive Notion of Non-Personal Data Is Counterproductive to Data Innovation' 44 *European Law Review* 605. For a comparison with the notion of personal data in the US see ML Montagnani and M Verstraete, 'What Makes Data Personal?' (2023) 56 *UC Davis Law Review* 101.

[54] As a starting point of the debate on anonymisation, see Article 29 Data Protection Working Party, 'Opinion 05/2014 on Anonymisation Techniques', Adopted on 10 April 2014, 0829/14/EN WP216.

[55] This is the same principle adopted in Article 2(2) of the Regulation (EU) 2018/1807 of the European Parliament and of the Council of 14 November 2018 on a framework for the free flow of non-personal data in the European Union OJ L [2018] 303/59.

the DGA's provisions as a set of instructions on how PSBs can open up public data of personal nature in compliance with the GDPR. In doing so, the DGA complements – at least in principle – both the ODD and the GDPR, representing a specification on how PSBs should proceed if they decide to open up the personal data that they hold.

As a matter of fact, the DGA does not impose an obligation on PSBs to make available for re-use data that were not already 'openable' pursuant to the ODD. Under this latter instrument, PSBs could decide to open up data of personal nature insofar as they do it in accordance with the GDPR. On this point, the EDPB-EDPS Joint Opinion on the proposal for the DGA clearly states that 'the rules of the Open Data Directive along with those of the GDPR provide already for mechanisms allowing the sharing of personal data held by the public sector bodies in a manner consistent with the requirements governing protection of individuals' fundamental rights'.[56]

Nonetheless, considering the complexity in complying with the GDPR, PSBs are unlikely to open up public personal data unless they are given clear indications on how to proceed and strong incentives. The DGA seeks to provide the former, that is the set of measures to follow when opening up data of personal nature, but fails to generate the latter.

For the above reasons, we may conclude that the DGA regime – albeit sound in principle – fails to meet the reality of PSBs' functioning.

On the one hand, some of the obligations are not clear in their practical implications, such as the duty of supporting re-users in seeking consent of the data subjects or permission from the data holders whose rights and interests may be affected by such re-use, where this is feasible without placing a disproportionate burden on the PSB.[57]

On the other hand, the set of obligations – consider for example the duty of vigilance, requiring PSBs to verify the results of the data processing undertaken by the re-user – assumes the availability of relevant resources for PSBs, which is not the situation in all Member States. This might imply that the goal of harmonising public data availability within the EU internal market achieves the result of an increasing geographical differentiation in the access to PSI, depending on PSBs' funding.

On a more general level, the impracticability of the DGA could be traced back to the controversial distinction between personal and non-personal data,[58] that compels PSBs, any time they are evaluating the opening of a dataset for re-use,

[56] EDPB-EDPS (n 41) para 71.

[57] A possibility may be the introduction of mechanisms allowing data subjects to choose what personal data PSBs can distribute, to whom and for which purpose. In this direction, Bart van der Sloot proposes to let everyone register their own privacy settings with the government, for example by registering an account on the website through which the government distributes public sector information, fellow citizens, companies, nonprofit organisations, other governments etc; see B van der Sloot, 'On the fabrication of sausages, or of Open Government and Private Data' (2011) 3 *JeDEM* 149.

[58] Which, as mentioned, underpins all the legislative instruments that the EU institutions have over the years adopted to govern data. See I Graef and R Gellert, 'The European Commission's proposed Data Governance Act: some initial reflections on the increasingly complex EU regulatory puzzle of stimulating data sharing' (2021) *TILEC Discussion Paper No. DP2021-006*, dx.doi.org/10.2139/ssrn.3814721.

to distinguish the data at hand (unless they are inextricably linked) and apply the required regime.

Moreover, in the case of personal data, the required regime hinges on anonymisation, that is currently deemed to be the main tool which makes re-use possible without infringing a data subject's rights and privacy. However, it is well-known that anonymisation raises many concerns as to its fallibility.[59] This further aggravates the status of PSBs that are also required, pursuant to Article 5(4) DGA, to take measures to preserve the integrity of the functioning of the technical systems of the secure processing environment used or to verify the process, the means and any results of processing of data undertaken by the re-user to preserve the integrity of the protection of the data.

Although the DGA presents a certain operational complexity, it is to be considered an advancement in the relationship between open data policies and data protection as it entails a significant interpretative tool for GDPR compliance. In other words, it builds a bridge between the ODD and the GDPR and provides useful guidance to PSBs.

Yet, as mentioned in the introduction of this chapter, this bridge is rather slippery and better guidance would certainly come from the adoption of guidelines on the technical tools that PSBs can actually deploy to make public data as open as possible – in compliance with data protection rules. The same DGA at paragraph 7 of its preamble asks Member States to provide support to PSBs to make optimal use of techniques enabling analyses on databases that contain personal data beyond anonymisation. These techniques include differential privacy, the use of synthetic data or similar methods that are the state-of-the-art privacy-preserving methods capable of contributing to a more privacy-friendly processing of data.[60]

Differential privacy, in particular, has recently emerged as the leading technique in computer science to allow for accurate data analysis in compliance with data protection.[61] It can provide a system for publicly sharing data by describing patterns of groups within a dataset while withholding information about individuals in the dataset.[62] The idea behind differential privacy is to introduce 'noise' into statistical procedures so as to hide the contribution of any single individual, while preserving statistical properties of data in the aggregate form. Introducing noise into any calculation of interest guarantees that the results do not leak too much information that is specific to any individual participant in the underlying database and entails only a negligible loss of accuracy.[63]

[59] See Article 29 Data Protection Working Party, 'Opinion 05/2014' (n 54) 10–11.

[60] For an overview of the diverse privacy-enhancing technologies see E Curry, S Scerri, and T Tuikka (eds), *Data Spaces: Design, Deployment and Future Directions* (Springer Nature, 2022).

[61] C Dwork, N Kohli and D Mulligan, 'Differential privacy in practice: Expose your epsilons!' (2019) 9 *Journal of Privacy and Confidentiality*, journalprivacyconfidentiality.org/index.php/jpc/article/view/689.

[62] A Belghiti and A Angrisani, 'Bridging the gap between technology and policy in GDPR compliance: the role of differential privacy' (2022) *Conference: Privacy 2.0-Interdisciplinary Perspectives on Privacy in the Digital Age, Hans Böckler Foundation*, hal.science/hal-03752824v1/file/DP_GDPR.pdf.

[63] V Feldman, K Kakaes, K Ligett, K Nissim, A Slavkovic and A Smith, 'Differential privacy: Issues for policymakers' (2020), simons.berkeley.edu/news/differential-privacy-issues-policymakers. The authors

In conclusion, now that the DGA significantly contributes to further shaping the framework for the opening up of public data, the next steps will require guidance as to the technical side so that hybrid solutions can become more available for PSBs. This entails the integration of legal and technical approaches, a complex task, only possible when legal specifications such as those of the GDPR are correctly interpreted, a task that the DGA tries to perform.

provide the example of a database of household incomes of students. If a researcher wants to know the average income, she might be given the average, under the assumption that the average does not disclose information about any individual student. However, when a new student is added to the database, the researcher could calculate the new arrival's household income from the difference between the previous and the new averages. Under differential privacy, instead, any query for the average income would return the actual average plus some tolerable degree of inaccuracy, preventing an operation such as the one just depicted.

6

Regulation of Machine-generated Data between Control and Access

ANDREAS WIEBE

I. Emerging Framework of Data Governance Regulations

For many years, there were intense debates on the protection of personal data and its scope, culminating in the adoption of the General Data Protection Regulation (GDPR) in 2016. In recent years, the focus has shifted to the governance of non-personal or machine-generated data (MGD) due to the enormously rising importance of data in the digital economy.

While in 2017 creation of a new exclusive right on data was contemplated,[1] it was soon realised that data with its special characteristics does not lend itself easily to concepts of exclusive rights in light of its design and consequences.[2] Stakeholders were not definite on their interests and it soon showed that the problem was not the lack of incentives but more the factual control over data that could not be broken up by property rights. As a result, the whole discussion moved away from the creation of exclusive rights and shifted more into the direction of providing access and how to implement this in regulation.

Following the 2017 Communication, the European Commission took different regulatory initiatives that slowly emerged as a patchwork of different regulations with data at the centre. The Data Governance Act (DGA)[3] is aiming at supporting data sharing also through non-legal measures, eg by providing public bodies with the option of imposing an obligation of using secure processing environments to access data in Article 5(4) DGA. It also supports the establishment of data intermediation services as a new business model that could be essential to

[1] See Commission, 'Building a European Data Economy' (Communication) COM (2017) 9 final.

[2] A Wiebe, 'Protection of industrial data – a new property right for the digital economy?' (2016) *GRUR Int.* 877 et seqq; J Drexl, 'Designing Competitive Markets for Industrial Data' (2017) 8 *JIPITEC* 257, 272 et seqq.

[3] Regulation (EU) 2022/868 of the European Parliament and of the Council of 30 May 2022 on European data governance and amending Regulation (EU) 2018/1724 (Data Governance Act) [2022] OJ L152/1.

alleviate data sharing and aims at promoting data altruism as well. The Digital Markets Act (DMA) aims at creating open markets by sector-specific regulation of obligations of core platform services and especially providing portability of and access to data generated through gatekeeper platforms.[4] In addition, the Free Flow of Non-Personal Data Regulation[5] seeks to ensure that non-personal data can be stored, processed and transferred anywhere in the EU. The Platform-to-Business Regulation[6] imposes transparency obligations and requires platforms to describe for business users the data generated through the provision of the service. The Data Act Proposal was published on 23 February 2022 and the final version was adopted by the EP on 27 November 2023.[7] The Data Act's general objective is to make more data in the EU usable to support sustainable growth and innovation across all sectors in the data economy to tackle the problem of inefficient and insufficient availability of data. Moreover, a couple of sector-specific access rules for data[8] reflect the approach of the European legislator to combine general horizontal regulation with sector-specific rules.

The policy objectives of data access and transfer in the emerging European digital economy, including improving access to anonymous machine-generated data and avoiding disclosure of confidential data, were laid down in different documents.[9] In the 2020 European Data Strategy, the concept of a 'single European data space' was promoted that includes rules for access to and use of data and clear and trustworthy data governance mechanisms.[10] The European Council in October 2020 stressed 'the need to make high-quality data more readily available and to promote and enable better sharing and pooling of data, as well as interoperability'.[11]

Against the background of these policy objectives, the chapter will analyse the different regulatory initiatives. Overlaps, gaps and inconsistencies will be identified. Moreover, possible solutions will be discussed. At the centre of attention will be the question of whether the emerging legal framework for MGD can still function as a coherent body of law.

[4] Regulation 2022/1925 of the European Parliament and of the Council on contestable and fair markets in the digital sector (Digital Markets Act) [2022] OJ L 265/1, Article 6(10).

[5] Regulation (EU) 2018/1807 of the European Parliament and of the Council of 14 November 2018 on a framework for the free flow of non-personal data in the European Union [2018] OJ L303/59 (Free Flow of Non-Personal Data Regulation).

[6] Regulation (EU) 2019/1150 of the European Parliament and of the Council of 20 June 2019 on promoting fairness and transparency for business users of online intermediation services [2019] OJ L186/57 (Platform to Business Regulation).

[7] European Parliament legislation resolution of 9 November 2023 on the proposal for a regulation on harmonised rules on fair access to and use of data (Data Act) (COM (2022) 0068) (hereinafter 'Data Act').

[8] See section IV(D), below.

[9] Commission, 'Building a European Data Economy' (Communication) COM (2017) 9 final; Commission, 'A Digital Single Market Strategy for Europe' (Communication) COM (2015) 192 final.

[10] Commission, 'A European strategy for data' (Communication) COM (2020) 66 final.

[11] See Commission, 'Proposal for a Regulation of the European Parliament and of the Council on harmonised rules on fair access to and use of data (Data Act)' COM (2022) 68 final, Explanatory Memorandum, pp 1 et seq.

II. Definition of MGD and Scope of Legislation

In its 2017 Communication 'Building A European Data Economy', the European Commission defined MGD as data 'created without the direct intervention of a human by computer processes, applications or services, or by sensors processing information received from equipment, software or machinery, whether virtual or real'.[12] Commentators pointed to the fact that some human intervention might always be present and used a broader definition of MGD as data generated by 'connected devices', being connected to other devices or persons.[13]

In the Study on the Database Right accompanying the Data Act Proposal, the following working definition of MGD has been used:

> MGD is defined as data recorded, collected, or generated independent of direct and economically significant human intervention by:
>
> - sensors processing information received from equipment, software or machinery, whether virtual or real
> - computer processes, applications or services.
>
> Sensor-generated data in IoT environment would include:
>
> - data generated by sensors about the sensor and machine itself, e.g. data on machine performance;
> - data generated/observed by sensors observing the environment in which sensors and machines operate, e.g. information on the soil recorded by sensors in smart tractors;
> - the data resulted from the aggregations and processing of the two types of data above.[14]

While this definition was not intended to be used a statutory definition, it clarifies the types of data included and the function of sensors. It also clarifies that the definition may include some pre-processing activities that are done directly by the sensor, such as data compression, data encoding, or transmission of raw data directly to the cloud structure. Data already structured in data warehouses and ready to be used for deriving insights should not be included in the definition of MGD.

The statutory definitions of data in Article 2(1) DGA, Article 2(1) Data Act, and Article 2(24) DMA are identical:

> 'data' means any digital representation of acts, facts or information and any compilation of such acts, facts or information, including in the form of sound, visual or audiovisual recording.

[12] Commission (n 1).

[13] J Drexl, 'Connected Devices – an Unfair Competition Law Approach to Data Access Rights of Users' (2021) Max Planck Institute for Innovation and Competition Research Paper No. 20–22, 6.

[14] C Moreno et al, 'Study to support an impact assessment for the review of the Database Directive, Final Report' (Brussels, 2022) pp 32 et seqq.

One issue regarding the scope of data included in the Data Act relates to the phase between generation of data and aggregation. In practice, raw data even if produced by machines are immediately refurbished or in other ways formatted or processed by machines or sensors or just collected and categorised and this 'curation' or formatting can hardly be separated from the generation process.[15] In addition to including primary data, the Data Act also includes pre-processed data 'for the purpose of making it understandable and useable prior to further processing and analysis', as recital 15 clearly states. Even data collected from a single sensor or a connected group of sensors would be included, for the purpose of making the collected data comprehensible for wider use-cases. The inclusion of pre-processed data in the scope of legislation was necessary to achieve the respective objectives.[16] It also benefits legislative coherence.

However, recital 15 of the Data Act excludes derived and aggregated data from the scope that were included in the broader definition stipulated above. The line is crossed if proprietary, complex algorithms are used and information derived by means of sensor fusion 'which infers or derives data from sensor fusion, collected in the connected products'. The reason pursuant to recital 15 seems to be that new investment is needed to produce the derived data. However, this not only leads to frictions as other sector-specific access rights are not limited, eg, in the automotive sector pertaining to repair and maintenance information which include all data necessary for the function,[17] it also is an overly restrictive limitation on access rights necessary for promoting innovation.

It is important to note that MGD is a broader concept than the reference to data generated by connected Internet of Things (IoT) devices suggests. Additional categories are: data generated by internal IT business systems, mainly containing information about products, services, sales, logistics, customers, partners or suppliers (CRM, etc); data generated through external interaction with users (ie, cookies, web tracking, logs); and data generated from crowdsourcing or web collaboration.[18] Whether these types of data are covered by the Data Act is not clear; recital 15 claims that data recorded as the result of user actions would also be included. This would cover data recorded as an intentional or indirect result of user action. Access to this data may also be necessary to support innovation. Pursuant to recital 16, data generated by a product when the user recorded, transmitted or displayed content would not be included, nor the content itself.

[15] Accompanying Study (n 14).

[16] See also R Podszun and C Pfeifer, 'Datenzugang nach dem EU Data Act: Der Entwurf der Europäischen Kommission' (2022) *GRUR* 953, 961.

[17] See Regulation (EU) 2018/858 of the European Parliament and of the Council of 30 May 2018 on the approval and market surveillance of motor vehicles and their trailers, and of systems, components and separate technical units intended for such vehicles, amending Regulations (EC) No 715/2007 and (EC) No 595/2009 and repealing Directive 2007/46/EC [2018] OJ L151, Article 61.

[18] Everis Benelux, 'Study on data sharing between companies in Europe', carried out for the European Commission, Final Report (Brussels, 2018), data.europa.eu/doi/10.2759/354943.

III. Protection of MGD and Alignment with the Data Act

As no special intellectual property regime exists for data, and protection under general civil law – though possible in some countries – would be deficient and systematically flawed,[19] the systems closest to protection of non-personal data are the database *sui generis* right and trade secret protection.

A. Database Right

1. *Exclusion of MGD*

The database right under Article 7 of the Database Directive 96/9/EC was designed to protect the investment into databases. The Directive was criticised from the beginning for being very vague and incomplete. The application of the database right to databases containing MGD was fraught with uncertainty due to four key judgments of the CJEU.[20] These judgments established the distinction between generation of data and collection of data. The Court narrowly interpreted the Directive to only consider investments separately shown as relating to the collection of data, while excluding investments into the generation of data. The discussion and subsequent case law demonstrated considerable uncertainties as to the extent to which MGD would be covered by the database right. The CJEU judgments could be interpreted as indirectly resulting in excluding MGD from the scope of the database right, since it could be argued that most investments of MGD producers go into the 'creation' of this data.[21] In the often cited *Autobahnmaut* case, the German Supreme Court considered registering lorry data at terminals as being directed at data that pre-existed and constituting collection of data – although you could make an argument in this case that the data was generated at the terminals.[22]

To avoid these uncertainties that could seriously hinder data sharing, the European Commission considered it the best option to exclude MGD completely

[19] See A Wiebe, 'Protection of industrial data – a new property right for the digital economy?' (2016) *GRUR Int.* 877 et seqq.

[20] Case C-203/02 *The British Horseracing Board Ltd and Others v William Hill Organization Ltd* ECLI:EU:C:2004:695, [2004] ECR I-10415; Case C-46/02 *Fixtures Marketing Ltd v Oy Veikkaus AB* ECLI:EU:C:2004:694, [2004] ECR I-10365; Case C-338/02 *Fixtures Marketing Ltd v Svenska Spel AB* ECLI:EU:C:2004:696, [2004] ECR I-10497; Case C-444/02 *Fixtures Marketing Ltd v Organismos prognostikon agonon odosfairou AE (OPAP)* ECLI:EU:C:2004:697, [2004] ECR I-10549.

[21] JIIP and technopolis, 'Study in support of the evaluation of Directive 96/9/EC on the legal protection of databases, carried out for the European Commission', Final Report (Brussels, 2018) p 20.

[22] BGH GRUR 2010, 1004 – *Autobahnmaut*.

from the database right. In Article 43 of the Data Act the following clause was included:

> Databases containing certain data
>
> The sui generis right provided for in Article 7 of Directive 96/9/EC shall not apply when data is obtained from or generated by a product or related service falling within the scope of this Regulation, in particular in relation to Articles 4 and 5 thereof.

The wording is not clear and subject to interpretation.[23] It could be regarded as a confirmation that MGD do not fulfill the substantial investment criteria.[24] However, the wording that was changed in the legislative process now seems to imply that the database right should not be exercised only where cases of concrete conflict with the access rights established by the Data Act occur.[25] Such an interpretation could create new uncertainties as it would not exclude application of the database right in cases of access based on other grounds than Chapter II of the Data Act. Hence, it is preferable to consider the provision as an exception from the scope of protection of the database right with respect to databases containing data covered by the Data Act.[26] This seems to be confirmed by the last sentence of recital 84 that leaves room for the database right with respect to databases not covered by the Data Act.

2. *Uncertainties and Inconsistencies Stemming from the Data Act*

However, even under such an interpretation uncertainties remain with respect to the exclusion of mixed databases containing MGD and other types of data. An analogy could be drawn to the 2019 Guidance for the free flow of non-personal data in the EU that concerns a similar problem relating to the mixture of personal and non-personal data by introducing a requirement that database protection would be excluded if MGD and other data were 'inextricably linked'.[27]

[23] Data Act (n 7) recital 112: '[…] it should be clarified that the *sui generis* right does not apply to such databases. That does not affect the possible application of the *sui generis* right under Article 7 of Directive 96/9/EC to databases containing data falling outside the scope of this Regulation provided the requirements for protection in accordance with Article 7(1) of that Directive are fulfilled'.

[24] See M Leistner and L Antoine, 'IPR and the use of open data and data sharing initiatives by public and private actors, Study requested by European Parliament's Committee on Legal Affairs (JURI)' (Brussels, 2022) 120. Favouring such a solution with the side effect of overturning the *Ryanair* Decision of the CJEU: E Derclaye and M Husovec, 'Sui Generis Database Protection 2.0: Judicial and Legislative Reforms' (2022) 11 *LSE Law, Society and Economy Working Papers* 15, papers.ssrn.com/sol3/papers.cfm?abstract_id=4138436.

[25] See J Drexl et al, 'Position Statement of the Max Planck Institute for Innovation and Competition of 25 May 2022 on the Commission's Proposal of 23 February 2022 for a Regulation on harmonised rules on fair access to and use of data (Data Act)' (2022) Max Planck Institute for Innovation and Competition Research Paper No 22-05, para 256 et seqq, considering the clause as an expression of the lex specialis character of the Data Act.

[26] See also A Metzger and H Schweitzer, 'Shaping Markets: A Critical Evaluation of the Draft Data Act' (2023) *ZEuP* 82 et seqq.

[27] Commission, 'Guidance on the Regulation on a framework for the free flow of non-personal data in the European Union'(Communication) COM (2019) 259 final 9.

In addition, a rebuttable presumption could be adopted according to which mixed databases are excluded from protection, unless the database holder can show that the database mostly consists of non-MGD.

The desirability of including aggregated/derived data into the scope of application of the Data Act has already been discussed. Extending the scope to aggregated and derived data would result in excluding the application of the database right with respect to this data included in a database accordingly. This would serve the purpose of data sharing and also avoids frictions with sector-specific regulations.

3. *Uncertainties and Inconsistencies Stemming from the Database Directive*

Other inconsistencies of the database right are of minor importance for MGD, but nevertheless can play a role in some cases. One issue relates to the narrow exceptions in Article 9 of the Database Directive that are not even mandatory. To avoid frictions with general copyright law, the copyright limitations should be extended to the database right as well.[28] The newly introduced limitation on text and data mining followed this path already and alleviated many concerns of the research community.[29] Adoption of general copyright limitations could provide more systematic clarity, although not all limitations appear to be useful in the database context. For example, extending the private copying exception to electronic databases could have a positive effect regarding access for users. Making the research exception to the database right mandatory could increase harmonisation of the legal framework and alleviate research activities in a digital environment that extends across borders.[30]

In the emerging patchwork of data regulations, one of the oldest pieces is the Public Sector Information (PSI) or Open Data legislation.[31] It has been long criticised that public bodies are not explicitly excluded from holding database rights, which led to diverging decisions in the Member States. While the European Commission thinks that the Open Data legislation had settled the issue, the Open Data Directive (ODD) leaves ownership of the database right by public bodies untouched.[32]

[28] Moreno et al (n 14) 77 et seqq.

[29] Directive (EU) 2019/790 of the European Parliament and of the Council of 17 April 2019 on copyright and related rights in the Digital Single Market and amending Directives 96/9/EC and 2001/29/EC (DSM Directive) [2019] OJ L130/92, Articles 3, 4.

[30] See L Guibault and A Wiebe (eds), *Safe to be open – Study on the protection of research data and recommendations for access and usage* (Göttingen University Press, 2013) 118 et seqq.

[31] Directive 2003/98/EC of the European Parliament and of the Council of 17 November 2003 on the re-use of public sector information [2003] OJ L345; Directive 2013/37/EU of the European Parliament and of the Council of 26 June 2013 amending Directive 2003/98/EC on the re-use of public sector information [2013] OJ L175/1; Directive (EU) 2019/1024 of the European Parliament and of the Council of 20 June 2019 on open data and the re-use of public sector information [2019] OJ L172/56.

[32] See Directive (EU) 2019/1024 of the European Parliament and of the Council of 20 June 2019 on open data and the re-use of public sector information [2019] OJ L172/56, Article 1(6).

So the database right is not completely excluded for public bodies and this may lead to some unwanted effects that could be avoided by explicitly stripping public bodies of the database right.[33]

Open Data legislation restricts the right to use to the limits set by the ODD (Article 1(6) ODD), but still leaves room for restrictions on the re-use in accordance with Article 1(6) ODD. This would be a potential source of uncertainty and could lead to challenging discussions in each case on whether the limits are kept and thus produce transaction costs. Moreover, ODD is limited to the 're-use' of public documents while acts infringing on *sui generis rights* may also relate to access to public documents that do not necessarily amount to 're-use'. To avoid any disputes on the scope of the ODD, the complete exclusion of public bodies from being right-holders would provide a clear and certain solution. Introducing a separate provision into the Database Directive could be regarded as a coherent and systematically sound regulation aligning database law to general copyright. As the *sui generis* is an economic right protecting investment, the general exclusion of public bodies is in line with open data policies.

B. Trade Secret Law

1. Trade Secret Protection of MGD

Until in 2016 when the Trade Secrets Directive was adopted, trade secret protection was regulated on a national level in Europe only.[34] MGD may be protected as trade secrets as well. Even single datasets may contain relevant pieces of information that can be potentially retrieved from it. The chance for protection increases down the value chain where data is aggregated and derived, thus adding value and meaning. Any further requirements for protection may be met as well. Key to this is that the information has to have commercial value because of the secrecy. Surely the aggregation of data and datasets and their combination with other data generates value as it may be unique.[35] Secrecy may be maintained due to organisational and contractual access restrictions, but encryption technology may be at the core of reasonable measures to protect trade secrets in an IoT-environment.[36] Protection against unlawful acquisition presupposes that the relevant objects containing the secret must be 'under the control of the trade secret holder' (Article 4(2)(a) Trade Secrets Directive). Control may be reduced

[33] See also Moreno et al (n 14) 85 et seqq.

[34] Directive (EU) 2016/943 of the European Parliament and of the Council of 8 June 2016 on the protection of undisclosed know-how and business information (trade secrets) against their unlawful acquisition, use and disclosure [2016] OJ L157/1.

[35] See also Leistner and Antoine (n 24) 87.

[36] See also A Wiebe and N Schur, 'Protection of trade secrets in a data-driven, networked environment – Is the update already out-dated?' (2019) 14 *Journal of Intellectual Property Law & Practice* 814, 820 doi.org/10.1093/jiplp/jpz119.

if the information is stored in the cloud but can still be preserved by contractual agreement.

2. Conflicts with the Data Act and Possible Solutions

With the Data Act introducing an obligation to share data, a conflict arises with the interest to secure trade secrets and not to lose valuable business assets. The Data Act acknowledges the precedence of access rights and includes some provisions to emphasise and secure the need to protect trade secrets as much as possible while preserving the precedence of access rights. The legislator did not exclude MGD from trade secret protection, as was done in Article 43 concerning the database right. A complete exclusion could hardly be justified in the light of the objectives of trade secret law, and would encroach upon the fundamental right of property that covers trade secrets.

At this point it may be worth taking a closer look at the extent of possible conflicts between trade secrets and access rights.[37] Moving from raw data to aggregated and derived data, the chances that trade secret law will apply are higher, and possible areas of conflict increase.[38] However, the Data Act excludes aggregated and derived data from its scope. This would go a long way towards minimising possible conflicts between the two regulations. However, drawing a dividing line seems hardly feasible from a practical side. Even if the generation of data and its aggregation and further processing may be perceived separately in theory, this would very often not be possible in practice. Consequently, aggregated and derived data should have been included not to severely limit the effectiveness of access rights.

The core of the Data Act is the establishment of access rights. The regulation distinguishes rights of users from access by third parties. The right of the user to access data produced by a connected product is established in Article 4 of the draft. The drafters tried to alleviate the conflict with trade secret protection by including some explicit safeguards. Pursuant to Article 4(6) Data Act, trade secrets shall only be disclosed if all necessary measures are taken to preserve the confidentiality of trade secrets, in particular with respect to third parties. It is not clear which measures are necessary not to consider such data as generally accessible with the consequence of trade secret protection being lost.[39] This will be left for the courts to decide. The Data Act points to the option of contractual agreements, model contracts, access controls, technical standards and Codes of Conduct. Additional safeguards are included but will face practical problems. Article 4(10) prohibits the user from developing a competing product from the data obtained. Offering

[37] See also A Wiebe, 'The Data Act Proposal – Access rights at the Intersection with Database Rights and Trade Secret Protection' (2023) *GRUR Int.* 227 et seqq.

[38] See also J Drexl, *Data Access and Control in the Era of Connected Devices – Study on Behalf of the European Consumer Organisation BEUC* (Brussels, 2018) 94.

[39] B Lorenzen, 'Geschäftsgeheimnisschutz und Data Act' (2022) *ZGE* 251, 256.

additional services on secondary markets for the user in competition with the data holder is not precluded and opens the way for free riding.[40] In addition, Article 4(13) prohibits the data holder from using such data generated to undermine the commercial position of the user. This seems to be a reasonable rule to preserve trade secret interests, but it may be hard to prove that the commercial position of the user is undermined.

Problems may also arise from the obligation of the data holder to make the data available to a third party upon request of the user pursuant to Article 5 Data Act. Article 5(9) attempts to preserve trade secrets in these cases by limiting disclosure to the extent 'strictly necessary' for the purpose agreed between user and third party and demanding 'all proportionate measures' to be taken by the third party to preserve the confidentiality of the trade secrets in an agreement between data holder and third party. But by defining a wide purpose, the trade secret interests of the data holder can be seriously impaired. Article 6 tries to put some limits relating to the use of the data by the receiving third party and the making available of the data for another third party. Interestingly, the limitation also covers aggregated and derived data although they seemed not to be covered by the scope of the Data Act.

On the other hand, while the obligation to identify the data which constitute trade secrets in Articles 4(6) and 5(9) Data Act protects the user and third party against blunt claims of trade secret protection, during the legislative process new exceptions favouring trade secret holders were introduced. Pursuant to Articles 4(8) and 5(11), access to data may be denied in exceptional circumstances with the potential of resulting in serious economic damage to the trade secret holder in case of infringement.[41] This 'emergency break' provision has the potential to seriously damage the effectiveness of the access rights and creates incentives for 'overclaiming' of trade secret rights. This danger is slightly alleviated by the right of the user to file a complaint to the competent authority or refer to dispute settlement pursuant to Articles 4(9) and 5(12). However, there is still a considerable barrier for the user that may seriously hamper data access rights. Further uncertainty is created by the right to withhold access in case of lack of agreement on certain measures or if the user or third party 'undermines' the confidentiality of trade secrets pursuant to Articles 4(7) and 5(10).

The same is true for the exception for safety requirements 'when such processing could undermine security requirements of the connected product, as laid down by Union or national law, resulting in a serious adverse effect on the health, safety or security of natural persons' introduced in the final version in Article 4(2).[42] Even if the user in this case has a right to redress as well, the exception creates considerable uncertainties as to when these conditions would be met and invites

[40] See also Lorenzen (n 39) 262; Leistner and Antoine (n 24) 88, pleading for further clarification and questioning the prohibition on developing competing products.

[41] Data Act (n 7).

[42] See Article 4(1a) Data Act (n 7).

the use of this clause as a general defence against access rights. It appears that a hard priority rule is necessary in the relationship between trade secret protection and data access rights to preserve a proper balance and secure the efficacy of the Data Act. This is increasingly true as precautions for protection of trade secrets are taken. In addition to the measures mentioned above, recitals 8 and 22 of the Data Act refer to *in-situ* access as a way to comply with data access obligations. *In-situ* data access means that the data no longer leave the manufacturer's systems but are accessed or processed by a third party on the server or network of the manufacturer under the latter's control. This method is increasingly emerging as a protection measure to secure countervailing rights and is already included in Article 5(3) Data Governance Act relating to access granted by public bodies.[43] This could be considered a 'proportionate measure' and there might even be an obligation to avail oneself of such mechanisms. However, this method gives the data holder considerable insights by monitoring the use of the accessing party and a chance to exploit this information for its own commercial purposes. Further specifying regulation might be needed.

A general limitation to further sharing of the data down the line is included in Article 11(2) Data Act. If the recipient has used the data for unauthorised purposes, it is obliged to destroy the data and end marketing of products or services unless there is no significant harm to the data holder, or it would be disproportionate. These limitations established by the Data Act would also determine the scope of protection against use or disclosure under Article 4(3) Trade Secrets Directive, especially as to subsequent uses.[44] Here the Data Act can be aligned with the Trade Secrets Directive. However, in light of the enormous importance of this issue for the preservation of trade secrets, further clarification seems inevitable at least as to the purposes of access and use.

3. *Divergent Roles*

In general, it is foreseeable that allocation of the statutory roles of data holder and user will be very hard to do in complex value chains. There may be situations relating to connected machines or cars as well as smart factories where the data holder and trade secret owner are different persons. The question arises whether with respect to an IoT product the data holder is equivalent to the trade secret holder in case the IoT product includes storage or processing of data as trade secrets. Article 2(13) of the Data Act refers to the data holder as the person who has the right or obligation to use or make available the generated data. Article 2(2) Trade Secrets Directive (EU) 2016/943 defines the trade secret holder as 'any natural or legal

[43] Regulation (EU) 2022/868 of the European Parliament and of the Council of 30 May 2022 on European data governance and amending Regulation (EU) 2018/1724 (Data Governance Act) [2022] OJ L152/1.

[44] See also Leistner and Antoine (n 24) 88.

person lawfully controlling a trade secret'. While lawful control and right to use or make available is not completely congruent in practice, the concepts will result in the same person being trade secret and data holder with respect to the data generated constituting the trade secret.

In cases of implementation of devices by third party service providers in smart factories, the processing of pre-existing trade secrets allocated to the factory or business owner may be more relevant. In these cases, data holder and trade secret holder may diverge. The data holder may be the person that has control over the device collecting and generating the data, while the trade secret holder may be the person controlling the information represented by the data and preserving their secret by contractual and organisational measures. The Data Act also does not cover the situation where the trade secret holder is another third party. Here protection is left to the contract between trade secret holder and data holder.

C. GDPR

In many cases, MGD will include personal data as well. Thinking of the data processing in the car, most data generated will also provide some information on the driver or owner of the car. Even in smart factories, data could still be connected to the performance of the remaining employees. This uncertainty is further enhanced by the concept of personal data that is not completely clear in theory, nor in its practical application.

1. *General Rule of Conflict*

While the interests of access to data and of the data subjects in protection of their data may be congruent in some ways, in cases of overlap tensions may arise between data sharing and the fundamental right to data protection (Article 8 Charter of Fundamental Rights). The latter focuses on the data sovereignty of the individual, acts as a protective instrument in favour of the data subject and is characterised by the guiding principle of data minimisation.[45] Against this background, there is a risk that the limitations imposed by data protection law could significantly curtail data access provisions.

The Data Act addresses the question of the concrete relationship between data protection and data economy law through the competition clause in Article 1(5), according to which the Regulation is without prejudice to data protection law. The

[45] *cf* L Specht-Riemenschneider and A Blankertz, 'Lösungsoption Datentreuhand: Datennutzbarkeit und Datenschutz zusammen denken' (2021) *MMR* 369, according to which data usability and data protection have so far largely been thought of as opposites; L Specht-Riemenschneider, 'Das Verhältnis möglicher Datenrechte zum Datenschutzrecht' (2017) *GRUR Int.* 1040, 1041; H Schweitzer, 'Datenzugang in der Datenökonomie: Eckpfeiler einer Informationsordnung' (2019) *GRUR* 569, 571.

rights under the Data Act should complement the data subject's rights under the GDPR and in cases of conflict the GDPR should prevail. Both the GDPR and the ePrivacy Directive 2002/58/EC apply without restriction.[46] In this respect, the Data Act can be considered as a supplement to the GDPR with respect to such data generated by the use of a product or related service. In line with this conception, no provision of the Data Act should be applied or interpreted in such a way as to diminish or limit the right to the protection of personal data or the right to privacy and confidentiality of communications (recital 7). As a consequence, the Data Act cannot be seen as a *lex specialis* to the GDPR and does not alter its level of protection.[47] In all areas of application of the Data Act in which personal data are also affected, the interaction between the Data Act and the GDPR is characterised by additional requirements.[48]

That does not solve the problem, however, as legal uncertainty remains in case there are contradictory provisions between the legal acts. In view of the indeterminate competition clause, from which no consistent competition doctrine has yet emerged, it is therefore recommended that in the event of conflict, a legal clarification be provided which explicitly states which law takes precedence.[49]

2. *Intersections*

Article 3(2) Data Act obliges companies to provide the user with certain minimum information in a clear and comprehensible format before concluding a contract for the purchase, rent or lease of a product or a related service. According to the Commission's intention, this obligation provides transparency over the data generated and enhances the easy access for the user (recital 24 Data Act). The obligations of Article 3(2) Data Act are in addition to the obligations under Article 13 and 14 GDPR (recital 24 Data Act) and require a separate provision.[50]

In case of data transfers from companies to consumers and between companies, the Data Act clarifies that users who, as natural persons, also act in the role of data subjects under data protection law, can both pursue the data access claims

[46] See also recitals 7, 8, 30, 36 and 39 Data Act (n 7).

[47] See in this respect L Specht-Riemenschneider, 'Der Entwurf des Data Act – Eine Analyse der vorgesehenen Datenzugangsansprüche im Verhältnis B2B, B2C und B2G' (2022) *MMR* 809, 811.

[48] Specht-Riemenschneider (n 47) 809, 811; M Hennemann and B Steinrötter, 'Data Act – Fundament des neuen EU-Datenwirtschaftsrechts?' (2022) *NJW* 1481, 1482.

[49] EDPB, EDPB-EDPS Joint Opinion 2/2022 on the Proposal of the European Parliament and of the Council on harmonised rules on fair access to and use of data (Data Act), adopted 4 May 2022, para 26; in this sense also Specht-Riemenschneider (n 47) 809, 810.

[50] *cf* on the information obligations pursuant to Article 3(2) Data Act (n 7) as well as the danger of an 'information overload' of the individual. GK Ebner, 'Information Overload 2.0 – Datenwirtschaftsrecht IV: Die Informationspflichten gem. Article 3 Abs. 2 Data Act-Entwurf' (2022) *ZD* 364; Specht-Riemenschneider (n 47) 809, 817 et seq.

established in Article 4(1) and Article 5(1) Data Act against the data holder, as well as claim against the data controller the data portability right under Article 20 GDPR (*cf* Article 1(5) Data Act).[51] The right to direct transferal in Article 20(2) GDPR is in line with Article 5(1) Data Act. As a supplement and extension to Article 20 GDPR,[52] the user has a right under Article 4(1) or Article 5(1) Data Act to have data made available not only once and upon request, but without undue delay, free of charge and, where applicable, continuously and in real-time.

The assumptions in Article 20 GDPR that the data subject had previously provided the data himself and the processing is based on consent or a contract, no longer apply for the application of the Data Act as no legal ground is expressly required.[53] In contrast to Article 20(1) GDPR, there is no reservation of technical feasibility within Article 5 Data Act.[54] In addition to Article 17 GDPR, the third party must delete the data as soon as they are no longer needed for the agreed purpose (Article 6(1) Data Act). With regard to the design of data access, recital 22 Data Act indicates that the user's right to data access is not a right to data portability, which includes the actual transfer of data to the user, but can be designed as a mere *in-situ right*.[55] In this respect, the information rights in Article15 GDPR that would allow the data subject to claim a 'copy' of the data stored with the data controller may be even broader – although the exact design of this provision is still not clear. All in all, the Data Act broadens the portability right of the GDPR as to personal data without creating frictions.

3. *Legal Grounds in Data Protection Law – Problem and Solutions*

While the principles of data minimisation[56] and privacy by design (eg by pseudonymisation and anonymisation) are to remain 'unaffected', access claims will generally require the identification of the user or a third party. This begs the question as to the proper legal ground for data processing. In the event that a user, who at the same time acts in the role of a data subject under data protection law, requests data access to themselves or to a third party, the data access may be based on consent pursuant to Article 6(1)(a) and Article 7 GDPR. Consent could be expressed impliedly in the data access request.[57] Conversely, if the user is not the data subject, the data controller may only provide personal data generated by the

[51] See J Klink-Straub and T Straub, 'Data Act als Rahmen für gemeinsame Datennutzung' (2022) *ZD-Aktuell* 01076.

[52] See recital 31 Data Act (n 7).

[53] *cf* Klink-Straub and Straub (n 51).

[54] As to this problem see Drexl et al, Position Statement 2022 (n 25) para 300 et seqq, suggesting to extend the interoperability obligation to data holders.

[55] See W Kerber, 'Governance of IoT Data: Why the EU Data Act Will not Fulfill Its Objectives' (2022) *GRUR International* 5, doi.org/10.1093/grurint/ikac107; also Specht-Riemenschneider (n 47) 809, 816.

[56] As to its implementation see Drexl et al, Position Statement 2022 (n 25) para 305.

[57] Specht-Riemenschneider (n 47) 809, 810.

use of a product or related service to the user if there is a valid legal basis. Legal obligations of the controller within the meaning of Article 6(1)(c) GDPR must be taken into account. Article 6 (1)(c) GDPR is in turn to be understood as a kind of mirror provision[58] to Article 6(1)(e) GDPR, on the basis of which public bodies process the personal data they receive on the basis of the obligations of the Data Act (Article 14 et seqq) in conjunction with Article 6(1)(c) GDPR.[59] Where there is a legal basis other than consent under the GDPR, the Data Act goes further by requiring a contract under Article 4(13) with the user for transfer of data. In case of a mixture of personal and non-personal data in a dataset, the data protection issues in the contract could be separated from other issues to be regulated under the Data Act.[60]

In the event that sensitive data are included, Article 9 GDPR has to be taken into account as well. The opening clauses in Article 9(2) (g–j) GDPR relating to public interest, public health as well as scientific and archival purposes could be activated with respect to the data access obligations of the Data Act.[61] Beyond that, only consent of the data subject[62] remains to legitimise data processing. The European legislator generally attaches a high interest in the right of access to data but also can be assumed to at least have given equal priority to the data protection interests when fulfilling the data access claim.[63]

A third, particularly problematic scenario occurs when a user who is not a data subject requests data access for a third party under Article 5 Data Act. It is important to note that the Data Act itself does not create a legal basis under the GDPR for the data holder to provide access to personal data or make it available to a third party when requested by a user that is not a data subject (recital 7 Data Act). Hence, the data access obligations of the Data Act cannot be read as a legal basis within the meaning of Article 6(1)(c) GDPR or Article 9(1)(g) GDPR.[64] In these cases, only consent of the data subject or recourse to the balancing clause of Article 6(1)(f) GDPR can be taken, which is, however, limited to non-sensitive data. It remains unclear whether a data protection-related legitimation is necessary for Article 3(1) Draft Data Act.

To obtain valid consent will, however, be difficult from a practical point of view. Technical systems (PIMS) or inclusion of a data trustee may alleviate implementation of valid consent. As another possible solution to the conflicts mentioned

[58] See on the relationship between Article 6(1)(c) GDPR and Article 6(1)(e) GDPR: B Buchner and T Petri, 'Article 6 DS-GVO' in J Kühling and B Buchner (eds), *Datenschutz-Grundverordnung/BDSG*, 3rd edn (CH Beck, 2020) para 78.

[59] *cf* Specht-Riemenschneider (n 47) 809, 810f.

[60] See also Drexl et al, Position Statement 2022 (n 25) para 298.

[61] In this sense Specht-Riemenschneider (n 47) 809, 811, according to which the guarantee of data access to the user could be in the substantial public interest in view of the overall societal objectives pursued by the Data Act.

[62] See on the problem of consent in the Big Data context, Specht-Riemenschneider (n 45) 1040, 1042 et seq.

[63] Specht-Riemenschneider (n 47) 809, 811.

[64] Specht-Riemenschneider (n 47) 809, 811; Metzger and Schweitzer (n 26).

it was suggested to amend the Data Act and to recognise Articles 4(1) and 5(1) as relevant obligations of Union law, to which the data holder is subject, and hence provide a legitimate ground under Article 6(1)(c) GDPR.[65] This could have provided clarity, although it might result in personal data to be processed by product users and third parties in an extensive way.[66] This has the potential to create an imbalance between access rights and data protection interests.

However, in line with data protection principles a workable solution would be to require data holders, users and third parties to use anonymisation technologies as early as possible in the process, favourably before sharing the data.[67] The implementation of respective measures will also be acknowledged in the balancing process relating to Article 6(1)(f) GDPR. The requirements of anonymisation in the GDPR are also related to reasonableness with respect to economic efforts.[68] Recital 8 mentions encryption in general terms and also points to technologies for 'algorithms to be brought to the data'. The Data Act could have been even more explicit on this point, although the required interpretation may already be inferred from application of data protection law.

Overall, the inclusion of personal data in the scope of data covered by the Data Act creates considerable frictions that are not dealt with in the Act. Uncertainties exist especially in relation to the general rule of conflict and the alignment with the legal grounds for personal data processing of the GDPR. While technical measures may alleviate the problem, clarifications would be needed to create the right level of legal certainty.

IV. Further EU Regulations, with Special Emphasis on Access Rights

Beyond the regulations discussed above that directly engage with non-personal data, other regimes apply to MGD as well. These regimes further complicate the regulatory framework. Although inconsistencies seem limited, coordination about how the regimes relate to each other may still be required.

A. Data Governance Act

The Data Governance Act[69] (DGA) is aiming at partly supporting data sharing by non-legal measures. Article 5 seeks to support data sharing by creating secure

[65] Leistner and Antoine (n 24) 91.
[66] See Metzger and Schweitzer (n 26).
[67] See also Drexl et al, Position Statement 2022 (n 25) para 307; Metzger and Schweitzer (n 26).
[68] See C-582/14 *Breyer / Deutschland* ECLI:EU:C:2016:779, [2017] 2 CMLR 3, paras 45–49.
[69] Data Governance Act (n 3).

processing environments controlled by the public sector for data access and obliging Member States to name competent bodies to grant technical support. Article 8 provides for a central single information point as a one-stop-shop that is vested with taking applications for data access and giving advice.

The DGA also supports the establishment of data intermediation services as a new business model and aims at promoting data altruism. Chapter 4 provides measures to increase trust in sharing personal and non-personal data and lower transaction costs linked to B2B and C2B data sharing by creating a notification regime for data sharing providers. These providers will have to comply with a number of requirements, in particular the requirement to remain neutral as regards the data exchanged. They cannot use such data for purposes other than facilitating data exchanges. In the case of providers of data sharing services offering services for natural persons, the additional criterion of assuming fiduciary duties towards the individuals using them will also have to be met. For example, a platform trading data from sensors from farming equipment is not allowed to use the data for developing their own products.

The approach is designed to ensure that data sharing services function in an open and collaborative manner, while empowering natural and legal persons by giving them a better overview of and control over their data. In this respect, the DGA is complementary to the Data Act that grants users and third parties access to MGD.[70] Recital 39 of the Data Act explicitly mentions data intermediation services as recipients. Data intermediation services could play an important role as to the further marketing of the data by the user. Consequently, the function of data intermediaries does not include the aggregation of data that would create additional interests on the side of the aggregator. From this angle, it is congruent with the proposal to include aggregated data into the scope of the Data Act stipulated above. Data marketplaces will be included, however.[71]

A competent authority designated by the Member States will be responsible for monitoring compliance with the requirements attached to the provision of data intermediation services. This could help in establishing trust and promoting data sharing by the users with safeguards for their neutrality as a prerequisite to act in fairness towards the user.[72] In a similar vein, the idea of employing neutral data trustees is gaining momentum.[73]

Further chapters of the DGA relate to data altruism and data sharing by public bodies. While these will probably not be very relevant as to MGD, it is worth noting that the section relating to public bodies addresses practical measures to support data sharing by organisational means, especially in cases where IP rights, trade

[70] See also Metzger and Schweitzer (n 26).

[71] On further issues of delineation see D Tolks, 'Die finale Fassung des Data Governance Acts' (2022) *MMR* 444, 446.

[72] Critical and supporting a voluntary certification system, see Tolks (n 71) 444, 447; Specht-Riemenschneider and Blankertz (n 45) 369, 370.

[73] See L Specht-Riemenschneider and W Kerber, *Designing Data Trustees – A Purpose-Based Approach* (Konrad-Adenauer-Stiftung, 2022).

secret protection or data protection applies. In this respect, it is again complementary to the main acts on PSI/Open Data. Beyond this, the provisions in Chapter V of the Data Act establish obligations for data sharing where public bodies are the beneficiaries in cases of emergency. Within the small range of overlap, no inconsistencies can be identified.

B. DMA

The Digital Markets Act (DMA)[74] aims at creating open markets by specific regulation of obligations of core platform services based on Article 114 TFEU. It entered into force in May 2023. Basically, the DMA complements competition law and provides graduated and overall fairly strict regulatory provisions.

Considering the objective of the DMA, data is affected mostly indirectly by its provisions. A direct relationship is established by Article 5(3) Data Act that excludes gatekeeper platforms from receiving data as a third party from the user or a data holder under the data access right of the Data Act. Beyond that, an overlap of both Acts may arise if the core platform services were to be considered data holders of connected devices. Comparing the definition of core platform services in Article 2(2) DMA and of connected products and related services in Article 2(5) and (6) Data Act, it is possible that core platform services would be provided in the operation of connected devices and then also be covered by the Data Act. Article 2(5) Data Act relates to data concerning the use or environment of a connected product and the access rights refer to data generated by the use of a connected product or related service. It cannot be excluded that this data could also constitute a service in the sense of Article 2(2) DMA that includes online search engines, operating systems, web browsers and virtual assistants. Following the broad definition of MGD, the data generated by their operation could be included in the scope of the DMA. An example would be data generated by virtual assistants or operating systems in a connected car and provided on big platforms.

The area of overlap appears to be small, however, and considerably limited by the threshold for applying the DMA in Article 3. As for the remaining cases, general rules of interpretation have to be applied. It follows that the rules on gatekeepers would have to be regarded as the more specific rules, as they only apply to a limited group of services with a specific competition law objective. The approach of Article 43 Data Act to exclude databases containing MGD from *sui generis* database protection could be applied to the DMA by analogy. This would mean that the *sui generis* database right cannot stand in the way of exercising the data access rights of the DMA.

[74] Regulation 2022/1925 of the European Parliament and of the Council of 14 September 2022 on contestable and fair markets in the digital sector and amending Directives (EU) 2019/1937 and (EU) 2020/1828 (Digital Markets Act) [2022] OJ L265/1.

In case of overlap, access rights in both pieces of legislation run parallel with respect to the obligation for gatekeepers under Article 6(10) DMA to grant access for business users as to data generated by the users or through the services they provide.[75] To the extent the platform is also considered to be a data holder, the access obligation goes beyond Articles 4 and 5 Data Act as the access has to be real-time and aggregated data is also included, which is of enormous relevance. Further obligations established by the DMA would be complementary to the Data Act. Article 6 Data Act contains provisions limiting use of data to compete on the primary markets for products, while the DMA does not include similar provisions for third parties getting access to data. Conversely, Article 6(2) DMA limits the gatekeeper's use of data generated on the platform in competition with users. If the gatekeeper were to be considered to be a data holder under the Data Act as well, this obligation goes beyond Article 4(10) Data Act where the data holder is only kept from using the generated data to obtain insights about the user's business.

Both obligations under the DMA provide for supplementary obligations with respect to the Data Act that are well-founded in competition law objectives. Their respective scopes of application differ, which may require further coordination in practice. Deviating from the rule of speciality it seems appropriate to apply the stricter rule respectively to achieve practical concordance.

C. P2B Regulation

The Platform to Business Regulation[76] imposes transparency obligations and requires platforms to describe for business users the data generated through the provision of the service. It is specifically applicable to online intermediation services (ie platforms that put different users in contact with each other for the purpose of conducting a transaction) and search engines. The objective is to reduce imbalances of power between business users of platforms and the platform itself. As to access to data, the general conditions must include a description of the technical access that the platforms will have to the personal data provided by the business users or consumers for the provision of the online intermediation service.

To the extent that data generated by the provision of services on the platform can be regarded as MGD, the Regulation supplements the Data Act as far as the platform can be regarded as data holder and the service provider as user. As to the transparency for platforms about personal data of business users and consumers provided in the course of use of the service, it supplements the GDPR that will fully apply to the platform. No inconsistencies can be perceived.

[75] Article 6(10) Digital Markets Act (n 4).

[76] Platform to Business Regulation 2019/1150 (n 6).

D. Sector-specific Rules

Some sector-specific access rules for data reflecting the approach of the legislator to combine general horizontal regulation with sector-specific rules are already in place. Just to give an overview:

- The Electricity Directive and Regulation[77] provide for eligible parties to access data on consumption, require certain actors in the sector to share network data and give customers access to metering and other data required for switching between providers.
- The Payment Services Directive 2 (PSD2)[78] enables third party providers to access an individual's account holder data at their request.
- For vehicles, the Type Approval Regulation[79] requires Original Equipment Manufacturers (OEMs) to make repair and maintenance information available to dealers and repair services, and CO_2 regulations permit OEMs to share data on CO_2 emissions.
- The ITS Directive and its Delegated Regulations[80] establish specifications in particular for data sharing in the field of road transport and multimodal travel information services.

[77] Directive (EU) 2019/944 of the European Parliament and of the Council of 5 June 2019 on common rules for the internal market for electricity and amending Directive 2012/27/EU [2019] OJ L159/125; Regulation (EU) 2019/943 of the European Parliament and of the Council of 5 June 2019 on the internal market for electricity [2019] OJ L158/54.

[78] Directive (EU) 2015/2366 of the European Parliament and of the Council of 25 November 2015 on payment services in the internal market, amending Directives 2002/65/EC, 2009/110/EC and 2013/36/EU and Regulation (EU) No 1093/2010, and repealing Directive 2007/64/EC [2015] OJ L337/35.

[79] Regulation (EU) 2018/858 of the European Parliament and of the Council of 30 May 2018 on the approval and market surveillance of motor vehicles and their trailers, and of systems, components and separate technical units intended for such vehicles, amending Regulations (EC) No 715/2007 and (EC) No 595/2009 and repealing Directive 2007/46/EC [2018] OJ L151/1.

[80] Directive 2010/40/EU of the European Parliament and of the Council of 7 July 2010 on the framework for the deployment of Intelligent Transport Systems in the field of road transport and for interfaces with other modes of transport Text with EEA relevance [2010] OJ L207/1; Commission Delegated Regulation (EU) No 885/2013 of 15 May 2013 supplementing ITS Directive 2010/40/EU of the European Parliament and of the Council with regard to the provision of information services for safe and secure parking places for trucks and commercial vehicles Text with EEA relevance [2013] OJ L247/1; Commission Delegated Regulation (EU) No 886/2013 of 15 May 2013 supplementing Directive 2010/40/EU of the European Parliament and of the Council with regard to data and procedures for the provision, where possible, of road safety-related minimum universal traffic information free of charge to users Text with EEA relevance [2013] OJ L247/6; Commission Delegated Regulation (EU) 2015/962 of 18 December 2014 supplementing Directive 2010/40/EU of the European Parliament and of the Council with regard to the provision of EU-wide real-time traffic information services [2015] OJ L157/21; Commission Delegated Regulation (EU) 2017/1926 of 31 May 2017 supplementing Directive 2010/40/EU of the European Parliament and of the Council with regard to the provision of EU-wide multimodal travel information services [2017] OJ L272/1.

- The Responsible Mining Regulation[81] requires EU importers to disclose information on their supply chain with suppliers.
- The Vessel Traffic Monitoring and Information System Directive[82] provides for maritime data collection and sharing.
- The European Statistical System (ESS) Regulation[83] provides the central legal framework for the development, production and dissemination of European statistics.
- The proposal for a European Health Data Space Regulation (EHDS)[84] contains very detailed provisions on access to health data in different circumstances.

Article 1(4) EHDS explicitly states that the rules are 'without prejudice' to access rights and data sharing under the DGA and the Data Act. However, the regulations listed above constitute sector-specific access rules that can be regarded as *lex specialis* with regard to the Data Act. The rules of the EHDS create very detailed access rights for users as well as for third parties and are more specific. This does not exclude supplementary application of the more general regulations as long as it does not conflict with the specific provisions.

Another example for the relationship between the sector-specific regulations and the Data Act is the Type Approval Regulation.[85] Preceding the Data Act by many years, it established a narrow but efficient access regime to certain types of data relating to car maintenance. It differs from the Data Act in several ways. It applies to all data needed for the purpose of maintenance and especially creates direct real-time access rights by the third party service providers against the data holder. So it deviates from the user-centric approach the Data Act is taking. In this respect, it is not compatible with the Data Act.

However, the Data Act is intended to be a baseline regulation, open for sector-specific rules. It makes sense to tailor the obligations of the Data Act to the

[81] Regulation (EU) 2017/821 of the European Parliament and of the Council of 17 May 2017 laying down supply chain due diligence obligations for Union importers of tin, tantalum and tungsten, their ores, and gold originating from conflict-affected and high-risk areas [2017] OJ L130/1.

[82] Directive 2009/17/EC of the European Parliament and of the Council of 23 April 2009 amending Directive 2002/59/EC establishing a Community vessel traffic monitoring and information system [2009] OJ L131/101.

[83] Regulation (EC) No 223/2009 of the European Parliament and of the Council of 11 March 2009 on European statistics and repealing Regulation (EC, Euratom) No 1101/2008 of the European Parliament and of the Council on the transmission of data subject to statistical confidentiality to the Statistical Office of the European Communities, Council Regulation (EC) No 322/97 on Community Statistics, and Council Decision 89/382/EEC, Euratom establishing a Committee on the Statistical Programmes of the European Communities [2009] L87/164.

[84] Commission, 'Proposal for a Regulation of the European Parliament and of the Council on the European Health Data Space' COM (2022) 197 final.

[85] Regulation (EU) 2018/858 of the European Parliament and of the Council of 30 May 2018 on the approval and market surveillance of motor vehicles and their trailers, and of systems, components and separate technical units intended for such vehicles, amending Regulations (EC) No 715/2007 and (EC) No 595/2009 and repealing Directive 2007/46/EC [2018] OJ L151/1. See W Kerber and D Gill, 'Access to Data in Connected Cars and the Recent Reform of the Motor Vehicle Type Approval Regulation' (2019) *Journal of Intellectual Property, Information Technology and Electronic Commerce Law (JIPITEC)* 244.

specifics of a sector and if necessary supplement them. In this sense, no inconsistencies would arise from different sector-specific rules although they would partly displace the fundamental access rules.

E. Open Data Legislation

A special regulation is in place for data held by public sector bodies. The Open Data Directive[86] does not create access rights but presupposes them. Instead, re-use of data is regulated in a way that it should be open to anybody on fair, reasonable and non-discriminatory (FRAND) terms. Pursuant to Article 1(2), information to which access is excluded by IP rights, trade secret law or data protection law is exempted from the scope of application is information.[87] Hence, in these cases conflicts are regulated by the Open Data Directive.

The right to re-use data under Open Data legislation is supplemented by Article 5(3)–(6) DGA that establishes practical ways of access to the data while at the same time preserving data protection and trade secret interests. This includes *in-situ* access, contractual measures and practical assistance. These more organisational measures can support the finding of practical concordance between conflicting interests and could serve as a model in different contexts. Overall, the open data framework appears to be well balanced.

While in theory the Data Act may be applicable to such public sector data as well, there seems to be no practical overlap as the Data Act is limited to data produced by connected devices that will not constitute public sector information. No conflict is perceivable in this respect. In case the public sector body could be regarded as data holder, the Data Act could be regarded as *lex specialis* in relation to the Open Data Directive, especially as it has a quite narrow area of practical application as to MGD.

V. Emerging Principles in European Data Law

Despite the current uncertainties stemming from the parallel application of the different regulations discussed above, some common rules or concepts can be identified as emerging out of the patchwork of regulatory activities. These areas of commonality are relevant to MGD, but could also be regarded as principles of the law of the data economy more generally.[88]

[86] Directive (EU) 2019/1024 of the European Parliament and of the Council of 20 June 2019 on open data and the re-use of public sector information [2019] OJ L172/56.

[87] *cf* A Wiebe, 'Open Data und Urheberrecht im Konflikt?' in V Fischer, G Nolte, M Senftleben and L Specht-Riemenschneider (eds), *Festschrift für Thomas Dreier* (Beck, 2022) 629, 635 et seqq.

[88] J Drexl, framed it in terms of 'path dependency' in a presentation on a conference of the EIPIN network in Alicante on 4 November 2022; see also Drexl et al, Position Statement 2022 (n 25) para 190.

A. Data Portability

The first principle is aiming at data portability in the interest of competitive markets. Article 6(9) DMA requires the gatekeeper to provide effective portability of data generated through the activity of a business user or end user and shall, in particular, provide tools for end users to facilitate the exercise of data portability, in line with the GDPR, including by the provision of continuous and real-time access.

As already mentioned, the rules on access to data in Articles 3 and 5 Data Act clarify some issues left open in the data portability right in Article 20 GDPR. The provisions on switching in Articles 23–26 Data Act include detailed provisions on the contractual and technical side of switching of data processing services.[89] Recital 70 explains that the efforts in the Free Flow of Non-Personal Data Regulation[90] to establish a self-regulatory framework for switching were not really successful and did not lead to the development of open standards and interface. Therefore, the aim of the Data Act is to establish a minimum of obligations to eliminate contractual, economic and technical barriers to switching. These quite detailed rules supplement and broaden the right of data portability in Article 20 GDPR, which is more or less limited to an obligation to provide the personal data in a certain format. The scope of the Data Act, however, is more limited as it applies only to data generated by a connected product.

The DGA in its section on data intermediation services is also aiming at facilitating data sharing by establishing a framework for data intermediation services. The DGA clearly emphasises the importance of interoperability that can be regarded as an important technical element of data portability. Article 12(i) DGA requires the service to ensure interoperability and refers to commonly used standards. Articles 30, 33–36 Data Act stipulate essential technical requirements of interoperability for data, data sharing and data processing services in detail and can be regarded as complementary. They complement the respective provisions in Article 6 of the Free Flow of Non-personal Data Regulation and Articles 26 and 27 DGA. The scope of application of a data processing service, covered by Article 2(8) Data Act, is broader, though, and not completely congruent with that of a data intermediation service, covered by Article 2(11) DGA.[91]

B. Safeguards for International Access and Transfer

Article 32 Data Act concerns international transfers of non-personal data by data processing providers and limits such transfers and governmental access if in conflict

Of course, introducing new rules in innovative regulations tends to establish a certain degree of precedence for later regulations. However, I would consider it to be more a common appropriate regulatory approach that fits in different areas of regulation.

[89] As to the differences to the DMA see Leistner and Antoine (n 24) 113.

[90] Free Flow of Non-Personal Data Regulation (n 5).

[91] See also Drexl et al, Position Statement 2022 (n 25) para 172.

with EU or national law. It very much resembles Article 44 et seqq. GDPR. Trade secrets and other 'commercially sensitive data' are explicitly mentioned as a ground for refusal.[92] Article 32 Data Act establishes safeguards against access and transfer of data in the international context and allows the transfer only if certain legal standards of European or Member States law are met. The parallel to Article 44 et seqq. GDPR is striking. Article 32(3) Data Act in particular requires an evaluation of the foreign legal system comparable to that under the *Schrems II* judgment of the CJEU for the GDPR.[93] A similar provision is included for data sharing services in Article 31 DGA.

There has been strong criticism as to these provisions, especially directed at Article 32(1) Data Act, referring to the different nature of the Data Act that does not involve personal interests but pursues the opposite objective of promoting data sharing.[94] One of the concerns is that it could have the effect of a data localisation rule that would be against the objective of the Free Flow of Non-Personal Data Regulation.[95] Moreover, experience of the GDPR shows that the respective requirements are almost impossible to comply with in practice. With respect to non-personal data, the effects of such a provision may be even more severe due to the widespread worldwide exchange of non-personal data. In addition, Article 32(1) Data Act may also be in conflict with the limited liability rules laid down in the DSA.[96] Due to these problems, the recommendation was to delete Article 32(1) Data Act and thereby to prevent the implied equivalence test from becoming a principle of European data law.[97]

C. Broader Governance Approach: Creating Sector-specific Data Spaces

In addition to the emerging legal framework, the European Commission increasingly focuses on a more holistic approach of establishing a more general governance framework for data. To facilitate data sharing and remove legal and technical barriers, the concept of Common European Data Spaces was introduced. Their objective is to increase control over and access to data and support data sharing by establishing an infrastructure. This infrastructure would include tools and data governance structures to improve the quality and interoperability of data. The design of the data spaces will be based on certain principles,[98] building upon

[92] Article 32(3) Data Act (n 7).

[93] Case 362/14 *Maximilian Schrems v Data Protection Commissioner* ECLI:EU:C:2015:650, [2016] 2 WLR 873; Case C-311/18 *Data Protection Commissioner v Facebook Ireland Ltd, Maximilian Schrems* ECLI:EU:C:2020:559, [2021] 1 WLR 751.

[94] See Drexl et al, Position Statement 2022 (n 25) para 190.

[95] See Drexl et al, Position Statement 2022 (n 25) para 197 et seqq. Free Flow of Non-Personal Data Regulation (n 5) focuses on eliminating intra-EU data localisation.

[96] See Drexl et al, Position Statement 2022 (n 25) para 206.

[97] See also Drexl et al, Position Statement 2022 (n 25) para 214.

[98] Commission Staff Working Document on Common European Data Spaces, SWD(2022) 45 final of 23.2.2022, 3.

and aligning with the different legal instruments discussed above. Data Spaces are planned for 12 different sectors.[99]

A proposal was already published for the health sector.[100] Article 33 et seqq of the Proposal on the European Health Data Space includes obligations to provide data and introduces rules for its secondary use. This regulation provides a balanced approach considering the relevant interests, especially regarding data protection. On this level, the legislator itself provides a sector-specific solution to conflicting interests that will supplement and complement the pertinent legislative instruments. The framework for the health data space would be complementary and specific, especially with respect to the more general rules of the DGA and the Data Act. This approach of combining general regulations with sector-specific frameworks can contribute to consistency by creating a comprehensive governance framework for the most relevant sectors, for example, a key governance feature is the provision of secure processing environments. Building on Article 5 DGA, the concept is now also integrated into Article 50 of the European Health Data Space Regulation Proposal.

VI. Conclusions and Perspectives

The emerging patchwork of regulations concerning data, data processing services and other types of intermediation services cover MGD to a certain extent and create a considerable level of uncertainty. The regulations have different scopes of applications and different rules apply in overlapping areas. Conflict rules inserted into the regulations are trivial and leave wide room for interpretation. Hence, recourse to general rules of interpretation will be taken, and in most cases the *lex specialis* rule will have to be applied. As far as possible, practical concordance in interpretation should be sought as long as there is no outright incompatibility arising from legislative conflicts.

As to the regulation of MGD, frictions arising from this patchwork approach are not so large as one would expect. An important step is the common definition of 'data' as part of determining the scope of application of the different regulatory instruments. With intellectual property protection being almost irrelevant to MGD, the main conflict in this field arises between rights to access data and trade secret protection of data. As the latter mostly applies only to aggregated data and these would be excluded from the Data Act, it is largely a theoretical question. With the safeguards built into the Data Act concerning trade secret protection, a legislative balance is provided. From a policy point of view, the narrow exception for denying access rights appears to be questionable.

[99] See ibid 12 et seqq.

[100] Proposal for a Regulation on European Health Data Space, COM(2022) 197 final of 3.5.2022, eur-lex.europa.eu/procedure/EN/2022_140.

The biggest friction was found between access rights and data protection legislation. Being applicable to personal data as well, the Data Act in fact amends the GDPR while pretending that both pieces of legislation are in harmony. Compatibility is still welcome from the legislator as interpretation alone will not suffice. Consent as a basis for access rights is shaky, especially with respect to third parties, and difficult to effectuate in practice. The preferable option would have been to establish access rights in the Data Act as a legal basis in the sense of Article 6 GDPR, combined with an accentuated obligation of anonymisation at an early stage.

Further legislative clarifications would have been worth including in the Data Act. While a broad general concept of 'data' is emerging in the definitions of the different regulations, a narrower concept of MGD is stipulated especially in the Data Act. It would have been desirable to extend its scope of application beyond data produced by connected products insofar as specific other regulations do not cover these other types of data. Moreover, the Data Act could have covered aggregated and derived data to be in line with other data-related legislation and sector-specific rules.

While the Data Act is taking centre stage as to the legal framework for MGD, European legislation is aiming at creating a broader governance framework that also includes technical and organisational measures. In this respect, compatibility with the DGA can be observed. Because of its different legal objectives, the Data Act is also compatible with the DMA and other competition-oriented legislation like the P2B Regulation. While these include a higher degree of regulation and administrative oversight, the Data Act aims at establishing a legal framework for the market process resulting in increased provision of data. These approaches are complementary. However, the Data Act as the centrepiece of MGD regulation does risk creating technical overprotection. Moreover, the architecture of the Data Act will be subject to a reality check. If it will not work in practice, new competition problems may arise, creating a need for new instruments and increased enforcement of competition law rules.

In perspective, it appears inevitable to supplement the horizontal approach of the Data Act with sector-specific rules that could be adapted to the specifics of the sector.[101] In light of future specific legislation, the appropriateness of a general Data Act may well be questioned again and its rules may be replaced. Further coherence has to be provided by judicial and academic interpretation and development. Frictions can be smoothed over in most cases. Moreover, distilling principles from the patchwork of legal rules and obligations can make visible a basis for the emerging order of data governance that constitutes an important factor for developing data markets and promoting innovation. For the most relevant areas of data access and use, the concept of European data spaces may be a promising way of establishing a data framework that could provide for concordance of different legal interests in a consistent way.

[101] See W Kerber, 'Data Governance in Connected Cars: The Problem of Access to In-Vehicle Data' (2018) 9 *JIPITEC* 310, 325f; W Kerber, 'Data-sharing in IoT Ecosystems and Competition Law: The Example of Connected Cars' 15(4) (2019) *Journal of Competition Law & Economics* 381, 394.

PART IV

Legal Consistency between EU and Member State Law

7

The Implementation of the GDPR in Member States' Law and Issues of Coherence and Consistency

MARK D COLE AND CHRISTINA ETTELDORF

I. Introduction

Replacing the former Data Protection Directive[1] of the European Union, the General Data Protection Regulation (GDPR)[2] was and still is a milestone for a harmonised and strong protection of personal data and thus also of the fundamental right to privacy across the EU. But even beyond the borders of the EU, the GDPR has implications for a global level of data protection. On the one hand, on the legislative level, many new data protection instruments in other countries follow the EU blueprint[3] or States adapt their existing data protection laws or related rules in order to obtain an adequacy decision from the European Commission for data transfers from the EU to third countries. On the other hand, at practice level, globally operating companies align their data protection policies with the standards set

[1] Directive 95/46/EC of the European Parliament and of the Council of 24 October 1995 on the protection of individuals with regard to the processing of personal data and on the free movement of such data [1995] OJ L 281/31.

[2] Regulation (EU) 2016/679 of the European Parliament and of the Council of 27 April 2016 on the protection of natural persons with regard to the processing of personal data and on the free movement of such data, and repealing Directive 95/46/EC (General Data Protection Regulation) [2016] OJ L 119/1.

[3] For example, the California Consumer Privacy Act (oag.ca.gov/privacy/ccpa) which came into force in January 2020 (see on that N Witzleb and S Hünting, 'The Influence of the GDPR on Protection of Young People's Privacy: New developments in China, California and Australia' (2023) *European Data Protection Law Review* 239–50), the Japanese Act on the Protection of Personal Information of 2018 (see on that H Iwase, 'Overview of the Act on the Protection of Personal Information' (2019) *European Data Protection Law Review* 92–98), the Brazilian Lei Geral de Proteção de Dados Pessoais (www.planalto.gov.br/ccivil_03/_ato2015-2018/2018/lei/l13709.htm) which has taken effect in August 2020 (see on that O Filipec et al, 'Personal Data Protection in Brazil: How Much Europeanization?' (2022) 2 *International and Comparative Law Review* 81–104), or the new Indonesian Law on the Protection of Personal Data (www.dpr.go.id/dokakd/dokumen/K1-RJ-20220920-123712-3183.pdf) which was approved in October 2022.

by the GDPR and do so not only for their activities in the EU, thereby giving the GDPR provisions international weight – the result often being referred to as the 'Brussels effect'.

As a Regulation the GDPR is directly applicable in all Member States and it features a high degree of harmonisation, in particular containing detailed rules about general principles, obligations, rights, supervision and sanctioning tools. One could therefore assume that questions of coherence and consistency of a national 'implementation' do not even arise, as there is no direct transposition obligation in contrast to the situation with Directives and as it formerly existed for the Data Protection Directive. However, three characteristics of the GDPR in particular mean that such an assumption is not true in a general and absolute manner: (1) the GDPR does not have an exhaustive scope of application, ie it does not apply to all types of data processing and leaves regulatory space to national law for the areas not covered; (2) the GDPR contains a number of opening clauses or margins for manoeuvre that can be (and have been) taken up by the Member States through domestic specific law; and (3) even within its scope of application, the GDPR contains margins for interpretation that are regularly (and at least initially) fleshed out by the competent data protection authorities and courts of the Member States. In order to answer questions about the consistency of the legal framework and possible legal tensions arising in the described setup, this contribution briefly analyses the scope of application of the GDPR and, associated with this, the remaining national scope for regulatory action, illustrates by means of a few selected areas how differences in data protection rules at the legislative level within the EU result from the use of such leeway,[4] addresses questions of different interpretation and their possible approaches to solutions within the case law of the Court of Justice of the European Union and the coherence mechanisms of the GDPR, and finally draws conclusions from this concerning the degree of a (potential) regulatory fragmentation.

II. GDPR: Scope and Margin(s) of Manoeuvre

The scope of application of the GDPR is limited in material and territorial terms by Articles 2 and 3 respectively. Only the processing of personal data is addressed. Personal data means any information relating to an identified or identifiable natural person, and processing activities are covered if carried out either automatically or in a filing system and not exclusively for family or household purposes. Data processing by the police and judiciary, in the framework of the Common Foreign and Security

[4] The Reports Section of the European Data Protection Law Review (EDPL), which the authors of this contribution are responsible for, has been hosting a special segment under the title 'GDPR implementation series' since 2017, in the context of which national implementation reports have been published on almost all Member States (including the UK) until date. This article also draws on the findings of this series.

Policy, and by Union institutions, bodies, offices and agencies is excluded from the scope of the GDPR, as specific legal acts exist for these areas. In territorial terms, processing activities which are neither carried out by EU-based undertakings nor concern EU citizens (which is the case if they do not offer goods/services to them or monitor their behaviour) are excluded. Overall, the GDPR nonetheless covers a broad spectrum of diverse economic activities within the Union.

Irrespective of this finding, Chapter 9 of the GDPR is a further limitation of the scope of the GDPR as it gives Member States additional leeway for provisions in the context of specific processing situations. This concerns processing in a variety of different areas such as public access to official documents, the national ID number, employment, archiving, scientific, historical, statistical or research purposes, purposes of academic, artistic or literary expression as well as religious activities. An illustrative example of the possible range of these special provisions is Article 85 GDPR, often referred to as the 'media privilege'. It applies to data processing for journalistic purposes, which can cover a wide range of constellations in practice.[5] The consequences that the GDPR ties to such specific processing activities vary in nuances, but essentially focus on either obliging (as a mandate to foresee such provisions) or at least enabling the Member States (in the meaning of a margin of manoeuvre) to enact their own specific national rules in these areas.

On top of that, the GDPR contains numerous opening clauses, some count up to 70,[6] allowing for the Member States to derogate from the regulatory substance of the GDPR or to adopt additional provisions. This can be seen as a result of a compromise in moving from a Directive to a Regulation in further developing the data protection rules on EU level. Consequently, there may be local differences even where the situation in question falls within the scope of the GDPR. This may come in the form of stricter, more liberal or more detailed rules. Notably, these leeways partly concern essential elements of the data protection regime such as the requirements for the designation of a data protection officer in data processing entities, the age level of minors for giving consent or data breach notification obligations.[7]

Finally, more specific provisions may arise, for example, from the Directive on privacy and electronic communications[8] (Article 95 GDPR) including national transpositions or from international agreements existing before 2016

[5] According to the Court of Justice, journalistic activities are those which have as their purpose the disclosure to the public of information, opinions or ideas, irrespective of the medium which is used to transmit them (see, to that effect, Case C-73/07 *Satakunnan Markkinapörssi and Satamedia* ECLI:EU:C:2008:727, [2008] ECR I-9831, para 61.

[6] See for a detailed overview E Miscenic and A-L Hoffmann, 'The Role of Opening Clauses in Harmonization of EU Law: Example of the EU's General Data Protection Regulation (GDPR)' (2020) *EU and comparative law issues and challenges series* 44–61.

[7] On the latter see generally MD Cole and S Schmitz, 'The Interplay Between the NIS Directive and the GDPR in a Cybersecurity Threat Landscape' (2020) *University of Luxembourg Law Working Paper* No. 2019–017.

[8] Directive 2002/58/EC of the European Parliament and of the Council of 12 July 2002 concerning the processing of personal data and the protection of privacy in the electronic communications sector (Directive on privacy and electronic communications) [2002] OJ L 201/37.

(Article 96 GDPR), which remain unaffected by the GDPR, at least in the conception of the GDPR provisions.

An overall look at these provisions shows, even if one takes a cursory glance, that there is no (and there might not be an intention for) full harmonisation of data protection law at EU level. Whether this leads to a fragmentation and, if so, which practical effects this has, depends on whether and to what extent a use of the possibilities at national level results in different sets of rules and behaviours of data processing entities.

III. Specific Processing Activities: The Example of the 'Media Privilege'

A. Context of Article 85 GDPR

As mentioned, the GDPR contains a number of exceptions for specific processing activities that require horizontal rules for certain sectors or elements of data processing. The reasons for such national specificities may vary – for example, processing in the employment context might depend on an alignment with national labour law or, in the religious context, on the status of churches and faith communities in the national legal system. An in-depth analysis of the 'implementation of the GDPR' in light of issues of coherence would therefore require, on the one hand, a consideration of all the areas mentioned and, on the other hand, possibly also a consideration of the regulatory 'network' in which data protection-specific rules operate.[9] None of this can be provided in the context of this contribution, instead an exemplary look at the aforementioned media privilege of Article 85 GDPR will be taken. This is interesting for two reasons. First, although the legal nature of this provision as either a binding mandate or offering a voluntary leeway to Member States has not been finally resolved, Article 85 GDPR is formulated more strongly ('shall' instead of 'may') and detailed in the way it addresses the Member States compared to the other provisions of Chapter 9, thus indicating a more pressing need for the adoption of national rules. This is set against the background of fundamental rights when it comes to securing the specific role of journalistic work.[10] Second, the media privilege concerns an area that is strongly characterised by different cultural traditions, also within the Union, and falls in the cultural prerogative of the Member States as far as the allocation of powers between Member States and the EU are concerned.[11]

[9] For the employment context see eg HH Abraha, 'A pragmatic compromise? The role of Article 88 GDPR in upholding privacy in the workplace' (2022) 4 *International Data Privacy Law* 276–96.

[10] See for an analysis and further references C Etteldorf, 'Media Privilege' in M Capello (ed), *Journalism and Media Privilege* (European Audiovisual Observatory, 2017).

[11] Extensively on this MD Cole, J Ukrow and C Etteldorf, *On the Allocation of Competences between the European Union and its Member States in the Media Sector – An Analysis with particular Consideration of Measures concerning Media Pluralism* (Nomos, 2021) doi.org/10.5771/9783748924975.

On a more general note, Article 85(1) of the GDPR states that Member States shall by law reconcile the right to the protection of personal data with the right to freedom of expression and information. More concretely, Article 85(2) of the GDPR adds that for processing carried out for journalistic purposes, Member States shall provide for exemptions or derogations from Chapters II–VII and IX if they are necessary to reconcile the right to the protection of personal data with the freedom of expression and information. This is accompanied by a notification obligation vis-à-vis the Commission (Article 85(3) of the GDPR).[12] Most of the Member States have taken up this task (or opportunity) by providing specific rules in their national media law.[13]

B. Lithuania

For example, very extensive protection in the context of journalistic work is provided for in Lithuania.[14] According to Article 4 of the Lithuanian Law on Legal Protection of Personal Data,[15] Articles 8, 12–23, 25, 30, 33-39, 41–50 and 88–91 of the GDPR do not apply in their entirety when personal data is processed for journalistic purposes. In addition, the notion of journalistic purposes, which is not defined by law, is interpreted broadly on national level[16] and is not bound to further requirements such as an assessment of whether the application of the GDPR would lead to an interference with journalistic freedom. Furthermore, the supervision in these cases does not lie with the data protection authority, as in all other cases, but with the Office of the Inspector for Journalist Ethics whose competences are limited to specifically this area.

C. Germany

The latter aspect of supervision is even more detailed in Germany when it comes to the legislative framing of the media privilege. Due to the federal structures of

[12] Notifications are available at commission.europa.eu/law/law-topic/data-protection/data-protection-eu/eu-member-states-notifications-european-commission-under-gdpr_en#:~:text=Under%20the%20General%20Data%20Protection,(Article%2085(3)).

[13] For a detailed overview *cf* TIPIK Legal, *Report on the implementation of specific provisions of Regulation (EU) 2016/679*, as published on 6 January 2021 by the European Commission, www.dataguidance.com/sites/default/files/1609930170392.pdf; N Bitiukova, 'Journalistic Exemption under the European Data Protection Law' (2020) *Vilnius Institute for Policy Analysis, Policy Paper Series*, www.vilniusinstitute.lt/wp-content/uploads/2020/02/VIPA_Bitiukova_2020_v5_LTsum_f.pdf.

[14] N Bitiukova 'GDPR implementation series: Lithuania' (2021) *European Data Protection Law Review* 108, 110 et seq.

[15] Law on Legal Protection of Personal Data (No I-1374 of 11 June 1996), e-seimas.lrs.lt/portal/legalAct/lt/TAD/ef70b5d2f14811e78f3dc265493430ae.

[16] N Bitiukova, 'Lithuanian Supreme Administrative Court Undertakes a Legitimate Interests Assessment in a Seminal Case on Journalistic Expression' (2022) *European Data Protection Law Review* 128–33; Bitiukova (n 13).

the country allocating relevant competences for media law and institutional structures on the level of the German Länder, supervision of data protection law lies in principle with 16 data protection authorities of the Länder. In case of journalistic activities, the rules are way more complex and multiplied.[17]

In essence, a distinction is made between different media categories (press, broadcasting and journalistic-editorial online media) with regard to data processing for journalistic purposes, for each of which different rules arise from various (around 50(!)) state laws and inter-state treaties. For the press, supervision lies partly with the data protection authorities, but in some Länder it can be transferred to the German Press Council if the press company adheres to this institution of voluntary self-regulation.

A similar approach is taken for journalistic online media. For commercial broadcasting, in most Länder the data protection authorities are in principle in charge of supervision, but then combined with the involvement of the national regulatory authorities for the media (*Landesmediananstalten*, state media authorities) in various ways (eg responsibility for complaints, notification obligations, rights of control or objection, etc). In other Länder, specific data protection commissioners at the respective state media authorities are competent altogether. For public service broadcasting, supervision is not carried out by an administrative authority, but by a broadcasting data protection commissioner within the broadcasters themselves.

With regard to the substantive rules, the respective state laws do not declare certain rules of the GDPR inapplicable, as is the case in Lithuania and many other Member States, but conversely only make certain rules applicable (usually Articles 5(1) and (2), 24, 32, 33, Chapter VII with special provisions on data secrecy, Chapters VIII, X and XI). Some particularities concern the possibility of deviating from the rules by means of codes of conduct and include special provisions on the right to information in the event of violations of personal rights.

D. Cyprus

Cyprus is another interesting candidate for a closer look at the national shape of the media privilege.[18] According to Section 29(1) of Law 125(I)2018,[19] the processing of any kind of personal data carried out for journalistic purposes is

[17] For a detailed overview of the system C Etteldorf, 'Synopse zu den Änderungen landesrechtlicher Regelungen zur Umsetzung des 21. RÄndStV und der DS-GVO' (2018) *Archiv für Medienrecht und Medienwissenschaft (UFITA)* 170–95.

[18] C Markou, 'GDPR Implementation Series: Cyprus: A Look into the Law for the Effective Application of the GDPR' (2019) *European Data Protection Law Review* 389, 395.

[19] Law providing for the Protection of Natural Persons with regard to the Processing of Personal Data and for the Free Movement of such Data of 2018 (Law 125(I)/2018), unofficial English version available at www.dataprotection.gov.cy/dataprotection/dataprotection.nsf/All/2B53605103DCE4A4C225826300362211.

lawful provided that the purposes for which processing takes place are proportionate to the objective pursued and respect the substance of the rights in the Charter of Fundamental Rights of the EU, the European Convention of Human Rights and Part II of the Cypriotic Constitution. This provision explicitly mentions that the processing of personal data or special categories of personal data or personal data relating to criminal convictions and offences is allowed for such purposes. Section 29(2) clarifies that Articles 14 and 15 GDPR apply to the extent that they do not affect freedom of expression and information as well as the journalistic privilege, which is intended to inter alia safeguard journalists against the risk of having to disclose their sources.

Other provisions of the GDPR are not addressed explicitly. Furthermore, there are no specific provisions in the supervisory system governing this area, as in other sectors, supervision is carried out by the Cypriot Data Protection Commissioner. However, there are some special rules in media law as well as binding guidance from the media authority, which relate to data processing in the context of the violation of personal rights.

E. Slovakia

In contrast, for example, Slovakian legislation is rather cautious when it comes to the media privilege settling with a more general provision without providing detailed rules on the applicability of the concrete provisions or chapters of the GDPR.[20] Section 78(2) of Act no. 18/2018[21] stipulates, derogating from the wording ('journalistic purposes') of the GDPR, that the controller may process personal data without consent of the data subject where this processing is necessary to inform the public by mass media means and where the personal data are processed by a controller based on its field of activity (eg press, a press agency, a broadcaster or similar subjects). However, this shall not apply where a controller violates the right of a data subject to the protection of their person or the right to privacy, or where such processing without consent of a data subject is excluded by a special regulation or an international treaty binding upon the Slovak Republic.

F. Comparative Assessment

As a result, it can be observed that even in a cursory overview of a few Member States, the implementation of the media privilege is very diverse and characterised

[20] M Mesarčík, 'GDPR Implementation Series Slovakia: On the Way to Accountability?' (2019) *European Data Protection Law Review* 537, 541.

[21] Act no. 18/2018 on personal data protection and amending and supplementing certain Acts, unofficial English version available at www.dataprotection.gov.sk/uoou/sites/default/files/2019_10_03_act_18_2018_on_personal_data_protection_and_amending_and_supplementing_certain_acts.pdf#overlay-context=sk/content/182018#overlay-context=sk/content/182018%22.

by different national approaches, which must be adapted to the legal context (here: the media law) in the respective Member State. This concerns on paper only a small excerpt of the GDPR, but in reality it involves a multitude of issues, since it is about a very essential form of data processing: journalistic investigations and reporting, which are essential for democratic decision-making processes. However, news coverage is increasingly global, especially online, where national borders and language barriers play only a subordinate role, and is shaped not only by traditional media protagonists, but also by distribution channels via intermediaries such as search engines, social networks or video-sharing platforms. From the point of view of both these actors and the data subjects concerned, the different implementations of the media privilege, which is deliberately allowed or even required by the GDPR, means that a different level of protection applies depending on the country of residence or distribution. This ranges from the question of whether they are covered by the privileges at all to the question of which supervisory authorities are responsible. It should also be pointed out here that the sectoral authorities (such as in Lithuania or Germany) are regularly not involved in finding coherent approaches to issues of international relevance within the framework of the European Data Protection Board.

IV. The GDPR and the Opening Clauses

In order to assess possible tensions stemming from a fragmentation of the regulatory framework for data protection, the use of the GDPR's opening clauses has to be taken into consideration, but cannot be provided in an all-encompassing manner within the scope of this contribution. However, there are some opening clauses dealing with issues that are particularly significant in cross-border data processing which in turn is a major aspect for questions of coherence and consistency: namely, the relevant age for giving consent for data processing and the processing of special categories of personal data such as biometric data. In an era of technological evolution, these two aspects can also coincide within one and the same daily life situation. One could think, for example, of age verification mechanisms for the protection of minors in the media that work with AI-based facial recognition software and are offered by globally operating companies for a variety of different online services.

A. Age of Consent

While the GDPR in several places acknowledges the importance of protecting children's personal data, it does not provide for a definition of a 'child' or an age limit. However, Article 8(1) GDPR does include such a limit when it comes to the requirements for lawful consent in relation to the offer of information society services under data protection law or when such consent can be given by the data subject themselves or when it is necessary to obtain it from the legal representative. The GDPR sets a minimum age of 16 years, but opens up the possibility for Member States (sentence 3) to provide by national law for a lower age concerning such purposes provided that the lower age chosen is not below 13 years. The majority of Member States (18 out of 27) have taken up this possibility, while the age of 16 years remains relevant in Germany, Croatia, Hungary, Luxembourg, the Netherlands, Poland, Romania, Slovakia, and, importantly, Ireland.[22] For the rest, the age limit in the EU is widely spread from 13 (Belgium, Denmark, Estonia, Finland, Latvia, Malta, Portugal, Sweden) and 14 (Austria, Bulgaria, Cyprus, Spain, Italy, Lithuania), to 15 (Czech Republic, Greece, France).

This divergence is primarily due to the fact that data protection law is also based on an assessment of whether the data subject, depending on their development, is capable of making a decision on their own responsibility, the implications and consequences of which they are fully aware of. Such aspects are also familiar to other, much older areas of law, such as civil and criminal law, when it comes to questions of liability or the ability to enter into contracts. Since such areas of law are not harmonised in the EU, or only in minor partial aspects, they have developed independently and differently, thus regularly providing for different standards in the Member States. The situation is similar in the law on the protection of minors in the media in which age thresholds for media content such as films, video games or other publications are regularly established by national law, media regulatory authorities or independent review bodies to protect children from content that is impairing their development (through labelling, broadcasting time restrictions or access controls). These thresholds also vary widely across Member States.

Against this background, the different approaches to Article 8(1) GDPR are not surprising. What is surprising, however, is that this topic seems to have been one of the most hotly debated in many Member States during the implementation process. In Slovakia, the age of consent was one of the focus areas of the debate during the parliamentary session focusing on the 'mental ability' of persons younger than 16 to apprehend the peculiarities of how information society services provided to them use their personal data. Although in the end Slovakia chose to stick to the age limit of 16, there were voices calling for a lower threshold opening up the way for further discussions in future.[23] In Sweden, the proposal of the Governmental Committee suggesting to lower the age limit to 13 was viewed rather critically by the Swedish data protection authority arguing that this would contradict the former practice of 15 years of age for giving consent in Sweden. In the end, the counterargument that a higher age limit would exclude children from participating in online activities prevailed.[24] This argument was also one of the decisive

[22] TIPIK Legal, Implementation Report (n 13) 5 et seq.

[23] Mesarčík (n 20) 537, 541.

[24] C Storr and P Storr, 'GDPR Implementation Series Sweden: Quantitative (but Qualitative?) Changes in Privacy Legislation' (2018) *European Data Protection Law Review* 97, 101 et seq.

aspects in discussions in Finland together with arguments that children have a right to self-development, they are today more accustomed to information society services and that a higher limit would lead to more circumvention of age verification systems.[25] It is remarkable that especially the Nordic countries with lower age limits have more confidence in children in the digital space and give them more leeway in their self-development. Bulgaria, on the other hand, not only lowered this age limit to 14 but in addition did not limit it to consent vis-à-vis information society services but introduced a general rule for the digital and analogue world.[26]

Western EU Member States, on the other hand, are perceived as being more 'conservative' in their view of minors and exposure to content, including Ireland. Ireland has to be mentioned in the present context because the most popular information society services, especially among children, such as various applications from Google or Meta, TikTok or Twitter, have their European headquarters in Dublin, which makes Irish law particularly relevant, including the responsibility of the Irish Data Protection Commissioner as lead supervisory authority. One may, therefore, assume that these services would be guided by the Irish implementation in their terms of use and therefore provide for a minimum age of 16 for the use of the platforms as part of the registration process. It is true that the registration process is basically of a civil law nature. However, it has become an open secret that the registration process for services such as Facebook, Instagram or TikTok also includes 'consent' (only in some cases through a separate consent button) to a number of data uses for which (real) consent is regularly required. Nevertheless, the majority of these services set the minimum age in their terms at 13 years, ie the minimum age of the GDPR, which actually only applies in eight Member States and not in Ireland. It is, of course, not surprising that the platforms choose the most favourable alternative for them – conversely, they are obliged to ensure the capacity of the individual to consent (Article 8(3) GDPR). But even a hypothetical will to establish a harmonised level of protection would be difficult to implement because the ideas and traditions as well as the legal bases are so diverse across the Union.

B. Processing of Biometric Data

According to Article 9 GDPR, special categories of personal data receive a higher protection due to their sensitive nature by inter alia limiting the legal bases for processing such types of data. In most cases, consent is required without the possibility of relying on other grounds such as contracts or legitimate interests. Article 9(4) GDPR, in a rather wide approach, states that Member States may maintain or introduce further conditions in addition to those provided in Article 9(1)–(3)

[25] P Korpisaari, 'GDPR Implementation Series Finland: A Brief Overview of the GDPR Implementation' (2019) *European Data Protection Law Review* 232, 234 et seq.

[26] M Zahariev and R Makshutova, 'GDPR Implementation Series Bulgaria' (2020) *European Data Protection Law Review* 424, 428.

GDPR, including limitations, with regard to the processing of certain kinds of special categories of personal data, namely of genetic data, biometric data or data concerning health.

Certainly, in light of the pandemic, the processing of health data and the question of whether there are any special applicable national rules has taken on particular weight in recent years. This concerned in particular the compatibility of containment measures and the use of related means, such as corona warning apps, information obligations of infected persons or access restrictions such as fever tests.[27] However, since the processing of health data is somewhat more closely linked to public health and therefore often also (but not only) follows sector-specific rules in an administrative context, a closer look will be taken in the following paragraphs at special rules for the processing of biometric data. This is interesting from the perspective of the most diverse sectors, because it can be utilised in a variety of ways.

Biometric data are, for example fingerprints, facial recognition, DNA, iris or retina recognition, but even an odour or voice can be categorised as such data. Processing of such data takes place in many different areas, such as law enforcement, identity or age verification, mobile payment methods or access security (unlocking smartphones, securing buildings, operating personal voice assistants, etc). Many of these areas of application have the advantage that they can also be used in the digital sector through existing technologies on end devices, for example by accessing the camera on a laptop or using sensors on a smartphone, and can deliver the desired results with a fair degree of certainty. This makes them particularly interesting in a cross-border context.

However, most Member States – except Austria, the Czech Republic, Denmark, Sweden and Slovakia[28] – went a step beyond the rules of the GDPR and used the opening clause to restrict the possibilities of utilisation for data controllers and processors or to provide more security to data subjects. The specifications are quite different. Some states already limit the persons authorised to access data by law, describe their role and define their confidentiality obligations (eg Belgium), limit the legally permitted purposes (eg Luxembourg), require written consent (eg Portugal), limit storage periods (eg Latvia) or define whose biometric data may not be processed (eg Bulgaria with regard to minors).[29]

What is particularly noteworthy is the role assigned to data protection authorities. Italy, for example, according to Article 2-septies of Legislative Decree No. 101 of 10 August 2018,[30] follows the approach of transferring substantive statutory powers to the data protection authority, which shall regulate all further conditions. In particular, this involves required security measures, including technical

[27] See on this in detail C Etteldorf, 'EU Member State Data Protection Authorities Deal with Covid-19: An Overview' (2020) *European Data Protection Law Review* 265–80.

[28] TIPIK Legal, Implementation report (n 13) 5 et seq.

[29] ibid 8.

[30] Legislative Decree No. 101 of 10 August 2018 (GU no. 205 of 04.09.2018).

measures for encryption and pseudonymisation, data minimisation measures, specific modalities for selective access to the data and for the provision of the information to and rights of data subjects, in legally binding guidelines.[31] Such binding guidance was already issued by the authority in 2014,[32] but at the time of writing has not yet been updated (the new 2018 law requires an update every two years). In addition to exceptional cases of lawful processing of biometric data, for example in the banking and tax sectors, as well as in critical infrastructures to enable security measures, relevant input in Poland[33] also comes from the Polish data protection authority. In a communication, the authority points out that biometric data may only be processed with restraint and in exceptional cases and also gives advice on some specific cases (discrimination and children's data).[34] French law also relies strongly on concretisations by the data protection authority. According to Article 8(2)(c) of the French Data Protection Act,[35] the authority shall, in consultation with the public and private representative bodies of the actors concerned, determine particular technical and organisational measures for the processing of biometric data.[36] In 2019, the authority followed up on this with guidelines on standard regulations for the implementation of devices for the purpose of controlling access by biometric authentication to premises, equipment and IT applications in the workplace.[37]

Hence, this analysis also shows that data controllers in the EU may have to comply with different rules across Member States, with some being more lenient and some being stricter in comparison with the baseline established in the GDPR.

V. Interpretation and Application of the GDPR

Even where there are no specific provisions in national law falling within the scope of application of the GDPR, questions of coherence and consistency can be raised. This concerns primarily issues of interpretation of the law and thus also regarding the sanctioning of infringements of GDPR rules. In this context, it is important

[31] G Finocchiaro, 'GDPR Implementation Series Italy: The Legislative Procedure for National Harmonisation with the GDPR' (2018) *European Data Protection Law Review* 496, 497 et seq.

[32] General Application Order Concerning Biometrics – 12 November 2014, www.garanteprivacy.it/web/guest/home/docweb/-/docweb-display/docweb/3590114.

[33] A Kobylańska and M Lewoszewski, 'GDPR Implementation Series Poland: A Brief Overview Concerning the Implementation of the GDPR' (2017) *European Data Protection Law Review* 507, 510 et seq.

[34] See press release of the data protection authority (09.08.2021) in English with further references to the Guidance, www.uodo.gov.pl/en/553/1283.

[35] Loi n° 78-17 du 6 janvier 1978 relative à l'informatique, aux fichiers et aux libertés, consolidated version available at www.cnil.fr/fr/la-loi-informatique-et-libertes.

[36] O Tambou, 'GDPR Implementation Series France: The French Approach to the GDPR Implementation' (2018) *European Data Protection Law Review* 88, 91 et seq.

[37] Délibération n° 2019-001 du 10 janvier 2019 portant règlement type relatif à la mise en œuvre de dispositifs ayant pour finalité le contrôle d'accès par authentification biométrique aux locaux, aux appareils et aux applications informatiques sur les lieux de travail, www.cnil.fr/sites/default/files/atoms/files/deliberation-2019-001-10-01-2019-reglement-type-controle-dacces-biometrique.pdf.

to recall two fundamental characteristics of the GDPR. First, due to the character of the GDPR as a Regulation, the Court of Justice has the interpretative sovereignty, generally speaking. Second, although all supervisory authorities of the Member States are in principle competent for matters on their territory (Article 55), the concept of lead supervisory authority applies in matters with a cross-border dimension (Article 56), which is linked to the cooperation mechanisms established by creation of the European Data Protection Board (EDPB). Without going into the details of EU and procedural law at this point, these characteristics essentially lead to the situation that, when assessing compliance with the GDPR, it is initially the views of the national (potentially lead) supervisory authorities and courts that are decisive. These views may well differ between Member States.[38] Supranational consistency can then be established in a second step, either when the procedural mechanisms provided for by the GDPR come into play within the EDPB, or when it comes to proceedings before a court and the court decides to refer the matter to the Court of Justice (which it is obliged to do in certain circumstances). In the latter case, the judgment of the Court of Justice must be subsequently observed by the respective Member State. In what follows, these two mechanisms will be briefly discussed by way of examples.

A. Consistency Through the European Data Protection Board

Following their mandate (Article 60 GDPR), the national supervisory authorities, associated within the EDPB, initially cooperate in a general manner. This has already led to a number of Guidelines, Recommendations and Best Practices on a wide range of topics and processing activities, which also guide the individual national authorities in the performance of their tasks.[39] These initiatives result in a further degree of harmonisation. However, the consistency mechanisms provided for in Article 63 et seq are much more important, as they provide for the formal involvement of the EDPB in cross-border cases and thus of all national authorities. Within this framework, the lead supervisory authority is obliged to transmit its draft decision to the EDPB members thereby opening up the possibility of comments from other affected authorities. Following the prescribed procedural mechanisms, the EDPB can either publish an Opinion,[40] which the lead authority

[38] The pandemic, or rather reactions of the data protection authorities determining what measures are allowed and not allowed under data protection measures, very well demonstrated differences on national approaches. The guidance which had to be very quick in light of the time pressure for containment measures remained very strict in terms of data protection in some places, and turned rather 'soft' in others. See Etteldorf (n 27).

[39] An overview is available at www.edpb.europa.eu/our-work-tools/general-guidance/guidelines-recommendations-best-practices_en.

[40] The EDPB issued 31 of such Opinions so far. An overview is available at www.edpb.europa.eu/our-work-tools/consistency-findings/opinions_en.

shall then 'take utmost account' of in its final decision, or, in certain cases of particular relevance and in the event of divergent opinions between the authorities, even issue a Binding Decision which can be asked for also in an urgent procedure.

The first Binding Decision under this procedure was issued on 9 November 2020 and concerned the draft decision of the Irish supervisory authority against Twitter.[41] It was about a data breach which arose from a bug in Twitter's design. If a user on an Android device changed the email address associated with their Twitter account, the protected tweets became unprotected and therefore accessible to a wider public (and not just the user's followers) without the user's knowledge. This bug appeared from 2014 until 2019. From the period 2017 to 2019, it affected, according to Twitter's estimation, 88,726 users in Europe.[42] After an investigation *ex officio*, the Irish supervisory authority as lead authority (because Twitter's main establishment is in Dublin) triggered the consistency mechanism and submitted its draft decision to the other supervisory authorities because Twitter users across the territory of those Member States were also affected. In its May 2020 Draft Decision, the Irish supervisory authority proposed to impose a fine (set between $150.000- and $300.000, ie approximately €139.000–€277.000) for breaching Articles 33(1) and (5) GDPR. However, many of the other data protection authorities concerned were not satisfied with the draft decision, to say the least. They raised strong concerns in their responses, which ultimately led to the EDPB's Binding Decision after the relevant procedure had been carried out.

Criticism was raised in particular against the assessment of the Irish authority in light of its competence, the qualification of the roles of TIC and Twitter, Inc., the infringements that had been identified which were regarded as a too narrow reading of the GDPR, the lack of a reprimand and finally, and most importantly, the calculation of the proposed fine which the others regarded as being too low. In its 47-page analysis of the situation, the EDPB concluded that not all the concerns could be dealt with. This was because some concerns did not meet the requirements of a relevant and reasoned objection as defined in Article 4(24) GDPR or sufficient facts were not available to the Board for a decision. However, the Board 'at least' required the Irish authority to re-assess the elements it relied upon to calculate the amount of the fixed fine and to amend its Draft Decision by increasing the level of the fine in order to ensure it fulfils its purpose as a corrective measure and meets the requirements of effectiveness, dissuasiveness and proportionality. The Irish authority followed up in its final decision one month later by imposing a fine 'of €450.000 on Twitter as an effective, proportionate and dissuasive measure' (sic).[43]

[41] Decision 01/2020 on the dispute arisen on the draft decision of the Irish Supervisory Authority regarding Twitter International Company under Article 65(1)(a) GDPR (09.11.2020), www.edpb.europa.eu/sites/default/files/files/file1/edpb_bindingdecision01_2020_en.pdf.

[42] For a more detailed description and assessment of the whole case see L Mustert, 'The First Article 65 Decision – Correct and Consistent Application of the GDPR Ensured?' (2021) *European Data Protection Law Review* 94–100.

[43] See the press release of the Irish authority (15.12.2020), www.dataprotection.ie/en/news-media/press-releases/data-protection-commission-announces-decision-twitter-inquiry.

Thus, the concerns were addressed, at least to a certain degree, but the EDPB also indicated in its final remarks that a resolution of the other concerns could be possible in principle in subsequent proceedings in the future. However, it took time to get to this point – from the launch of the investigation in January 2019, to the communication of the draft decision in May 2020, to the EDPB decision in November 2020, to the final announcement of the penalty in December 2020.

The first EDPB Urgent Binding Decision of 12 July 2021, on the other hand, was taken in a much faster procedure reflecting the characteristic of the urgency procedure. It dealt with a request under Article 66(2) of the GDPR from the Hamburg Supervisory Authority (one of the German Länder supervisory authorities) for ordering the adoption of final measures regarding Facebook.[44] In short, it was about the amendment of WhatsApp's terms of use in May 2021, requiring users to consent to the merging of their data of the different services and use for various purposes (including marketing) by the entire Facebook group (now Meta). The Hamburg authority felt compelled to take immediate measures due to the urgency of the case, so that it issued a provisional prohibition against WhatsApp. Facebook had already announced this change of the terms of service to the Irish supervisory authority in December 2020. Although the Irish authority had been urged by the German authorities to take countermeasures after having communicated the information to the other national authorities within the information exchange mechanism, it had not acted by that date. The EDPB's decision was rather sobering. The Board decided that no final measures had to be taken by the Irish authority because, on the one hand, no particular urgency could be established and, on the other hand, although there was a high likelihood that Facebook was already (unlawfully) processing data of WhatsApp users, the EDPB did not have sufficient evidence for this.

About two weeks later, however, the EDPB issued its next Binding Decision regarding WhatsApp, which, although it does not resemble exactly the facts of the Urgent Binding Decision, at least addressed also the processing of data within the Facebook group.[45] Based on numerous 'reprimands', the EDPB acted against the Draft Decision of the Irish lead authority. Among others, the EDPB instructed the Irish authority to find that there has been an infringement of Article 13(1)(d) GDPR, which the authority so far had declined. This eventually led to a final fine against WhatsApp in the amount of 225 million euros coming from the Irish supervisory authority.[46]

[44] Urgent Binding Decision 01/2021 on the request under Article 66(2) GDPR from the Hamburg (German) Supervisory Authority for ordering the adoption of final measures regarding Facebook Ireland Limited (12.07.2021), www.edpb.europa.eu/system/files/2021-07/edpb_urgent bindingdecision_20210712_requesthh_fbireland_en.pdf.

[45] Binding Decision 1/2021 on the dispute arisen on the draft decision of the Irish Supervisory Authority regarding WhatsApp Ireland under Article 65(1)(a) GDPR (28.07.2021), www.edpb.europa.eu/system/files/2021-09/edpb_bindingdecision_202101_ie_sa_whatsapp_redacted_en.pdf.

[46] See on a detailed description of these decisions L Mustert, 'The EDPB's second Article 65 Decision – Is the Board Stepping up its Game?' (2021) *European Data Protection Law Review* 416–22.

As a result, it can be concluded that the consistency mechanism does provide some hurdles – both in terms of time and procedure. However, it is suited to contribute to coherence in both substantive and formal terms by integrating different views and reaching common compromises that are ultimately binding and thus also create more transparency in practice. The more Guidelines, Recommendations and Best Practices that are developed jointly by the authorities and are consequently also implemented by them, the less such contentious procedures between the authorities will perhaps have to be carried out in the future or at least the more predictable their findings will become.

As regards an improvement of (cross-border) enforcement and cooperation in light of challenges identified in the course of application of the GDPR, the EDPB has drawn up a list of procedural aspects that could benefit from further harmonisation at EU level to the European Commission's consideration in October 2022.[47] This development should be highlighted at this point, as the Commission has responded to this 'wish list' by proposing in July 2023 a Regulation laying down additional procedural rules relating to the enforcement of Regulation (EU) 2016/679.[48] The key element of this proposal is the harmonisation of procedural aspects to complement the GDPR with regard to the rights of complainants and litigants, as well as an expansion and concretisation of cooperation and conflict resolution mechanisms.

B. Consistency Through the Court of Justice of the European Union

Since the entry into force of the GDPR, the Court of Justice has already issued a significant number of judgments on the interpretation of the Regulation. In addition, the Court emphasised the continued validity of judgments rendered under the Data Protection Directive for interpreting the GDPR. Decisions on the concretisation of a central legal concept of the GDPR and its prerequisites can be referred to here as one example, namely the notion of consent.

In its judgment in *Planet49*, the Court of Justice stated that consent (under the former Data Protection Directive as well as under the GDPR) is not validly constituted if, in the form of cookies, the storage of information or access to information already stored in a website or a user's terminal equipment is permitted by way of a pre-checked checkbox that users must deselect to refuse their consent.[49]

[47] EDPB, letter to Commissioner Didier Reynders, (10.10.2022), Ref.: OUT2022 -0069, www.edpb.europa.eu/system/files/2022-10/edpb_letter_out2022-0069_to_the_eu_commission_on_procedural_aspects_en_0.pdf.

[48] COM/2023/348 final (4.7.2023), www.eur-lex.europa.eu/legal-content/EN/TXT/?uri=CELEX%3A52023PC0348. See for an overview L Mustert, 'The Commission Proposal for a New GDPR Procedural Regulation: Effective and Protected Enforcement Ensured?' (2023) *European Data Protection Law Review* 454–464.

[49] Case C-673/17 *Bundesverband der Verbraucherzentralen und Verbraucherverbände – Verbraucherzentrale Bundesverband eV v Planet49 GmbH* ECLI:EU:C:2019:801, [2020] 1 WLR 2248, para 65.

The Court confirmed and concretised this further in *Orange Romania* also for the offline context (a pre-ticked checkbox in a written contract). In particular, it is for the data controller to demonstrate that the data subject has, by active behaviour, given his or her consent and that he or she has obtained, beforehand, information relating to all the circumstances surrounding that processing, in an intelligible and easily accessible form, using clear and plain language, allowing that person easily to understand the consequences of the consent so that it is given with full knowledge of the facts.[50] According to the judgment in *Proximus*, informed consent does not necessarily require that the data subject is already aware of all data recipients, as long as the group of recipients is described in general terms.[51] The Court of Justice clarified in *Fashion ID* by whom consent is to be obtained, namely the entity that decides on the purposes and means of the processing, and only to the extent that it decides on them. This entity, however, can also be a website operator who embeds a Facebook plugin into its website and thereby becomes responsible for the social media giant's data machinery.[52]

The practical harmonising effects of the judgments of the Court of Justice can be observed every day when surfing the global web by way of compliant cookie banners and rather restrained implementation of social media plugins, at least on those websites that value privacy. This applies certainly to those areas within the scope of application of the GDPR where the Court of Justice made such clear and unambiguous statements as those referred to. If, on the other hand, one takes a look at areas in which there is substantial margin of manoeuvre at national level, as in the case of the media privilege discussed above, the practical effects of the judgments of the Court of Justice are not so clearly foreseeable.

In the *Satamedia* case, the Court of Justice laid down its broad understanding of the term 'journalistic activities' (then referring to the situation under the Data Protection Directive). Such activities have as their purpose the disclosure to the public of information, opinions or ideas, irrespective of the medium used to transmit them.[53] Nearly 10 years later in the *Buivids* case, the Court of Justice confirmed this by giving further details.[54] Whether special rules have to be applied in contrast to 'normal' data protection law rules depends on the definition of the term 'journalistic activities'. For this reason, the spectrum of this definition is of particular relevance, as it ultimately also decides on the scope of national competences for such special rules. The Court of Justice rightly sees it as a matter for the national courts to judge in the specific case whether a processing in a journalistic context has taken place. This can lead to nationally fragmented interpretations and applications to

[50] Case C-61/19 *Orange România SA v Autoritatea Națională de Supraveghere a Prelucrării Datelor cu Caracter Personal (ANSPDCP)* ECLI:EU:C:2020:901, [2022] 1 All ER (Comm) 195, para 52.

[51] Case C-129/21 *Proximus NV v Gegevensbeschermingsautoriteit* ECLI:EU:C:2022:833, para 49.

[52] Case C-40/17 *Fashion ID GmbH & Co. KG v Verbraucherzentrale NRW eV* ECLI:EU:C:2019:629, [2020] 1 CMLR 16, para 106.

[53] Case C-73/07 *Satakunnan Markkinapörssi and Satamedia* ECLI:EU:C:2008:727, [2008] ECR I-9831, para 61 et seq.

[54] Case C-345/17, *Sergejs Buivids* ECLI:EU:C:2019:122, [2019] 2 CMLR 24, para 53 et seq.

comparable situations, at least until an involvement of the Court of Justice. Although it is in principle up to the national court to assess whether data processing for journalistic purposes takes place in a specific case, 'the fact remains that the Court may provide the referring court with the elements of interpretation which are necessary for its assessment'. Consequently, the Court of Justice provided a number of assessment criteria in *Buivids*. For example, it is not the profession of the processor or the communication medium or dissemination channel that matters (even if it is a platform explicitly for user-generated content), but it is rather the intentions of the actor, such as informing society about relevant circumstances, that must be taken into account. However, in its *Google Spain* judgment, the Court of Justice assumed the existence of a clear dividing line between the traditional media, which it regarded to be covered by the media privilege, and the operators of search engines, which it did not recognise as performing any journalistic activity of its own that would be worthy of protection by the journalistic privilege rules.[55]

The jurisprudence of the Court of Justice in this regard cannot provide full legal clarity for every publication that conflicts with data protection interests, but again, as in the case with cookie banners, it ensures that Member States follow similar criteria when balancing the two conflicting fundamental rights of freedom of expression and freedom of the press against the fundamental right to privacy.

VI. Negative Fragmentation or Positive Diversification

The term 'fragmentation', when used to describe the state of a legal framework, can be regarded as a strong statement, as its common meaning is 'the act or process of breaking or making something break into small pieces or parts'.[56] The term suggests that something is damaged and thus unusable, or at least difficult to handle in practice, ie in a way has a negative connotation. In this direction, the European Commission used this term to justify both the creation of the Digital Services Act (DSA)[57] itself and the choice for a Regulation as the legislative instrument. In particular, the Commission argued that it is necessary 'to avoid and put an end to fragmentation of the internal market and to ensure legal certainty, thus reducing uncertainty for developers and fostering interoperability'.[58] This can

[55] Case C-131/12 *Google Spain SL, Google Inc. v Agencia Española de Protección de Datos (AEPD), Mario Costeja González* ECLI:EU:C:2014:317, [2014] 3 CMLR 50.

[56] Oxford Advanced Learner's Dictionary.

[57] Regulation (EU) 2022/2065 of the European Parliament and of the Council of 19 October 2022 on a Single Market For Digital Services and amending Directive 2000/31/EC (Digital Services Act) [2022] OJ L 277/1.

[58] Recital 4 of Regulation (EU) 2022/2065 of the European Parliament and of the Council of 19 October 2022 on a Single Market For Digital Services and amending Directive 2000/31/EC [2022] OJ L 1/277.

certainly not be stated in such an absolute way for data protection law. With the GDPR, we already have a Regulation with a fairly intensive degree of harmonisation. Nevertheless, in its first evaluation report on the GDPR, which was published in June 2020, about two years after the GDPR became applicable, the European Commission pointed out that there is a certain degree of fragmentation that needs to be continuously monitored.[59]

Against this background, there needs to be a much more nuanced consideration of consistency issues. These should be guided by the various aspects of margins of manoeuvre and opening clauses for the Member States as well as the evolution of the law by case law and the data protection authorities, which have already been addressed above.

A. Fragmentation Due to Specific National Rules

Only a few weeks after applicability of the GDPR, the European Parliament raised the question of whether the Commission sees a danger of European data protection law becoming fragmented as a result of the piecemeal use of the opening clauses in the GDPR.[60] Pointing out that it is too early for a final assessment and that the Member States were just submitting their notifications on the use of opening clauses, the Commission replied it would launch a study to evaluate the use of some of these clauses. Meanwhile, a report has been produced on behalf of the Directorate General for Justice and Consumers discussing the implementation of Articles 8(1), 9(4), 23(1)(c) and (e) as well as 23(2), 85(1) and (2) as well as 89(2–4) of the GDPR. These provisions cover three areas that the European Commission highlighted in its evaluation report as potentially leading to a negative fragmentation and which are addressed in this contribution too: namely differences in the age of consent, the reconciliation of the right to the protection of personal data with freedom of expression, and information as well as derogations from the general prohibition for processing special categories of personal data.[61]

With regard to the media privilege, this contribution highlighted that, indeed, there are very different approaches on a national level. However, it needs to be remembered that this concerns an area – media law – that in principle lies within Member State competencies and therefore developed very differently under different cultural traditions and in a different constitutional framework although

[59] Communication from the Commission to the European Parliament and the Council, Data protection as a pillar of citizens' empowerment and the EU's approach to the digital transition – two years of application of the General Data Protection Regulation, COM/2020/264 final (24.06.2020), www.eur-lex.europa.eu/legal-content/EN/TXT/?uri=CELEX%3A52020DC0264.

[60] Question for written answer P-003121-18 to the Commission (8.6.2018), www.europarl.europa.eu/doceo/document/P-8-2018-003121_EN.html.

[61] COM/2020/264 final (n 59) 7.

shaped by the European Convention on Human Rights[62] and the jurisdiction of the European Court of Human Rights.[63] This cultural leeway allows for adaptation to existing structures and traditions and should be preserved for the Member States, as this is precisely the reason why it was granted in the GDPR in the first place. The GDPR must therefore be open to accommodate the cross-sectoral idea, which prevents in certain areas an EU-wide one-size-fits-all solution for all Member States. In this light, such different approaches should be regarded as diversification and not fragmentation of the GDPR's application, as long as they respect the fundamental rights impacted as well as the limitations – as shown above – provided by the jurisdiction of the Court of Justice. The Member States are bound to do this anyway.

Questions relating to the age of consent are likewise interwoven with areas that have evolved differently in the Member States, eg the protection of minors in the media. The quite obvious differences in design at national level are particularly difficult in relation to information society services that regularly operate globally and whose business models are mostly based on the exploitation of personal data. In its evaluation report, the Commission pointed out that the different use of the relevant opening clause could create uncertainty for children and their parents as to the application of their data protection rights in the Single Market as well as lead to challenges for conducting business across borders and for innovation, in particular as regards new technological developments and cybersecurity solutions.[64] On the other hand, from the perspective of the Member States, a one-size-fits-all approach could lead to fragmentation at the national level. Because age limits exist in different areas of law (data protection law, civil law, criminal law, youth protection law), it may be more reasonable to check for consistency within the regulatory framework of one Member State rather than across the data protection frameworks of all Member States.

De facto, providers already partly follow a unified approach (whether lawful or not) as they offer services across borders according to the same organisational set-up. This can clash with the policies of Member States, which may not all follow the same direction or have reached the same level of implementation. As an example, the promotion of media and digital literacy can be mentioned here, which should ideally be linked to the lowering of the minimum age for consent that also depends on digital (understanding) skills. In Scandinavian countries where this may already be more advanced, maintaining the GDPR age limit would inhibit the progress there or, conversely, transferring the lower age limit from Scandinavia could overburden children in other Member States. In this context, it should also

[62] European Convention for the Protection of Human Rights and Fundamental Freedoms, as amended by Protocols Nos. 11 and 14 (4.11.1950), ETS 5.

[63] See on this aspect extensively MD Cole, J Ukrow and C Etteldorf, *On the Allocation of Competences between the European Union and its Member States in the Media Sector. An Analysis with particular Consideration of Measures concerning Media Pluralism* (Nomos, 2020).

[64] COM/2020/264 final (n 59) 7.

be mentioned that the Audiovisual Media Services Directive,[65] which incidentally also encourages Member States to promote media literacy, contains provisions on the protection of minors from harmful media and on the protection of children's data, but in doing so also does not set an EU-wide harmonised age limit.

Finally, a similar observation has to be made with regard to derogations for the processing of special categories of personal data. Genetic, biometric and health data especially concern data processing activities that play a major role in the public sector, in particular in research and development, administration, (national) security or health care. In the public sector, Member States tend to establish explicit and specific legal rules determining which authorities can process which types of special categories of personal data and under what conditions. In the private sector, on the other hand, there are often only general rules (outside the context of employment) which are and must be filled in by concretisations and guidance of data protection authorities. The extent of possible fragmentation therefore depends mainly on the effectiveness of cooperation mechanisms and guidance at supranational level.

B. The Role of Jurisprudence and Cooperation in Coherence

As already pointed out above, the jurisdiction of the Court of Justice has played and will continue to play an essential role in finding consistent approaches and to avoid a too far-reaching fragmentation of the legal framework. This is true with regard to the interpretation of the GDPR but also concerning general principles of EU law that have to be respected by the Member States when using their margins of manoeuvre.

However, mechanisms of cooperation seem to be even more relevant than gradual alignment by the Court of Justice. This does not only apply to individual cases, which can be brought to a (compromise) solution within the framework of the consistency procedures described and thus (should) also have a continuing effect on the decision-making of individual authorities. It is even more relevant that Guidelines for specific areas can be developed which are then reflected in the practical implementation of the GDPR by both data processors and data protection authorities. To stay with the examples given in the context of this contribution, initiatives by the EDPB exist, for example, in the area of the protection of minors.[66]

[65] Directive 2010/13/EU of the European Parliament and of the Council of 10 March 2010 on the coordination of certain provisions laid down by law, regulation or administrative action in Member States concerning the provision of audiovisual media services (Audiovisual Media Services Directive) [2010] OJ L 95/1. Consolidated version: www.eur-lex.europa.eu/legal-content/EN/TXT/?uri=CELEX%3A02010L0013-20181218.

[66] For example, the EDPB established a taskforce to coordinate potential actions and to acquire a more comprehensive overview of TikTok's processing and practices across the EU with regard to the protection of children's data. See EDPB, thirty-first Plenary session, www.edpb.europa.eu/news/news/2020/thirty-first-plenary-session-establishment-taskforce-tiktok-response-meps-use_en.

As regards biometric data, there are Guidelines on the use of facial recognition technology in the area of law enforcement[67] and on processing of personal data through video devices.[68] While such Guidelines will not (or cannot) lead to an absolute avoidance of differences in regulatory approaches, they do, however, contribute to the achievement of consistency.

This can be illustrated by the recent multitude of penalties imposed on the US company Clearview AI by various data protection authorities in the Member States. In this case, the one-stop-shop mechanism of the GDPR did not apply due to the lack of a European branch.[69] Although the decisions differ in nuances, they all come to the conclusion that the use of facial recognition software by this company was unlawful and imposed fines in the same amount of 20 million euros.[70] The decisions also refer to corresponding guidance issued by the EDPB.

In other areas, such as the media privilege, such cooperation can only exist to a lesser extent. This is due to the fact that the media regulatory authorities and bodies are typically entrusted with supervision or at least involved in supervision in many Member States. In addition, they are not incorporated in the EDPB.

C. Cross-sectoral Fragmentation

Cross-sectoral fragmentation of the regulatory framework is the 'elephant in the room', which has been mentioned in this contribution several times but not yet detailed further. The previously mentioned example underscores this. While data protection law in itself, in the opinion of the authors, cannot be described as fragmented, at least not in a negative sense that would give rise to an immediate need for adaptation, this statement is not so straightforward from the perspective of the overall regulatory network. Data protection law is a cross-sectoral matter, which means that it needs to be taken into account and adapted in many different sectoral areas of law. Data, including personal data, play a decisive role as the currency of the future and as an economic resource.

[67] Guidelines 05/2022 on the use of facial recognition technology in the area of law enforcement Version 1.0 (12.05.2022) www.edpb.europa.eu/system/files/2022-05/edpb-guidelines_202205_frtlawenforcement_en_1.pdf.

[68] Guidelines 3/2019 on processing of personal data through video devices Version 2.0 (29.01.2020) www.edpb.europa.eu/sites/default/files/files/file1/edpb_guidelines_201903_video_devices_en_0.pdf.

[69] The authorities in Italy in March 2022 (*Ordinanza ingiunzione nei confronti di Clearview AI – 10 febbraio 2022 [9751362]* www.garanteprivacy.it/web/guest/home/docweb/-/docweb-display/docweb/9751362), Greece in July 2022 (*Επιβολή προστίμου στην εταιρεία* Clearview AI, Inc, No. 35, www.dpa.gr/el/enimerwtiko/prakseisArxis/epiboli-prostimoy-stin-etaireia-clearview-ai-inc) and in France in October 2022 (Restricted Committee Deliberation No. SAN-2022-019 of 17 October 2022 concerning CLEARVIEW AI, www.cnil.fr/sites/default/files/atoms/files/deliberation_of_the_restricted_committee_no_san-2022-019_of_17_october_2022_concerning_clearview_ai.pdf) all imposed fines on Clearview AI amounting to 20 million euros.

[70] See on the Clearview cases G Pathak, 'Manifestly Made Public: Clearview and GDPR' (2022) *European Data Protection Law Review* 419–22.

It is therefore not surprising that many laws, both at national and EU level, contain special rules on data protection or special conditions for data processing. In addition, the regulatory framework is further expanding. By way of illustration, only a few recent legislative instruments out of many can be mentioned. Both the Regulation on addressing the dissemination of terrorist content online[71] and the proposed Regulation laying down rules to prevent and combat child sexual abuse[72] contain obligations for hosting services to combat illegal content, but also include rules on how to deal with the personal data that is affected in the execution of the obligations. The proposal for an Artificial Intelligence Act contains, inter alia, specific rules on the processing of biometric data or rather, on the use of remote biometric identification systems which due to its risky nature requires certain safeguards under the proposal.[73] The Audiovisual Media Services Directive states that personal data of minors collected or otherwise generated by media service providers by way of implementing protection mechanisms (such as age verification) may not be processed for commercial purposes, such as direct marketing, profiling and behaviourally targeted advertising. A similar rule can also be found in the DSA for online platforms, as well as regarding the prohibition of processing personal data of minors and special categories of personal data for the purpose of personalised advertising. The overlaps between the Digital Markets Act (DMA)[74] and the GDPR are even more intense, due to the fact that power over data and power in markets (which is the regulatory subject of the DMA) are closely linked.[75] For example, the DMA contains rules on when gatekeepers may (or may not) merge data within a company group and what purposes (or not) they may pursue with the processing. With regard to the relationship with (parallel applicable) data protection law, however, the aforementioned legislative instruments regularly limit themselves to stating that the rules of the GDPR shall remain unaffected or are 'without prejudice'. This may seem enough on paper, but will be challenging in legal practice. After all, such a general rule certainly cannot answer every practical collision case in terms of a clear priority relationship.

This is all the more risky considering that there are no formal cross-sectoral cooperation mechanisms in the DMA beyond the advisory role of the high-level

[71] Regulation (EU) 2021/784 of the European Parliament and of the Council of 29 April 2021 on addressing the dissemination of terrorist content online [2021] OJ L 172/79.

[72] Proposal for a Regulation of the European Parliament and of the Council laying down rules to prevent and combat child sexual abuse COM/2022/209 final (11.05.2022), www.eur-lex.europa.eu/legal-content/EN/TXT/?uri=COM%3A2022%3A209%3AFIN.

[73] Proposal for a Regulation of the European Parliament and of the Council laying down harmonised rules on Artificial Intelligence (Artificial Intelligence Act) and amending certain Union legislative Acts, COM/2021/206 final (21.04.2021), www.eur-lex.europa.eu/legal-content/EN/TXT/?uri=CELEX%3A52021PC0206.

[74] Regulation (EU) 2022/1925 of the European Parliament and of the Council of 14 September 2022 on contestable and fair markets in the digital sector and amending Directives (EU) 2019/1937 and (EU) 2020/1828 (Digital Markets Act) [2022] OJ L 265/1.

[75] See on this C Etteldorf, 'DMA – Digital Markets Act or Data Markets Act?' (2022) *European Data Protection Law Review* 255–61.

group for the Digital Markets Act, of which the EDPB and the European Data Protection Supervisor form part.[76] In the DSA, such mechanisms are controlled by the Digital Services Coordinator, which is supposed to serve as a single point of contact for providers that potentially are concerned by several competent national authorities. However, the DSA leaves cooperation rules as an option to the national level. The DMA deals with cross-sectoral issues by involving the EDPB at least in specific areas (mainly issues of profiling activities of gatekeepers) by foreseeing information of the Board.[77] However, fixed and recurring supranational and cross-sectoral cooperation structures are missing, as are information exchange obligations and conflict resolution mechanisms. In national law, too, such structures exist only in parts.

This can lead to different approaches for different sectors, including against a cross-border background. That consequence can again be exemplified by looking at the topic of biometric age verification. From the perspective of data protection law, the French data protection authority recently opined strictly against the use of biometric systems in age verification (here especially on pornography platforms).[78] From the perspective protection of minors in the media, on the other hand, the German Commission for the Protection of Minors in the Media, as the German media regulatory authority, declared such systems to be suitable for providing effective access restrictions to protect children from content that is harmful to their development only two months earlier and one country border away.[79]

As Advocate General Rantos rightfully underlined in his Opinion delivered in September 2022 in the *Meta Platforms* case dealing with the relationship between data protection and competition law, the GDPR and also other laws do not contain rules governing cooperation between different sectoral authorities.[80] Such cooperation could therefore only be derived from the duty to cooperate in good faith enshrined in Article 4(3) Treaty of the European Union[81] or from the principle of sound administration as a general principle of EU law, which includes, inter alia, an extensive duty of diligence and care on the part of national authorities. Whether these general principles are sufficient to effectively avoid fragmentation in the processing of personal data in the increasingly cross-border internal market landscape may be questioned. The Court of Justice in its judgment, however,

[76] Article 40 DMA.

[77] Articles 15(1) and 46(1)(g) DMA.

[78] Commission Nationale de l'Informatique et des Libertés, 'Online age verification: balancing privacy and the protection of minors' (22.09.2022), www.cnil.fr/en/online-age-verification-balancing-privacy-and-protection-minors.

[79] C Etteldorf, 'KJM approves age verification systems based on biometric age checks for the first time' (2022) *IRIS*, merlin.obs.coe.int/article/9561. For differing approaches in selected Member States on the protection of minors related to their personal data see extensively J Ukrow, MD Cole and C Etteldorf, *Stand und Entwicklung des internationalen Kinder- und Jugendmedienschutzes*, EMR/Script 6 (dco-Verlag, 2023), www.dco-verlag.de/wis/ebk/9783910513129.pdf.

[80] Opinion of Advocate General Rantos delivered on 20 September 2022, Case C-252/21 *Meta Platforms Inc., formerly Facebook Inc., Meta Platforms Ireland Limited, formerly Facebook Ireland Ltd., Facebook Deutschland GmbH v Bundeskartellamt* ECLI:EU:C:2022:704, para 27 et seq.

[81] Consolidated Version of the of the Treaty on European Union [2008] OJ C115/13.

confirmed the opinion of Advocate General Rantos in principle and highlighted that a sectoral (here: competition) authority, when applying data protection law, has a 'duty of sincere cooperation' with the competent data protection authorities in the course of which it has to follow their interpretation of data protection rules and, in case of doubt, must consult them and seek cooperation.[82] Therefore, strengthening and institutionalising cross-border cooperation is the first step in the necessary and right direction and, if needed, can be supplemented by legislative action as a second step.

VII. Concluding Remarks

The GDPR was and still is a milestone for a very high level of protection of personal data of Union citizens and a prime example of a comprehensive piece of legislation reaching beyond the borders of the EU. However, as this contribution has shown, even such a strongly harmonised legal framework does not automatically mean that it provides an unconditionally applicable standard that applies absolutely and equally across all different sectors and Member States. This is already obvious due to certain characteristics of the GDPR having a broad, but nonetheless limited scope of application, including opening clauses and margins for manoeuvre in the application by the Member States as well as leaving space for interpretation of provisions of the law.

In practice, this leads to differing rules for applications in certain areas – both cross-border and cross-sector. The need for these characteristics of the GDPR is attributable to the fact that data protection law is a cross-sectoral discipline, therefore responding to differences in Member States, sectoral specificities of data processing or the existence of different framework conditions. And data protection will always remain a cross-sectional matter.

Questions on a possible fragmentation must therefore be considered in a more differentiated way than in other more 'isolated' areas of law. It should not be considered a negatively connotated fragmentation in the sense of a shortcoming in legislation or practical implementation, if a differing treatment of data protection law in different sectors and/or different Member States has good reasons to be different. In the context of this contribution, journalistic data processing and the legal framework for the protection of minors were mentioned as examples for such justified diversity.

Rather, it is a question of coherence and consistency that must be posed in data protection law and answered in the endeavour to achieve a level of protection for the fundamental rights of data subjects that is as uniform as possible.

[82] Case C-252/21 *Meta Platforms Inc., formerly Facebook Inc., Meta Platforms Ireland Limited, formerly Facebook Ireland Ltd., Facebook Deutschland GmbH v Bundeskartellamt* ECLI:EU:C:2023:537, para 53 et seq.

This concerns cross-border, cross-sectoral and cross-legal-framework coherence. While the first two aspects have a solid foundation through the unifying jurisprudence of the Court of Justice and, above all, the work and cooperation of the data protection authorities gathered in the EDPB – which will be further strengthened by initiatives such as the proposed procedural Regulation for better enforcement – the creation of an overall consistent legal framework seems to prove challenging, but also needed. The complex 'network of rules', especially for the digital sphere, necessitate consistency with the GDPR. Such rules must be clear, unconditional and transparent and may require extensions of institutional (cooperation) structures. Otherwise, there is a risk that the level of protection envisaged by the GDPR will diminish, at which point we would be really talking about fragmentation – in that case in a negative sense.

8

Regulating Digital Platforms: Streamlining the Interaction between the Digital Markets Act and National Competition Regimes

INGE GRAEF

I. Introduction

The Digital Markets Act (DMA)[1] marks a turning point in the economic regulation of digital markets. After the European Commission and national competition authorities (NCAs) have taken on high-profile competition cases against big tech firms like Google, Facebook and Amazon,[2] the EU competition rules are now complemented by the DMA's regulatory obligations. These obligations target so-called gatekeepers, which are especially powerful providers of core platform services that meet certain criteria for which quantitative thresholds apply as presumptions.[3] The DMA contains an exhaustive list of core platform services including, among others, search engines, social networks, video-sharing platforms, web browsers, virtual assistants and advertising services.[4] The objective of the DMA is to complement EU competition law 'by laying down harmonised rules ensuring for all businesses, contestable and fair markets in the digital sector'.[5] Similarly, national legislators have been adopting stricter national competition rules.[6]

[1] Regulation (EU) 2022/1925 of the European Parliament and of the Council of 14 September 2022 on contestable and fair markets in the digital sector [2022] OJ L265/1 (Digital Markets Act).

[2] See for instance: Case T-612/17 *Google Shopping* ECLI:EU:T:2021:763, [2022] 4 CMLR 6; Case C-252/21 *Meta Platforms v Bundeskartellamt* ECLI:EU:C:2023:537; Press release Autorita' Garante della Concorrenza e del Mercato, 'A528 – Italian Competition Authority: Amazon fined over € 1,128 billion for abusing its dominant position', 9 December 2021, en.agcm.it/en/media/press-releases/2021/12/A528.

[3] Articles 3(1) and (2) DMA.

[4] Article 2(2) DMA.

[5] Article 1(1) DMA.

[6] See for instance *Law no. 4886/2022 'Modernisation of Competition Law for the Digital Era'*, amending the Greek competition framework, and the *Kartell- und Wettbewerbsrechts-Änderungsgesetz 2021*, amending the Austrian competition framework.

Germany is the pioneer in this regard with the adoption of a regime targeting undertakings of paramount significance to competition across markets in the 10th amendment to the German Competition Act in 2021 and the introduction of a market investigation tool in the 11th amendment in 2023, allowing the Bundeskartellamt (the German competition authority) to impose remedies in markets without the need to establish a competition violation.[7] These national initiatives go beyond the scope of the EU competition rules and the DMA.

The co-existence of different EU and national rules could pose risks to the legal consistency of the overall framework of economic regulation for digital markets, because it reduces the level of harmonisation across the EU. Nevertheless, the chapter argues that the parallel application of EU and national regulation for digital markets can be a welcome aspect of the current reality. There may be problematic practices that are not captured under the EU regime, which has its own legal and political restrictions by which national legislators may not be constrained. Rarely will all problematic conduct be covered by a single piece of legislation. To ensure that the overall regulatory framework remains future-proof and can capture as many problematic practices as possible, it may therefore be desirable to have a variety of rules in place at both EU and national level. This could especially be true for a regime like competition law, which mainly develops through complex and – often – resource-heavy and lengthy cases. In addition, it will rarely be possible for a single regulator to take up all possible ongoing violations. As with any regulator, the Commission has limited resources to enforce the DMA and the EU competition rules.[8] However, to ensure that the parallel existence of EU and national regulation is a strength rather than a weakness of the regulatory framework, the application and enforcement of the EU and national regimes have to be streamlined. This requires coordination. Against this background, the chapter comes up with some suggestions to ensure effective coordination between the DMA and national competition regimes, drawing from the experience with the interaction between EU and national competition enforcement.

To understand the dynamics between EU and national competition law, Section II provides a background of how the enforcement of the competition rules evolved from the moment of their inception in EU law. Section III discusses the relationship between EU and national competition law as laid down in Regulation 1/2003[9] and as applied in practice. Based on these insights, Section IV moves on to analyse whether a similar approach can be taken regarding the relationship between the DMA and national competition law. Section V concludes.

[7] Respectively, the 10th and 11th amendment to the German *Gesetz gegen Wettbewerbsbeschränkungen*.

[8] See A de Streel, R Feasey, J Krämer and G Monti, 'Enforcement and Institutional Arrangements', *CERRE DMA Issue Paper*, May 2021, 12, cerre.eu/wp-content/uploads/2021/05/CERRE_FOURTH-ISSUE-PAPER_DMA_European-Parliament-Council-recommendations_May-2021.pdf.

[9] Council Regulation (EC) No 1/2003 of 16 December 2002 on the implementation of the rules on competition laid down in Articles 81 and 82 of the Treaty [2003] OJ L1/1 (Regulation 1/2003).

II. How the Enforcement of EU Competition Law Evolved from the EU to the National Level and Now Back Again?

Regulation 17, adopted in 1962, was the first legislative instrument laying down how to implement and enforce the EU competition rules that are now contained in Articles 101 and 102 Treaty on the Functioning of the European Union (TFEU).[10] Regulation 17 concentrated the power to enforce the EU competition rules mainly at the European Commission. This changed with the entry into force of Regulation 1/2003, which provided NCAs with the opportunity to become involved in enforcing the EU competition rules.

A. The Centralised Enforcement System of Regulation 17

Until the entry into force of Regulation 17, Member States were required to apply the EU competition rules in accordance with their national laws.[11] With Regulation 17 coming into effect, the Commission was provided with the competence to apply and enforce Articles 101 and 102 TFEU,[12] and Member States only remained competent to apply the two prohibitions to a certain practice as long as the Commission had not yet initiated a procedure into the behaviour itself.[13] In particular, the opening of a procedure by the Commission relieved the Member States from their competence to apply the EU competition rules to the case. In addition, Regulation 17 provided the Commission with the exclusive power to grant exemptions pursuant to Article 101(3) TFEU to the prohibition of anticompetitive agreements laid down in Article 101(1) TFEU.[14] This meant that Member States were not allowed to apply the exemption of Article 101(3) TFEU at all. As such, Regulation 17 set up a centralised authorisation system under Article 101(3) TFEU by providing the Commission with a monopoly to assess whether restrictive practices qualified for an exemption.

The objective behind the creation of this centralised enforcement model was to help ensure a uniform interpretation of the EU competition rules at a time when Member States still had limited experience with competition enforcement. Until the adoption of the Treaty establishing the European Economic Community in 1957, cartels were still mostly seen as an acceptable business practice. To increase the awareness of competition harms, it was thus a logical choice to assign the

[10] Regulation No 17: First Regulation implementing Articles 85 and 86 of the Treaty [1962] OJ L13/204 (Regulation 17).

[11] As laid down by Article 88 Treaty establishing the European Economic Community.

[12] Article 9(2) of Regulation 17.

[13] Article 9(3) of Regulation 17.

[14] Article 9(1) of Regulation 17.

Commission as the main competition enforcer.[15] Although not all Member States were initially in favour of a centralised system, in the end all agreed to centralising powers within the Commission to prevent the competition rules from being applied less strictly in other Member States.[16]

The Commission published a White Paper on the modernisation of the EU competition system in 1999 to evaluate the functioning of Regulation 17, which had been applied for more than 35 years without major changes. The Commission argued that the centralised enforcement system of Regulation 17 had proven effective for establishing a 'culture of competition' at a time when competition policy was not yet widely known across the EU and the interpretation of the competition rules was still uncertain.[17] Moreover, Regulation 17 had allowed the Commission to build up a body of precedent to ensure a consistent interpretation of the competition provisions across the Member States.[18] While centralised enforcement by the Commission was a suitable choice at the inception of EU competition law, its disadvantages became clear with the expansion of the number of cases to be assessed by the Commission due to the enlargement of the EU from 6 to 15 Member States and the success of the internal market integration process as well as the effects of globalisation.[19] For this reason, the Commission proposed to abolish the centralised notification and authorisation system of Article 101(3) TFEU by making the latter's exemption to the prohibition of restrictive practices directly applicable without the need for a prior decision by the Commission and by allowing NCAs as well as national courts to enforce Article 101(3) TFEU.[20]

These proposals came as a surprise for most.[21] Because the Commission had held strongly onto its exclusive power to grant exemptions under Article 101(3) TFEU in the past decades, the changes were seen as a radical and revolutionary reform of the EU competition system.[22] The main objectives of the reform were to reduce the administrative burden on undertakings, who would no longer have to obtain an exemption under Article 101(3) TFEU from the Commission but would become able to self-assess the compatibility of their restrictive practices with EU competition law, and to allow the Commission to refocus its efforts on the most

[15] LF Pace and K Seidel, 'The Drafting and the Role of Regulation 17: A Hard-Fought Compromise' in KK Patel and H Schweitzer (eds), *The Historical Foundations of EU Competition Law* (Oxford University Press, 2013) 54, 55 and 59–61.

[16] ibid 54, 71.

[17] White Paper on Modernisation of the Rules Implementing Articles 85 and 86 of the EC Treaty, Commission Programme No 99/027, 28 April 1999), 4.

[18] ibid 29.

[19] ibid 19, 29–30.

[20] ibid 5.

[21] Wouter PJ Wils, 'Ten Years of Regulation 1/2003-A Retrospective' (2013) 4 *Journal of European Competition Law & Practice* 293, 294.

[22] In the words of CD Ehlermann, 'The Modernization of EC Antitrust Policy: A Legal and Cultural Revolution' (2000) 37 *Common Market Law Review* 537, 538: 'In [the Commission], the "natural" monopoly theory [i.e. regarding its exemption monopoly under Article 101(3) TFEU] was almost a religious belief. It constituted for four decades [the Commission's] main credo. Not to adhere to it was considered heresy, and could lead to excommunication'.

serious competition infringements.[23] As a result of its exemption monopoly, the Commission had become overwhelmed with notifications under Article 101(3) TFEU during the 1990s and this resulted in a backlog of sometimes thousands of cases requiring a Commission decision.[24]

B. The Decentralisation of Competition Enforcement in Regulation 1/2003

The changes proposed by the Commission in the 1999 White Paper were largely welcomed by industry, the European Parliament and Member States, who agreed to become more involved in the enforcement of EU competition law.[25] This led to the adoption of Regulation 1/2003, which repealed Regulation 17 and started applying from 1 May 2004.[26] As suggested in the 1999 White Paper, Regulation 1/2003 indeed replaced the notification and authorisation system for exemptions under Article 101(3) TFEU with a system of direct applicability and self-assessment of restrictive practices by undertakings. A prior decision of the Commission was no longer needed to exempt agreements from the prohibition of restrictive practices.[27] Based on the Commission's decision-making practice and the case law of the EU Courts, undertakings could now assess themselves whether their agreement or restrictive practice met the conditions laid down in Article 101(3) TFEU. More generally, Regulation 1/2003 assigned the Commission, NCAs, and national courts with parallel competences to apply Articles 101 and 102 TFEU.[28]

To ensure effective cooperation, the Commission and NCAs started coordinating cases, exchanging information and assisting each other in competition investigations within the European Competition Network (ECN).[29] The ECN is a forum where the Commission and the NCAs can discuss, exchange ideas and cooperate to foster competition enforcement. The ECN is built upon the principles of equality, respect and solidarity;[30] and it sets the rules for an efficient case allocation and assistance between the different enforcers. To further improve mutual assistance among NCAs and to harmonise the resources and powers of NCAs across the Member States, the ECN+ Directive was adopted in 2019.[31] It

[23] White Paper on Modernisation (n 17) 19.
[24] Ehlermann (n 22) 541.
[25] Summary of the Observations, 'Whiter Paper on Reform of Regulation 17', 29 February 29 2000, 3–4, ec.europa.eu/competition/antitrust/others/wp_on_modernisation/summary_observations.pdf.
[26] Articles 43 and 45 of Regulation 1/2003.
[27] Article 1(2) of Regulation 1/2003.
[28] Articles 4–6 of Regulation 1/2003.
[29] See Articles 11, 12, 20, 22 of Regulation 1/2003 and Commission Notice on cooperation within the Network of Competition Authorities [2004] OJ C101/43.
[30] Joint Statement of the Council and the Commission on the Functioning of the Network of Competition Authorities 15435/02, para 7.
[31] Directive (EU) 2019/1 to empower the competition authorities of the Member States to be more effective enforcers and to ensure the proper functioning of the internal market [2019] OJ L11/3 (ECN+ Directive).

must be said, however, that the Commission still retains a special role. Although the role of the NCAs has become more important in the EU competition system, the Commission still is 'the guardian of the Treaty' and has 'the ultimate but not the sole responsibility for developing policy and safeguarding consistency' regarding the application of EU competition law.[32] In particular, the Commission still has the power to remove a case from an NCA. The start of proceedings by the Commission namely relieves NCAs of their competence to apply Articles 101 and 102 TFEU and if an NCA is already working on a case, the Commission can launch proceedings itself after consulting the respective NCA.[33] Furthermore, before an NCA can adopt a decision applying the EU competition rules, it must provide the Commission with the envisaged decision.[34] Beyond this, Regulation 1/2003 also prevents NCAs and national courts from taking decisions running counter to a decision already adopted by the Commission against the same behaviour.[35]

C. From Proactive NCAs to the Commission as Sole Enforcer of the DMA

As such, Regulation 1/2003 paved the way for the Commission remaining the *primus inter pares* for the enforcement of EU competition law – even though NCAs and national courts have become fully competent to apply Articles 101 and 102 TFEU in parallel. In the last decade, however, NCAs have become increasingly active. Two particularly impactful national cases from the past years are discussed here as illustrations of such a possible trend.

The Bundeskartellamt (the German competition authority), held Facebook (now Meta) liable in 2019 for an abuse of dominance consisting of the imposition of unfair terms and conditions on its social network users.[36] Facebook did not leave users a choice but to agree to the combination of personal data in their Facebook account with data collected beyond the social network, including through Facebook-owned services such as WhatsApp and Instagram and on third-party websites, as a condition for being able to use Facebook's social network. The case is noteworthy because the Bundeskartellamt, in the absence of any precedent at the EU level used data protection law as a benchmark to establish a violation of the competition rules.[37] Following a preliminary reference from the Düsseldorf

[32] Commission Notice on cooperation within the Network of Competition Authorities [2004] OJ C101/43, para 43 (Commission Notice on cooperation).

[33] Article 11(6) of Regulation 1/2003 and Commission Notice on cooperation, paras 51–57.

[34] Article 11(4) of Regulation 1/2003 and Commission Notice on cooperation, para 44.

[35] Article 16 of Regulation 1/2003.

[36] Case B6-22/16, *Facebook – exploitative business terms*, 6 February 2019, www.bundeskartellamt.de/SharedDocs/Entscheidung/EN/Entscheidungen/Missbrauchsaufsicht/2019/B6-22-16.pdf?__blob=publicationFile&v=5.

[37] See V Robertson, 'Excessive Data Collection: Privacy Considerations and Abuse of Dominance in the Era of Big Data' (2020) 57 *Common Market Law Review* 161, 185.

court in the proceedings on appeal, the Court of Justice endorsed the approach of the Bundeskartellamt in its July 2023 judgment.[38]

Another example of a pioneering NCA is the imposition of interim measures in 2020 by the *Autorité de la concurrence* (the French competition authority) requiring Google to conduct negotiations in good faith with press publishers about the remuneration for the display of their content as protected by the neighbouring right of the Directive on Copyright in the Digital Single Market.[39] This Directive created a new ancillary or neighbouring right for press publishers such as newspapers and online news outlets, providing press publishers with the exclusive right to authorise or prohibit the display of their content by digital platforms such as search engines and news aggregators.[40] In response to the entry into force of the relevant French implementing legislation, Google unilaterally decided to no longer display content of French press publishers in its search results, unless the publishers authorised such displays free of charge. Even though the neighbouring right created by the Directive did not foresee a remuneration for the the reuse of press publications,[41] the Autorité argued that Google's application of a zero price amounted to abuse of dominance because it did not appear to constitute a reasonable measure under the competition rules.[42] The Autorité's decision was upheld by the Paris Court of Appeal in October 2020[43] and the Autorité imposed a 500 million fine on Google in July 2021 for not complying with several of the injunctions issued in its April 2020 decision.[44] As such, through its competition decisions the Autorité has increased the level of protection for press publishers in France beyond the level foreseen in the Directive on Copyright in the Digital Single Market.

Both cases involve practices against which the Commission had not yet taken action. While the Commission still is the main competition enforcer, national cases like these illustrate that NCAs are also able to play a leading and pioneering role in the development of competition law. This may indicate that the primacy of

[38] Case C-252/21 *Meta Platforms v Bundeskartellamt* ECLI:EU:C:2023:537.

[39] Directive (EU) 2019/790 of the European Parliament and of the Council of 17 April 2019 on copyright and related rights in the Digital Single Market [2019] OJ L130/92 (Directive on Copyright in the Digital Single Market).

[40] Article 15(1) of the Directive on Copyright in the Digital Single Market in conjunction with Articles 2 and 3(2) of Directive 2001/29/EC of the European Parliament and of the Council of 22 May 2001 on the harmonisation of certain aspects of copyright and related rights in the information society [2001] OJ L167/10.

[41] Article 15 of the Directive on Copyright in the Digital Single Market.

[42] Autorité de la concurrence, decision 20-MC-01 of 9 April 2020 on requests for interim measures by the Syndicat des éditeurs de la presse magazine, the Alliance de la presse d'information générale and others and Agence France-Presse, para 203.

[43] Paris Court of Appeal, 8 October 2020, www.autoritedelaconcurrence.fr/sites/default/files/appealsd/2020-10/ca_20mc01_oct20.pdf.

[44] Press release Autorité de la concurrence, 'Remuneration of related rights for press publishers and agencies: the Autorité fines Google up to 500 million euros for non-compliance with several injunctions', 13 July 2021, www.autoritedelaconcurrence.fr/en/press-release/remuneration-related-rights-press-publishers-and-agencies-autorite-fines-google-500.

competition enforcement is leaning more towards the national level, even though it remains to be seen whether NCAs remain as proactive as cases such as those discussed here suggest.

With the entry into force of the DMA, the balance between the Commission and NCAs may slightly change again. The enforcement of the DMA is fully in the hands of the Commission. While the DMA requires NCAs to cooperate with and support the Commission where relevant,[45] only the Commission can adopt decisions and impose sanctions for non-compliance under the DMA.[46] The DMA complements the competition rules and does not substitute them,[47] but many of the obligations it imposes on so-called gatekeepers build on past or ongoing competition cases. For instance, the restrictions regarding personal data combination (Article 5(2) DMA) stem from the German *Facebook* case discussed above and the prohibitions regarding self-preferencing in rankings and access to data (Articles 6(5) and (2) DMA) originate from, respectively, the Commission's *Google Shopping* and *Amazon* competition cases.[48]

Because of the overlap between the substance of the DMA and the EU competition rules, it may be that the DMA's centralised enforcement model brings the Commission to the forefront again as the main enforcement actor. At the same time, the DMA leaves room for Member States to impose their own obligations at the national level beyond those contained in the DMA.[49] To understand how the relationship between the Commission and NCAs may evolve within this framework of EU and national rules regulating gatekeepers, the next section explores the interaction between EU and national competition law as laid down in Regulation 1/2003. Analogies may be drawn from this interaction for the future relationship between the DMA and national competition law.

III. Relationship between the EU and National Competition Rules in the Books and in Action

As discussed in the previous section, Regulation 1/2003 makes the Commission and the NCAs responsible in parallel for the enforcement of the EU competition rules.[50] This is different under the DMA, where the Commission is the sole enforcer. Nevertheless, inspiration can be drawn from EU competition enforcement

[45] Articles 37 and 38 DMA.

[46] Articles 29–31 DMA.

[47] See the objective in Article 1(1) DMA: 'The purpose of this Regulation is to contribute to the proper functioning of the internal market by laying down harmonised rules ensuring for all businesses, contestable and fair markets in the digital sector across the Union where gatekeepers are present, to the benefit of business users and end users'.

[48] Case T-612/17 *Google Shopping* ECLI:EU:T:2021:763, [2022] 4 CMLR 6 and Case AT.40462 *Amazon Marketplace* and AT.40703 *Amazon Buy Box*, 20 December 2022.

[49] Article 1(5) and (6) DMA.

[50] Articles 4–6 of Regulation 1/2003.

to inform coordination between the Commission and the NCAs in the context of the DMA.

A. The Interaction between EU and National Competition Law in the Books

Member States are free to have national competition rules in place beyond the EU competition rules laid down in Articles 101 and 102 TFEU. To ensure consistency between the EU and national competition rules, Regulation 1/2003 requires NCAs and national courts to apply Articles 101 and 102 TFEU alongside the national competition rules when dealing with anticompetitive agreements or abuses of dominance falling within the scope of the EU competition rules.[51] Beyond this, Regulation 1/2003 limits Member States in applying national competition rules that are stricter than EU competition law. Article 3(2) of Regulation 1/2003 points out that national competition rules cannot prohibit agreements and concerted practices that comply with Article 101 TFEU. As a result, a single standard of assessment applies for agreements and concerted practices across the EU.[52]

This is different in the area of unilateral conduct where Article 3(2) of Regulation 1/2003 allows Member States to adopt and apply national laws that are stricter than Article 102 TFEU. During the adoption of Regulation 1/2003, several Member States insisted on including this exception to prevent them from having to take down national competition rules that prohibited behaviour not covered by Article 102 TFEU – for instance regimes protecting economically dependent businesses.[53] Similarly, the DMA to a certain extent leaves Member States free to have national rules in place that complement the EU's obligations applicable to gatekeepers.

According to Article 1(5) DMA, Member States are free to impose further obligations on gatekeepers as long as they do not relate to the objective of ensuring contestable and fair markets, fall outside the scope of the DMA, and do not result from the qualification of a firm as gatekeeper under the DMA. Article 1(6) DMA also specifies that national competition rules may prohibit other forms of unilateral conduct when they apply to firms other than gatekeepers or when they amount to the imposition of further obligations on gatekeepers. As discussed by commentators, the exact room for national rules to go beyond the DMA remains unclear and will likely be subject to litigation.[54] For instance, because contestability and

[51] Article 3(1) of Regulation 1/2003.

[52] Recital 8 of Regulation 1/2003. The European Commission referred to Article 3(2) of Regulation 1/2003 as the 'convergence rule' in its Report on the functioning of Regulation 1/2003, COM(2009)206, 29 April 2009, para 21.

[53] See recital 8 of Regulation 1/2003.

[54] J van den Boom, 'What does the Digital Markets Act harmonize? – exploring interactions between the DMA and national competition laws' (2023) 19 *European Competition Journal* 57, 65–68; M Cappai and G Colangelo, 'Applying ne bis in idem in the aftermath of bpost and Nordzucker: The case of EU

fairness are broad concepts,[55] it will be hard to determine at what point an obligation pursues a different purpose. Different interpretations are possible and time will tell how much room the DMA leaves for national rules. Whichever interpretation prevails, the key issue for our purposes here is how the DMA and national law can be applied in parallel in an effective way reinforcing each other without duplicating resources. Inspiration can be drawn from competition cases where the Commission and NCAs coordinated their enforcement actions.

B. The Interaction between EU and National Competition Law in Action

An example is the coordination in the Dutch *Apple* case. Following a market study into app stores for mobile phones, the Netherlands Authority for Consumers & Markets (ACM) launched an investigation into Apple's App Store in 2019 initially focusing on a possible abuse of dominance vis-à-vis Dutch apps for news media.[56] In June 2020, the Commission announced the opening of a competition investigation into Apple's App Store rules and their impact on competition in music streaming and e-books or audiobooks.[57] In April 2021, the Commission informed Apple of its preliminary view that the distribution of music streaming apps through its App Store amounted to an abuse of dominance because of the mandatory use of Apple's own in-app purchase mechanism and the restrictions applicable to app developers preventing them from informing Apple users of alternative and cheaper purchasing possibilities.[58] In December 2021, the decision of ACM was made public in which it ordered Apple to adjust the unfair conditions in its App Store applicable to dating-app providers.[59] Such parallel investigations raise the question of how to ensure coordination and avoid duplication or conflicts.

competition policy in digital markets' (2023) 60 *Common Market Law Review* 431, 451–54; O Brook and M Eben, 'Who should guard the gatekeepers: does the DMA replicate the unworkable test of Regulation 1/2003 to settle conflicts between EU and national laws?' (2022) December *Competition Policy International Antitrust Chronicle* 38–39.

[55] Recital 32 of the DMA defines contestability as 'the ability of undertakings to effectively overcome barriers to entry and expansion and challenge the gatekeeper on the merits of their products and services'. Recital 33 of the DMA defines unfairness as relating 'to an imbalance between the rights and obligations of business users where the gatekeeper obtains a disproportionate advantage'.

[56] Press release Netherlands Authority for Consumers & Markets, 'ACM launches investigation into abuse of dominance by Apple in its App Store', 11 April 11 2019, www.acm.nl/en/publications/acm-launches-investigation-abuse-dominance-apple-its-app-store.

[57] Press release European Commission, 'Antitrust: Commission opens investigations into Apple's App Store rules', 16 June 2020, ec.europa.eu/commission/presscorner/detail/en/ip_20_1073.

[58] Press release European Commission, 'Antitrust: Commission sends Statement of Objections to Apple on App Store rules for music streaming providers', 30 April 2021, ec.europa.eu/commission/presscorner/detail/en/IP_21_2061.

[59] Press release Netherlands Authority for Consumers & Markets, 'ACM obliges Apple to adjust unreasonable conditions for its App Store', 24 December 2021, www.acm.nl/en/publications/acm-obliges-apple-adjust-unreasonable-conditions-its-app-store.

In this regard, Article 11(6) of Regulation 1/2003 entitles the Commission to initiate proceedings into an issue on which an NCA is already acting after consulting with that NCA. The same provision states that the Commission, by opening its own investigation, may relieve NCAs of their competence to apply the EU competition rules.[60] However, the Commission rarely uses this power in practice. The Dutch *Apple* case forms an illustration of how the Commission instead lets NCAs run their own investigations in parallel. In June 2021, the ACM announced that its investigation could continue because it complemented the investigation of the Commission. As explained by the ACM, its case focused on the conditions applicable to apps not competing with Apple's apps (in particular, apps related to online dating in the Netherlands), while the Commission was investigating Apple's conduct vis-à-vis apps competing with its own apps (namely apps for music streaming).[61] The fact that the Commission did not ask the ACM to end the case against the Apple App Store signals that it welcomes NCAs to conduct parallel investigations as long as they are complementary to its own.

The Commission has a similar power under the DMA to relieve NCAs from their investigation powers. While the Commission is the sole enforcer of the DMA, NCAs may on their own initiative conduct investigations into possible non-compliance with the DMA's obligations in their own territory and report their findings to the Commission. However, the Commission can relieve NCAs of the possibility to conduct such investigations or end investigations that are already ongoing by opening its own proceedings.[62] Under the DMA, the interaction between the Commission and NCAs is slightly different from that in EU competition enforcement. NCAs do not have the power to establish a violation of the DMA; the Commission is the DMA's only enforcer. However, NCAs can still rely on any national rules applicable to gatekeepers in their territories to the extent Article 1(5) and (6) DMA allow them to do so. As a result, the Commission and NCAs can coordinate their enforcement actions under the DMA and relevant national rules in a similar manner as they already do in the context of EU competition enforcement.

A case illustrating how the Commission creates room for NCAs to conduct their own investigations under EU competition law in their own territories is the Italian *Amazon* case. The Italian *Autorita' Garante della Concorrenza e del Mercato* (AGCM – the Italian competition authority) opened proceedings against Amazon in April 2019, alleging that Amazon engaged in abusive discrimination by giving third-party merchants who also use Amazon's logistic services improved visibility,

[60] See also Commission Notice on cooperation, paras 51–57 and Case C-857/19 *Slovak Telekom* ECLI:EU:C:2021:139, [2021] 4 CMLR 19, para 30.

[61] Press release Netherlands Authority for Consumers & Markets, 'ACM can continue its investigation into the Apple App Store', 22 June 2021, www.acm.nl/en/publications/acm-can-continue-its-investigation-apple-app-store.

[62] Article 38(7) DMA.

higher search rankings and better access to consumers on its e-commerce platform.[63] In November 2020, the Commission announced the opening of a competition investigation into similar behaviour, focusing on the issue of whether the criteria used by Amazon to select the winner of the so-called Buy Box (which prominently shows the offer of one single seller for a chosen product) and to enable sellers to offer products to its loyal Prime users led to preferential treatment of Amazon's own retail business or of the sellers that use Amazon's logistics and delivery services. In its press release, the Commission stated that its investigation would cover the European Economic Area except for Italy, where the AGCM 'started to investigate partially similar concerns last year, with a particular focus on the Italian market'.[64] In December 2021, the AGCM imposed a fine of over €1,128 billion on Amazon for abusing its dominant position by harming its competitors in the market for e-commerce logistics services.[65]

The existence of parallel investigations by the Commission and the AGCM into similar practices of the same company is an odd situation, because Article 11(6) of Regulation 1/2003 precisely seems to aim at preventing this. To avoid the existence of parallel proceedings at the EU and Italian level, Amazon sought annulment before the General Court of the Commission's decision to exclude Italy from its investigation based on Article 11(6) of Regulation 1/2003. The General Court declared the action inadmissible and regarded the Commission's decision as a preparatory act that is not challengeable because it does not produce legal effects versus Amazon.[66] Nevertheless, the judgment of the General Court contains interesting insights on the substantive interpretation of Article 11(6) of Regulation 1/2003 in the context of parallel proceedings by the Commission and NCAs. The General Court referred to the 2021 judgment of the Court of Justice in *Slovak Telekom* arguing that the parallel application of the EU competition rules by an NCA and the Commission 'cannot be at the expense of undertakings' and that '[n]ational authorities being relieved of their competence makes it possible to protect the undertakings from parallel proceedings brought by those authorities and the Commission'.[67] However, the General Court also noted that the protection against parallel proceedings does not imply a right of an undertaking 'to have a case dealt with in its entirety

[63] Press release Autorita' Garante della Concorrenza e del Mercato, 'A528 – Amazon: investigation launched on possible abuse of a dominant position in online marketplaces and logistic services', 16 April 2019, en.agcm.it/en/media/press-releases/2019/4/A528.

[64] Press release European Commission, 'Antitrust: Commission sends Statement of Objections to Amazon for the use of non-public independent seller data and opens second investigation into its e-commerce business practices', 10 November 2020, ec.europa.eu/commission/presscorner/detail/en/ip_20_2077.

[65] Press release Autorita' Garante della Concorrenza e del Mercato, 'A528 – Italian Competition Authority: Amazon fined over €1,128 billion for abusing its dominant position', 9 December 2021, en.agcm.it/en/media/press-releases/2021/12/A528.

[66] Case T-19/21 *Amazon* ECLI:EU:T:2021:730.

[67] Case C-857/19 *Slovak Telekom* ECLI:EU:C:2021:139, [2021] 4 CMLR 19, para 32 as quoted in Case T-19/21 *Amazon* ECLI:EU:T:2021:730, para 41.

by the Commission'.[68] In the view of the General Court, the protective effect of Article 11(6) of Regulation 1/2003 'does not imply that the Commission is obliged to initiate proceedings in order to deprive the national competition authorities of their competence to apply Articles 101 and 102 TFEU'.[69] On appeal, the Court of Justice upheld the General Court's reasoning, leaving it to the Commission's discretion to exercise its power to relieve NCAs of their competence under Article 11(6) of Regulation 1/2003.[70]

While the Commission's decision to allow the AGCM to conduct its own investigation risks leading to duplication of resources and perhaps even conflicting outcomes if the Commission turns out to target exactly the same behaviour, the case shows that in practice the Commission leaves room for NCAs to conduct their own investigations. Provided that such parallel investigations are well coordinated and do not duplicate resources by focusing on the same conduct, this can lead to a more effective form of supervision by dividing responsibilities, expertise and attention. One should note, though, that interventions of NCAs have a legally binding effect only in their own territories, while Commission decisions apply across the EU. However, the outcomes achieved by NCAs may lead to novel insights that can be taken up at the EU level later on or are sometimes applied by the respective undertakings in other Member States as well. The latter for instance happened in the context of the commitments that the French, Italian and Swedish NCAs obtained from Booking.com to stop preventing hotels from offering more favourable prices and conditions on any other sales channel.[71] This also illustrates that initial divergence among Member States can lead to consolidation towards stronger results at the EU level in the longer term.

C. Relevance of the *ne bis in idem* Principle

Beyond these practical issues of the impact of parallel investigations, there are also legal risks. When investigations target similar behaviour of the same company, concerns relating to the principle of *ne bis in idem* may occur. In the words of the Court of Justice, this principle 'precludes an undertaking being found liable or proceedings being brought against it afresh on the grounds of anti-competitive conduct for which it has been penalised or declared not liable by an earlier decision

[68] Case T-19/21 *Amazon* ECLI:EU:T:2021:730, para 45.

[69] Case T-19/21 *Amazon* ECLI:EU:T:2021:730, para 49.

[70] Case C-815/21 P *Amazon* ECLI:EU:C:2023:308, [2023] 5 CMLR 5, para 34.

[71] See Press release Booking.com, 'Booking.com Announces Support of New Commitments in Europe', 21 April 2015, news.booking.com/bookingcom-announces-support-of-new-commitments-in-europe/: 'Booking.com intends to implement these commitments throughout the European Economic Area and is working with all other European National Competition Authorities towards this objective. Booking.com trusts that its commitments will set the tone for an industry wide solution which all European NCAs will endorse and safeguard'.

that can no longer be challenged'.[72] The *ne bis in idem* principle is laid down in Article 50 of the Charter of Fundamental Rights of the European Union[73] and its scope has been interpreted in various competition cases. For instance, the Court of Justice held that the principle of *ne bis in idem* does not apply when an NCA and the Commission take decisions targeting the same type of anticompetitive practices but applied in separate product markets, namely two margin squeezes conducted by the dominant player Slovak Telekom in different markets.[74] Another example is the finding of the Court of Justice that the *ne bis in idem* principle does not stand in the way of an NCA imposing two fines in the same decision combining a violation of national and EU competition law for the same behaviour as long as there is no repetition of proceedings and the fines taken together are proportionate to the nature of the infringement.[75] Even though *ne bis in idem* is a relevant legal constraint to take into account, these cases already illustrate that the protection it offers is not absolute. The way the *ne bis in idem* principle has been interpreted in the context of EU competition law is also relevant for understanding its role in situations of possible overlap between the DMA and national competition regimes.

Until 2022, the *ne bis in idem* principle was interpreted in EU competition law as being triggered only under the threefold condition of identity of the facts, offender and legal interest protected. In other words, the same undertaking could not be sanctioned more than once for a single unlawful course of conduct designed to protect the same legal asset.[76] In other areas of EU law, a different and less restrictive interpretation is followed whereby only the two conditions of identity of the facts and offender need to be met for the *ne bis in idem* principle to apply.[77] In its 2022 judgments in *bpost* and *Nordzucker*, the Court of Justice unified the conditions of *ne bis in idem* across EU law by stating that the legal interest protected is 'not relevant for the purposes of establishing the existence of the same offence' and that the scope of protection conferred by Article 50 of the Charter cannot 'vary from one field of EU law to another'.[78] This means that *ne bis in idem* protection will be triggered more easily than before in competition cases. It no

[72] Case C-17/10 *Toshiba* ECLI:EU:C:2012:72, [2012] 4 CMLR 22, para 94.

[73] Charter of Fundamental Rights of the European Union [2012] OJ C326/391. The provision states that: 'No one shall be liable to be tried or punished again in criminal proceedings for an offence for which he or she has already been finally acquitted or convicted within the Union in accordance with the law'.

[74] Case C-857/19 *Slovak Telekom* ECLI:EU:C:2021:139, [2021] 4 CMLR 19, paras 45–46.

[75] Case C-617/17 *Powszechny* ECLI:EU:C:2019:283, [2019] 4 CMLR 28, paras 32–38.

[76] Joined Cases C-204/00 P, C-205/00 P, C-211/00 P, C-213/00 P, C-217/00 P and C-219/00 P *Aalborg Portland and Others v Commission* ECLI:EU:C:2004:6, [2004] ECR I-123, para 338; Case T-322/01 *Roquette Frères v Commission* ECLI:EU:T:2006:267, [2006] ECR II-3137, para 278.

[77] In the area of freedom, security and justice, see Case C-436/04 *Van Esbroeck* ECLI:EU:C:2006:165, [2006] ECR I-2333, paras 27, 32 and 36. See also the discussion by Advocate General Kokott in Case C-17/10 *Toshiba* ECLI:EU:C:2011:552, paras 114–124 and by Advocate General Wahl in Case C-617/17 *Powszechny* ECLI:EU:C:2018:976, paras 24–49.

[78] Case C-117/20 *bpost* ECLI:EU:C:2022:202, [2022] 4 CMLR 10, paras 34–35 and Case C-151/20 *Nordzucker* ECLI:EU:C:2022:203, [2022] 4 CMLR 11, paras 39–40.

longer matters whether the legal interest protected is the same; the only conditions to be considered are the identity of the facts and offender.

In *bpost*, the Court of Justice was asked to answer questions referred to it by a national court about whether the principle of *ne bis in idem* stands in the way of the Belgian competition authority establishing an abuse of dominance by bpost in the Belgian postal market based on EU and national competition law after the Belgian postal regulator had already found that bpost's rebate system breached several sector-specific postal rules. After stating that only the identity of the facts and offender matter, the Court of Justice left it up to the national court to determine whether the facts under scrutiny in the two sets of proceedings were identical. If so, the duplication would constitute a limitation of the fundamental right of Article 50 of the Charter. Such a limitation can, however, be justified according to the Court.[79] A few conditions apply for such justification following Article 52(1) of the Charter, namely the limitation must be provided for by law, respect the essence of the fundamental right to *ne bis in idem*, and be made only if it is 'necessary and genuinely meets objectives of general interest recognized by the European Union or the need to protect the rights and freedoms of others'.[80]

The Court argued that the duplication of proceedings respects the essence of *ne bis in idem* when 'national legislation does not allow for proceedings and penalties in respect of the same facts on the basis of the same offence or in pursuit of the same objective, but provides only for the possibility of a duplication of proceedings and penalties under different legislation'.[81] While the Court stated that the two sets of legislation at issue in the case do pursue distinct legitimate objectives,[82] it left it up to the national court to verify that the duplication of proceedings did not exceed what was appropriate and necessary to attain the distinct objectives and that the duplication of proceedings could be justified by their 'complementary aims relating to different aspects of the same unlawful conduct'.[83] With regard to the necessity of the duplication of proceedings, the Court mentioned a number of aspects to be assessed: (1) whether there are clear and precise rules making it possible to predict which acts or omissions are liable to be subject to a duplication of proceedings and penalties, and also to predict that there will be coordination between the different authorities; (2) whether the two sets of proceedings have been conducted in a manner that is sufficiently coordinated and within a proximate timeframe; and (3) whether any penalty that may have been imposed in the proceedings that were first in time was taken into account in the assessment of the second penalty.[84]

[79] Case C-117/20 *bpost* ECLI:EU:C:2022:202, [2022] 4 CMLR 10, paras 38–40.
[80] ibid para 41.
[81] ibid para 43.
[82] ibid para 44.
[83] ibid paras 48 and 50.
[84] ibid para 51.

The Court admitted that a full assessment of necessity can only be taken ex post,[85] but did give the national court a few pointers on how to apply these three aspects to the case at hand, namely: (1) the existence of a provision of national law providing for cooperation and exchange of information among the concerned authorities would constitute an appropriate framework, with the caveat that it needs to be established that the coordination has in fact taken place;[86] (2) the file submitted to the Court of Justice in its view contained indications of a sufficiently close connection in time between the two proceedings in which decisions were adopted in July 2011 and December 2012, respectively;[87] (3) the fact that the second fine was larger than the first one did not show in itself that the duplication of proceedings was disproportionate given that they 'may constitute complementary and connected, but nevertheless distinct, legal responses to the same conduct'.[88]

These considerations about when there is a duplication of proceedings that can be justified under the Charter will also become of relevance in the context of the parallel application of the DMA and national competition law.[89] Applying the conditions set out by the Court in *bpost* can lead to the conclusion that there is still room for national competition regimes to target behaviour of gatekeepers regulated under the DMA as long as the national laws pursue an objective other than the DMA's objectives of contestability and fairness, and there is coordination among the Commission and the respective NCAs. However, gatekeepers are likely to start litigation against NCAs taking up own cases next to the DMA, along the lines of the *Amazon* case discussed above. The success of such litigation will mainly depend on how the courts interpret any similarity of objectives between the DMA and national competition regimes.[90] The *Nordzucker* case illustrates what are relevant boundaries to keep in mind for assessing such similarity between legislative objectives.

In *Nordzucker*, the Austrian competition authority found Nordzucker liable for a violation of Austrian competition law and Article 101 TFEU after the German Bundeskartellamt had already adopted a decision establishing that Nordzucker had infringed German competition law and Article 101 TFEU for the same behaviour. In assessing whether the proceedings of the two NCAs pursued complementary aims, the Court referred to Regulation 1/2003 that establishes a close link between Article 101 TFEU and national competition rules prohibiting restrictions of competition.[91] Article 3(1) and (2) of Regulation 1/2003 does not allow for the national competition rules applicable to agreements and

[85] ibid para 52.
[86] ibid para 55.
[87] ibid para 56.
[88] ibid para 57.
[89] Another relevant area of overlap to which the *ne bis in idem* principle may apply is the relationship between the DMA and EU competition law. This relationship is not analysed here, because of the chapter's focus on streamlining EU and national law.
[90] See also the discussion in Cappai and Colangelo (n 54) 446–48 and Van den Boom (n 54) 78–82.
[91] Case C-151/20 *Nordzucker* ECLI:EU:C:2022:203, [2022] 4 CMLR 11, para 53.

restrictive practices to achieve a result different from the outcome that application of Article 101 TFEU would have reached.[92] For this reason, the Court expressed the view that the two authorities would pursue the same objective of general interest if they took proceedings against the same facts to ensure compliance with Article 101 TFEU and the corresponding national provision.[93]

While the Court did not touch upon the relationship of Article 102 TFEU with national competition rules, the Advocate General distinguished Articles 101 and 102 TFEU from each other in his opinion. He pointed at the fact that there is a large but not a complete overlap for situations falling under Article 102 TFEU, because Article 3(2) of Regulation 1/2003 explicitly mentions the ability of Member States to adopt stricter rules complementing Article 102 TFEU.[94] This may mean that the parallel application of Article 102 TFEU and national law is justified when the national rules are stricter than Article 102 TFEU and the general interests protected by the EU and national rules can therefore be considered complementary. Following this reasoning, there would also be no breach of the *ne bis in idem* principle when national competition regimes go beyond the DMA to achieve another objective because this has been foreseen and explicitly enabled in Article 1(5) and (6) of the DMA. Again, future litigation will need to clarify the precise scope for national rules to complement the DMA without violating the *ne bis in idem* principle.

IV. Coordination between the DMA and National Competition Law

The above discussion about the relationship between EU and national competition law shows that in the books as well as in practice there is still quite some scope for national interventions alongside actions of the Commission. Even though the Court of Justice clarified that identity of the legal interest is no longer necessary for the *ne bis in idem* principle to be triggered in competition law, there is still room to justify the existence of parallel EU and national investigations when they are based on legal regimes pursuing different objectives. It is submitted here that a similar attitude is desirable in the context of the relationship between the DMA and national competition law.

The DMA covers a range of obligations and prohibitions relating to the conduct of digital platforms, but it is inherently selective in its scope and focus – as is any legislative instrument. The decentralisation of EU competition enforcement has shown that the involvement of NCAs can support the effectiveness of the overall

[92] ibid paras 54–55.
[93] ibid para 56.
[94] Opinion of Advocate General Bobek in Case C-151/20 *Nordzucker* ECLI:EU:C:2021:681, [2022] 4 CMLR 11, para 51.

system by involving additional capacity and expertise. The presence of national rules targeting conduct of digital platforms that is not regulated by the DMA or imposing stricter conditions on gatekeepers to pursue objectives beyond the DMA's focus on contestability and fairness can therefore be considered welcome to involve NCAs as enforcers and to keep learning about the impact of other interventions. This allows for an evaluation of whether such national 'deviations' are worth taking up at the EU level. In this regard, reference can be made to Articles 12 and 19 of the DMA that allow the Commission to conduct market investigations in order to examine, respectively, whether the list of obligations needs to be updated and whether any new core platform services need to be added. One way of ensuring that the scope of the DMA stays future-proof over time is by allowing Member States to test additional rules at the national level and to evaluate their effects. However, the parallel existence of EU and national interventions does give rise to risks as well – in particular relating to duplication of resources and clashing outcomes. So while there are benefits in allowing for experimentation at the national level, any parallel EU and national interventions should be streamlined to ensure complementarities and avoid conflicts. A couple of suggestions can be made here to ensure such a form of effective coordination and to uphold the legal consistency of the overall framework of economic regulation for digital markets.

First, it is important to facilitate learning by comparing approaches. When Member States go beyond the DMA, it is desirable to closely monitor and evaluate the different interventions. Ideally, such monitoring does not fully take place behind closed doors but also allows for input from market players and other stakeholders such as consumer organisations and academics. Because it is impossible to predict what the impact of a particular legislative approach or regulatory intervention will be, some degree of experimentation is arguably needed to learn over time what works best in particular market settings and to use such insights for designing future interventions.[95]

Second, conflicts between EU and national approaches need to be avoided. This implies that the priority for national interventions should be to complement the DMA rather than to impose stricter obligations on gatekeepers for conduct that is already regulated under the DMA. Even though Article 1(5) and (6) of the DMA allow Member States to do the latter following a literal reading of the text, this would lead to regulatory fragmentation for the same behaviour across Member States to the detriment of the harmonisation that the DMA aims to achieve – especially considering that Article 114 TFEU, the provision focusing on harmonisation of national laws, forms its legal basis.[96] Less clear-cut are situations where NCAs expand the scope of the DMA's obligations to services not covered by the DMA. This happened in the context of the commitments that the Bundeskartellamt

[95] For a more in-depth discussion about the need for experimentation, see I Graef, 'Future-Proofing Plural Antitrust Enforcement Models: Lessons from the United States and the European Union' (2023) 85 *Antitrust Law Journal* 339, 363–72.

[96] See van den Boom (n 54) 68–72.

obtained from Google in October 2023 regarding the combination of personal data across Google's services and from non-Google sources. Such restrictions are contained in Article 5(2) DMA, but on the basis of its competences under the 10th amendment to the German Competition Act the Bundeskartellamt obtained commitments from Google to also apply these restrictions to more than 25 other services outside of the DMA – including Gmail, Google News, Assistant, Contacts and Google TV.[97] On the one hand, this may be positive from the perspective of the protection of consumers and the desire to experiment with interventions of a wider scope. On the other hand, these commitments have a legally binding effect in Germany only and can thereby lead to regulatory fragmentation across Member States for the same conduct. To keep such divergences under control, they need be carefully monitored and evaluated.

Third, the European Competition Network (ECN) remains a key venue for the Commission and NCAs to exchange information and stay in close contact regarding how to divide resources and to do joint priority-setting in the context of the enforcement of the DMA and relevant national regimes. Article 38 DMA refers to the ECN and recital 86 mentions the principles of proportionality and *ne bis in idem* as relevant boundaries for the Commission and NCAs to take into account when acting against the same offender for the same facts. In the context of the commitments it obtained from Google as mentioned above, the Bundeskartellamt referred to the need for coordination in the ECN and stated that the case 'is a testament to the close cooperation between the Bundeskartellamt and the European Commission on the way to achieving more competition and fair markets in the digital sector'.[98] The ECN has so far functioned well in the context of coordinating competition enforcement and therefore offers the opportunity to achieve a similar form of constructive cooperation in the context of the enforcement of the DMA and relevant national regimes.

V. Conclusion

A reflection on how the division of action between the EU and national level evolved from the inception of the EU competition rules shows that different periods can be distinguished in which the balance between the Commission and NCAs continues to slightly shift. After Regulation 1/2003 decentralised competition enforcement by letting the Commission and NCAs apply the EU competition rules in parallel, the DMA may put the Commission back at the forefront as the sole enforcer of the obligations targeted at gatekeepers that provide core platform

[97] Press release Bundeskartellamt, 'Bundeskartellamt gives users of Google services better control over their data', 5 October 2023, www.bundeskartellamt.de/SharedDocs/Meldung/EN/Pressemitteilungen/2023/05_10_2023_Google_Data.html.

[98] ibid.

services. At the same time, Member States have shown an eagerness to retain a role in regulating the conduct of digital platforms by adopting national regimes complementing or going further than the DMA. These developments give rise to questions about how to balance the relationship between EU and national law in the area of economic regulation for digital markets in the future.

The chapter has shown that there is quite some leeway by law and in practice for NCAs to act alongside the Commission in the context of competition enforcement. It is submitted that a similar attitude is desirable in the framework of the DMA and national competition regimes as well in order to allow for learning-by-doing and help the overall regulatory framework stay future-proof. While coordination is needed to avoid duplication and regulatory fragmentation, NCAs should continue to be taken seriously as relevant actors able to monitor the behaviour of digital platforms and to develop the law alongside the Commission.

9

With a Little Help from My Friends: Harmony and Dissonance in Europe's Many Patent Laws

LÉON DIJKMAN

A book about regulatory fragmentation in Europe could not be complete without a chapter on patent law, which has a credible claim to 'original gangster' status in this regard. Because European patents are governed by international, regional, European Union (EU) and national law, the regulatory framework is rife with complementarities, gaps and tensions. What is more, these different legal instruments are applied in a range of different fora whose interpretations are often authoritative but rarely bind sister courts. Justine Pila has aptly characterised this plurality of norms and institutions as a 'crowded house' in search of a coherent methodology.[1] Although the 'judicial dialogue' among the tenants of the crowded house has been extensively chronicled, a coherent methodology remains elusive and it is perhaps best captured by a line from a Beatles song: 'Lend me your ears and I'll sing you a song / and I'll try not to sing out of key'.[2] This chapter invites readers to tune in to Europe's key players in the field of patent law and outlines the fragmented legal landscape that dictates the melody.

'European patent' typically refers to the grant, by the European Patent Office (EPO) headquartered in Munich, of a patent according to the European Patent Convention (EPC).[3] As many others have noted,[4] the term misleadingly suggests a right of pan-European scope when actually, upon grant, the European patent

[1] J Pila, 'Some Reflections on Method and Policy in the Crowded House of European Patent Law and their Implications for India' (2012) 24 *National Law School Review of India* 54, 61.

[2] The Beatles, 'With a Little Help from my Friends', first released on *Sgt. Pepper's Lonely Hearts Club Band* (1967).

[3] Convention on the Grant of European Patents (Munich, 5 October 1973) 13 ILM 268.

[4] For instance, J Brinkhof, 'Patent Litigation in Europe: Two Sides of the Picture' (2000) 9 *Federal Circuit Bar Journal* 467.

becomes a bundle of national rights, each valid only in the jurisdiction for which protection was requested. The consequences are that a 'single' European patent must be enforced in parallel in each jurisdiction where protection is sought; and that across those jurisdictions courts may reach different outcomes, even on identically worded patents. This state of affairs is not exactly in line with the ideal of a European single market and attempts to overcome it date back to the EU's earliest days but have always resulted in failure, primarily because of the political sensitivity of patent law.[5] Yet an important change has occurred: as of 2023, the so-called Unified Patent Court (UPC) has become operational.[6] This is a court common to several – but not all – EU Member States, devoted exclusively to patent law. A further change is the introduction, through Article 3 of Regulation 1257/2012 (the Unitary Patent Regulation), of the so-called European patent with unitary effect (unitary patent).[7] In contrast to the traditional European patent, a Unitary patent is not a bundle of national rights but a single right valid in all Member States that participate in the UPC, much like the European Union trade mark. The possibilities for protection of inventions offered by the UPC and the Unitary patent are complementary to, rather than a replacement of, national patents and enforcement fora. These possibilities thus add to, rather than mitigate, the fragmentation and complexity of the European patent landscape.[8] Thus, it will remain possible not only to apply for 'classic' European patents but also for national patents, granted by national patent offices.

There are many aspects of this system that could credibly be the focus of a contribution on the fragmentation of European patent law. This chapter addresses two as it discusses: (i) fragmentation of *the law as such*, in that substantive European patent law derives from diverse legal instruments, often with overlapping scopes; and (ii) fragmentation of *judicial authority*, in that there are now three main fora that apply the legal framework: the EPO, national courts, and the UPC. Sections I(A) and I(B), respectively, describe these phenomena, while Section I(C) suggests that part of the resulting fragmentation stems from *normative dissonance*, ie the application in patent disputes of sets of laws with conflicting normative justifications or policy objectives. Section II(A) outlines the longstanding practice of judicial dialogue in European patent law, which has traditionally been the main way to overcome fragmentation, while Section II(B) makes some observations on the role of scholarship in this endeavour.

[5] J Pila, 'The European Patent: An Old and Vexing Problem' (2013) 62 *International & Comparative Law Quarterly* 917, 937.

[6] See generally R Ballardini et al, 'European Patent Law: the Case for Reform' in R Ballardini et al (eds), *Transition in European Patent Law* (Kluwer International, 2015).

[7] Regulation (EU) No 1257/2012 of the European Parliament and of the Council of 17 December 2012 implementing enhanced cooperation in the area of the creation of unitary patent protection.

[8] L Dijkman and C Van Paddenburgh, 'The Unified Patent Court as Part of a New European Patent Landscape: Wholesale Harmonization or Experiment in Legal Pluralism?' (2018) 26 *European Review of Private Law* 97, 109.

I. A Brief Introduction to Europe's Many Patent Laws

A. National, European, and International Instruments Governing Patent Law

European patent law is influenced by a notably diverse suite of legal instruments, each with a different scope. The most important international instruments are the TRIPS Agreement,[9] the EPC, and the UPC Agreement.[10] The most important EU law instruments are the Biotechnology[11] and Enforcement[12] Directives, the Brussels I[13] and Unitary Patent Regulations, and the EU Charter of Fundamental Rights (CFR). Lastly, patent laws are governed by national patent laws and their enforcement is subject to national civil procedure. The coverage of these instruments is summarised in the table below.[14]

Table 1 Overview of main legal instruments governing European patents

	TRIPS	**EPC**	**EU Dirs**	**EU Regs**	**ECHR/ CFR**	**National procedural law**	**National patent law**	**UPC Agreement**
Patentability	X	X	X				X	
Scope of protection		X					X	X
Limitations and exceptions	X		X	X			X	X
Enforcement	X		X	X		X	X	X
Property aspects		X		X	X		X	

When European patents are enforced before national courts, as they traditionally have been, the courts apply national law, including in particular national patent law, which incorporates the standards laid down by the other international instruments. As we will see below, these common standards are nevertheless often

[9] Agreement Establishing the World Trade Organization (Marrakesh, 15 April 1994) 33 ILM 619, Annex 1C (Agreement on Trade-Related Aspects of Intellectual Property Rights).
[10] Agreement on a Unified Patent Court (Brussels, 19 February 2013) OJ C 175/1.
[11] Directive 98/44/EC of the European Parliament and of the Council of 6 July 1998 on the legal protection of biotechnological inventions.
[12] Directive 2004/48/EC of the European Parliament and of the Council of 29 April 2004 on the enforcement of intellectual property rights, OJ L 157/30.
[13] Regulation (EU) No 1215/2012 of the European Parliament and of the Council of 12 December 2012 on jurisdiction and the recognition and enforcement of judgments in civil and commercial matters (recast).
[14] The precise classification of each instrument's scope is debatable but the table is intended to give a high-level overview of the fragmented regulatory framework, not an exact characterisation of the contents of the cited instruments.

subject to different interpretations across jurisdictions. The UPC has created a parallel forum for the enforcement of patents whose jurisdiction is not limited to individual Member States but covers all Member States that have ratified the UPC Agreement, which at the time of writing number 17. The grey highlighted column in Table 1 shows that some issues nevertheless remain outside the UPC's jurisdiction (most property aspects of patents), while for others (patentability standards) the UPC will apply other instruments, notably the EPC. In the foreseeable future, Europe will therefore have two fora for enforcement of patents, each applying standards mostly derived from international or EU law instruments, which in the case of national courts are incorporated into national law and in the case of the UPC in the UPC Agreement, but only partially. Fragmentation is inherent in such a plurality of fora and some examples are discussed in the next subsection. I first discuss the fragmentation of the legal framework as such because as the table demonstrates, every aspect of patent law is governed by an overlapping set of legal instruments.

Patentability standards govern what can be patented, and on what conditions. The TRIPS Agreement (1994) achieved minimum harmonisation of these standards on a global scale. But two decades prior, patentability standards had already been harmonised across Europe through the EPC. The EPC established a shared patent office (the EPO) for these states and today counts 38 Member States, extending beyond the EU to important non-EU economies such as Switzerland and Turkey. So far, the EU has not intervened in patentability requirements, barring one important exception: the Biotechnology Directive. The Biotechnology Directive excludes from patentability a variety of products and processes primarily over bioethical concerns and offers a fine illustration of just how fraught and politically difficult legislating patentability of cutting-edge technologies can be.[15]

Scope of protection generally refers to the extent of the patentee's exclusive rights, which is first and foremost established by interpretation of the patent's claims.[16] Here, too, the EPC plays an important role as it lays down a uniform standard in Article 69. Diverging applications in, particularly, the Netherlands, Germany, and England resulted in the adoption of an explanatory protocol (2001), but significant differences remain.[17] The UPC Agreement stipulates the acts that may constitute infringement of a patent (Article 25) and lays down a standard for acts of so-called indirect infringement (Article 26). The scope of protection

[15] N Coghlan, 'Health Union and Bioethical Union: Does Hippocrates Require Socrates?' (2020) 11 *European Journal of Risk Regulation* 766, 772–73.

[16] In addition to a general description of the invention for which protection is sought, a patent contains claims which seek to concisely define the invention and the precise way in which they do is highly consequential for the scope of protection offered by the patent. As per Article 69 EPC: 'The extent of the protection conferred by a European patent or a European patent application shall be determined by the claims'.

[17] For an overview, see P England, *A Practitioner's Guide to European Patent Law*, 2nd edn (Hart Publishing, 2022) ch 2.

afforded to European patents is thus governed by two regional instruments: the EPC and the UPC Agreement. As of yet, there is no European legislation touching on this subject.

Limitations are statutory exceptions to the patentee's monopoly and have long remained fully within a country's national sovereignty.[18] To prevent perceived harms from protectionist application of these provisions, the TRIPS Agreement laid down, in Articles 30–31, harmonised (and quite strict) guidelines for their application, particularly as regards compulsory licensing. The UPC Agreement contains provisions on important limitations like prior and experimental use or exhaustion (see Articles 27–29). Whereas scope of protection is a subject typically left to patent law specialists, limitations offer a more obvious interface with public policy and it is therefore unsurprising that the EU has been more active in this respect. First, it introduced the so-called Bolar exemption in Directive 2001/83, which exempts from patent infringement conducting 'necessary studies and trials' to obtain market approval for a pharmaceutical.[19] Second, the Unitary Patent Regulation lays down special regimes for exhaustion and licences of right for Unitary patents. Third, further EU involvement may be on the horizon as the European Commission is contemplating a regulation that would introduce a harmonised framework and procedure for compulsory licensing of patents.[20]

The framework for enforcement of patents offers an example of legal regulation at its most fragmented. Subject again to minimum harmonisation through the TRIPS Agreement, which sets baseline standards for enforcement proceedings, enforcement modalities are governed by national procedural laws, which differ vastly. Because this was perceived as harmful to the EU's competitiveness, the Enforcement Directive introduced minimum harmonisation and made available to patent holders a uniform suite of enforcement remedies. In addition, the Brussels I Regulation fully harmonises rules on jurisdiction, an especially pertinent subject in patent practice as patentees understandably search for ways to consolidate proceedings to prevent the costs and uncertainties caused by parallel litigation. As might be expected, this chimera of national and partially or fully harmonised EU law gives rise to important differences between Member States when it comes to enforcement modalities. The European Court of Justice (ECJ)'s case law interpreting the Enforcement Directive and the Brussels I Regulation has offered some important guidance, but differences and open questions remain.[21]

[18] Pila (n 5) 927 (arguing that this sovereignty was an important reason the EPC proved politically viable).

[19] Directive 2001/83/EC of the European Parliament and of the Council of 6 November 2001 on the Community code relating to medicinal products for human use, Article 10(6).

[20] European Commission, 'Proposal for a Regulation of the European Parliament and the Council on compulsory licensing for crisis management and amending Regulation (EC) 816/2006' COM(2023) 224 final.

[21] See, in particular, on remedies: Case C-170/13 *Huawei Technologies* ECLI:EU:C:2015:477, [2015] 5 CMLR 14; and on jurisdiction: Case C-4/03 *GAT* ECLI:EU:C:2006:457, [2006] ECR I-6509; Case C-539/03 *Roche Nederland* ECLI:EU:C:2006:458, [2006] ECR I-6535; and Case C-616/10 *Solvay* ECLI:EU:C:2012:445.

The UPC must apply and respect both the Enforcement Directive and the Brussels I Regulation, though the UPC Agreement lays down special jurisdictional rules.

Last, patents as objects of property (such as rules for their transfer or pledging them as collateral) are governed by the national law of the country where they are registered. The Unitary Patent Regulation designates as the law applicable to Unitary patents the country where the applicant has its residence, while the EPC provides rules for patent applications. Here, too, fragmentation exists as transferring a 'single' European patent necessitates observing idiosyncrasies of national patent laws crucial to transferring each individual part of the bundle.[22] In addition, patents enjoy constitutional protection against arbitrary interference by the authorities, as per Article 1 of the First Protocol to the European Charter of Human Rights (ECHR).[23] This protection is now also incorporated into Article 17(2) CFR. Traditionally, these safeguards primarily set limits on government regulation of patent uses, surely a salient issue in the wake of a devastating pandemic.[24] In addition, the ECJ held that enforcement of IP rights may disproportionately interfere with competing Charter rights.[25] While it remains unclear how this line of cases affects patent law, it adds another layer of complexity to the enforcement of these rights.

B. Together Alone: The Crowded House of Europe's Patent Institutions

In addition to the various complementarities and overlaps in the governing legal instruments, a factor contributing significantly to fragmentation of the European legal framework for patents is the plurality of adjudication bodies tasked with application of this framework. It was already observed that national courts have long been the only forum for the enforcement of European patents. In addition, the EPO's Boards of Appeal hear oppositions against patent grants and have over time developed a vast jurisprudence covering the minutiae of the various patentability doctrines. So far, then, national courts and the EPO's Boards of Appeal have been far and away the most important institutions to drive the development of European patent law, but they are not the only ones. European patent law is further developed by, inter alia, national patent offices, deciding on objections to national patent grants; the ECJ, interpreting EU legal instruments relevant for patent law and deciding on patent law's relation to other fields of EU law; arbitration bodies

[22] D Van Engelen, 'The Assignment of a European Patent Portfolio: A Plea for a "Lex Proprietas"' in C Osterrieth et al (eds), *Patentrecht: Festschrift für Thomas Reimann* (Carl Heymanns, 2009).

[23] Eur. Comm. H.R., decision of 4.10.1990, *Smith Kline and French Laboratories Ltd v the Netherlands*, No. 12633/87. DR 66, p 89.

[24] M Husovec, 'The Fundamental Right to Property and the Protection of Investment: How Difficult is it to Repeal New Intellectual Property Rights?' in C Geiger (ed), *Research Handbook on Intellectual Property and Investment Law* (Edward Elgar, 2019) 393.

[25] Case C-324/09 *L'Oréal and others* ECLI:EU:C:2011:474, [2011] ECR I-6011, para 143.

such as the World Trade Organization's panels, interpreting obligations contained in trade agreements and ruling on the compatibility of national measures with those obligations; and competition authorities, which occasionally bring actions against patentees for allegedly abusive behaviours. Borrowing Pila's metaphor – and the name of an Australian rock band whose fourth studio album, *Together Alone* (1993), perfectly captures the mood of European patent institutions – this is a veritable 'crowded house' that is nevertheless on the brink of welcoming yet another tenant, the UPC. As we saw, the UPC provides a forum for patent enforcement parallel to national courts and with jurisdiction covering all signatory states.

The key observation here is that while these institutions all apply the same legal framework – sometimes even to the same set of facts – there is no hierarchical relationship between them, with the possible exception of the ECJ.[26] It is thus conceivable that different institutions reach different conclusions under the same patent, as has in fact occurred on several occasions. The most famous example is *Improver v Remington*, where the English court arrived at a different answer than other European courts to the question whether a slitted rubber rod was equivalent (in patent law terms) to a helical spring.[27] More recent examples also exist.[28] This type of divergence has been the basis for calls to further harmonise European patent law for decades.[29] Section II(A) addresses the dialogue that developed between European patent courts in the absence of such harmonisation or a centralised appeals court to definitively decide contentious cases. Reliance on these techniques will remain necessary with the advent of the UPC, notwithstanding its status as a centralised patent court common to a significant number of Member States. Its decisions, authoritative though they may be, will not formally bind national courts and therefore divergence will remain possible. Especially in countries that did not or cannot accede to the UPC Agreement, its rulings will have no more than persuasive authority.[30]

C. Normative Dissonance

It is interesting to consider in some detail what causes the diverging interpretations of common norms as happened in *Improver v Remington*. The first and most

[26] I write 'possible' because while from the perspective of EU law, it is established orthodoxy that the ECJ is hierarchically superior to national courts, this view does not appear to be universally accepted from the perspective of national law: BVerfG 5 May 2020, 2 BvR 859/15 (*Weiss II*).

[27] *Improver Corp v Remington Consumer Products* [1990] FSR 181 (finding no equivalence); the Dutch and German courts reached opposite conclusions, see [1993] IIC 832 (Netherlands) and 838 (Germany) respectively.

[28] R Arnold, 'Harmonization of European Patent Law' (2019) 14 *Journal of Intellectual Property Law and Practice* 657 refers to a decision by the District Court of Hague which went against prior decisions by English and German courts and even the Court of Appeal in the Hague. Arnold nevertheless concludes that 'There can be no dispute that, in so deciding, the District Court fully discharged its duty to act as an independent tribunal'.

[29] Brinkhof (n 4) 467.

[30] Dijkman and Van Paddenburgh (n 8) 112.

obvious cause is the divergence between national procedural laws.[31] These differences might preclude a court in one Member State from considering evidence deemed crucial in another Member State: the most salient example would be jurisdictions with so-called bifurcated systems, where infringement and validity claims are heard separately. In those jurisdictions, it is possible for infringement remedies to be issued on the basis of patents that later turn out to be invalid and that sister courts in other jurisdictions have previously invalidated.[32] The second cause is equally obvious: applying law is a subjective exercise and reasonable minds might differ on what the best application is. That is especially likely to hold true for patent law, the two key doctrines of which – inventive step and scope of protection – turn on inherently subjective evaluations of an invention's worth and have strong policy implications. This latter circumstance suggests differing views on the justification or normative basis of the applicable legal regime as a third cause. *Improver* is a case in point, as the differing decisions reached by the English courts on the one hand and the Dutch and German courts on the other reflected differing views of how patent claims ought to be read. Whereas the English tradition emphasised legal certainty for third parties and thus adhered to a strict reading of the claims, the Dutch and German courts traditionally emphasised a fair protection for the inventor and so were willing to look 'behind' the wording of the claim. That conflict of views was ultimately resolved by adding the aforementioned protocol to Article 69 EPC, although an individual judge's views of the patent system may well still influence how they apply the protocol's middle ground.

Whereas divergence on scope of protection may reflect different views on the normative anchor of a single shared provision (in *Improver*, that was Article 69 EPC), the fragmented legal landscape outlined under Section I(A) above may also result in overlaps of legal regimes that each have a different or even ostensibly conflicting normative bases. In these cases, we might speak of 'normative dissonance': the purpose of one legal instrument may point courts in one direction, whereas the purpose of an equally applicable different instrument might point in another. Although various justificatory theories exist for patents, today it seems commonplace in Europe to adopt a utilitarian view of patent law, according to which it exists to 'enhance social and economic welfare by stimulating innovation and diffusion of knowledge'.[33] The assumptions underlying this view are that: (i) exclusive rights over inventions are necessary because otherwise the risk of free-riding by others will cause the market to undersupply inventions, and (ii) that the static costs stemming from granting such rights (ie access restrictions

[31] Brinkhof (n 4) 468.

[32] L Dijkman, 'Does the Injunction Gap Violate Implementers' Fair Trial Rights Under the ECHR?' (2021) 70 *GRUR International* 215, 219.

[33] Cowan et al, 'Policy options for the improvement of the European patent system' (European Parliament / STOA commissioned report, 2007) 8. This formulation of the purpose of the European Patent Convention was arrived at by a collaboration of academics and EPO officials and can be considered representative of the mainstream European position. For an overview of the various theories justifying intellectual property, see M Spence, *Intellectual Property* (Oxford University Press, 2007) ch 2.

and monopoly pricing) are outweighed by 'dynamic' gains (ie the ultimate societal benefits from innovation).[34] Naturally, these assumptions may be – and have repeatedly been – challenged.[35] But for better or worse, these challenges have not resulted in the abolition of the patent system and so long as we have it, these twin assumptions are called upon to justify it.

It can readily be imagined that the exclusive rights called to life by patent law might clash with other bodies of law, especially Union law. An early example is the clash with the free movement of goods on the EU's internal market: could patents justify an exception to this rule? The ECJ held that it may indeed.[36] In so doing, it laid the basis for the European doctrine of exhaustion of IP rights, according to which rights holders may oppose imports of protected goods unless they were first put on the market in a Member State with their consent, even if no patent protection exists in that Member State.[37] Another example is the clash of patent law and competition law, which seeks specifically to prevent abuse of market dominance on the internal market. This has given rise to numerous decisions by the European courts. A recent and representative example is *Huawei Technologies*, where the ECJ formulated the licensing obligations that apply to dominant holders of so-called standard-essential patents, which disclose technology necessary to practice technological standards common in the IT and telecoms industries.[38] The interface between patent law and the free movement of goods and competition law, respectively, has been extensively documented elsewhere and I will not further address it here.[39] The point is rather that the outcome of these cases may well have been different and that the chosen outcome depends on the normative framework that takes precedence.[40] Almost invariably, the goal will be to reconcile the aims pursued by both legislative bodies which requires theorising their interface and the development of patent-specific doctrines.

New instances of normative dissonance can be expected as patents are embedded in the constitutional infrastructure of the EU, ie as rights with protected Charter status among other such rights. IP rights, including patents, have long

[34] D Booton, 'The construction of patent claims' (2020) 40 *Legal Studies* 651, 661.

[35] See eg P Drahos, *The Global Governance of Knowledge: Patent Offices and Their Clients* (Cambridge University Press, 2010) ch 11; and M Boldrin and D Levine, *Against Intellectual Monopoly* (Cambridge University Press, 2010) ch 8.

[36] Case 24/67 *Parke Davis & Co v Probel* ECLI:EU:C:1968:11, [1968] ECR I-81.

[37] Case 187/80 *Merck v Stephar* ECLI:EU:C:1981:180, [1981] ECR I-2063, para 11.

[38] *Huawei Technologies* (n 21).

[39] See generally I Calboli, 'The Intricate Relationship Between Intellectual Property Exhaustion and Free Movement of Goods in Regional Organizations' (2019) 9 *Queen Mary Journal of Intellectual Property* 22; and A Jones and R Nazzini, 'The Effect of Competition Law on Patent Remedies' in B Biddle et al (eds), *Patent Remedies and Complex Products: Towards a Global Consensus* (Cambridge University Press, 2019).

[40] Indeed, these issues have been decided differently in different jurisdictions. For instance, unlike EU law, US patent law allows contractual restrictions on exhaustion: Calboli (n 39) 32. At the same time, and again unlike EU law, holders of US Standard-essential patents almost never qualify for injunctive relief: Jones and Nazzini (n 39) 236.

been recognised in Europe as constitutionally protected property, but this was traditionally understood as protection against unlawful government interference or expropriation.[41] The ECJ's recent case law, however, suggests that when patents are enforced, national courts must ensure a fair balance between all interests concerned.[42] This language immediately calls to mind the ECJ's decisions on injunctions against intermediaries, according to which courts must strike a fair balance between 'the various fundamental rights protected by the Community legal order'.[43] It is far from clear, however, what striking this balance entails.[44] Some authors were quick to embrace the ECJ's fair balance case law as a means to create rights-based exceptions to exclusivity, especially in the field of copyright law.[45] A series of 2019 decisions by the ECJ appears to preclude this possibility.[46] At the same time, it seems clear that competing fundamental rights may influence the interpretation of EU law provisions on IP or place limits on the exercise of these rights at the stage of enforcement.[47] The latter limitation follows explicitly from Recital (32) of the Enforcement Directive, which states that it 'respects the fundamental rights … recognised in particular by the Charter of Fundamental Rights of the European Union'. Indeed, when it comes to patents, §139 of the German Patent Act (as recently revised) expressly states that a claim for injunctive relief is excluded insofar as this would cause disproportionate hardship to third parties, and European patent courts have acknowledged third party rights as a limitation on IP enforcement on several occasions.[48]

An increased sensitivity to third-party rights may well herald a major change in how patents are conceptualised. Traditionally, ad hoc conflicts with interests of third parties were considered subsumed in the utilitarian quid pro quo of the patent system. As we saw above, the short-term costs associated with reduced access to the patented technology and monopoly pricing are assumed to be outweighed by the longer-term gains in terms of increased innovation. Consequently, European courts would decline to consider interests of third parties, such as patients, during

[41] O-A Rognstad, *Property Aspects of Intellectual Property* (Cambridge University Press, 2018) 182.

[42] *Huawei Technologies* (n 21) para 55. See also the opinion of A-G Wathelet at 59: 'After all, the grant of an injunction sought by an action to cease and desist places a significant restriction on [the freedom to conduct a business, protected in Article 16 CFR] and is therefore capable of distorting competition.'

[43] Case C-275/06 *Promusicae* ECLI:EU:C:2008:54, [2008] ECR I-271, para 68.

[44] Rognstad (n 41) 192.

[45] C Geiger and E Izyumenko, 'Towards a European "Fair Use" Grounded in Freedom of Expression' (2019) 35 *American University International Law Review* 1, 11. Such reliance on competing rights as 'external' limitations on copyright exclusivity was seemingly accepted in *Ashby Donal v France* App no 36769/08 (ECtHR, 20 July 2004).

[46] See, among others, Case C-476/17 *Pelham* ECLI:EU:C:2019:624, [2019] Bus LR 2159, para 63.

[47] C Sganga, 'Multilevel Constitutionalism and the Propertisation of EU Copyright' in J Griffiths and T Mylly, *Global Intellectual Property Protection and New Constitutionalism* (Oxford University Press, 2021) 263, 265.

[48] See, for instance, *Edwards Lifesciences LLC v Boston Scientific* [2018] EWHC 1256 (Pat) and Tribunale Ordinario di Milano 29 October 2019 *Heraeus Medical GmbH v Biomet* No 9828/2019 (albeit concerning trade secrets).

patent enforcement.[49] The only way they could be considered was if they represented a *public* interest of sufficient importance to justify the grant of a compulsory licence.[50] Such an approach seems far removed from the apparent obligation on patent courts to decide, on a case-by-case basis, whether a fair balance is struck between all interests concerned. Whether this will change much in practice depends on the threshold one applies for a fair balance to be upset: some have argued that should be accepted only when competing interests would justify the grant of a compulsory licence, others have argued against this view.[51]

Importantly for the purpose of this contribution, embedding patent enforcement in the Charter will require reconciliation of patent law's quid pro quo with the logic underlying the Charter. There are various ways in which this logic might be at odds with the idea of an absolute right of exclusivity. Conflicts of Charter rights should be resolved according to Article 52 CFR, which essentially lays down a balancing mechanism in which Article 17(2) CFR would not seem to take any specific precedence. This suggests that courts may need to scrutinise more closely whether patent protection is justified in light of conflicting rights, rather than rejecting any conflicting claim by reference to patent law's quid pro quo. In fact, the content of the quid pro quo could change as patents may come to be recognised not simply as economic rights that seek to foster innovation in some abstract sense and which are shielded from the influence of competing values and rights, but rather as serving more broadly 'the interests and needs that citizens identify through the language of human rights as being fundamental'.[52] Such a shift of perspective would clearly imply a lower threshold of intervention where patent laws fail to serve the public interest, expressed in the Charter in the form of competing fundamental rights.

Equally complicated issues of normative reconciliation are raised by the so-called proportionality defence, which is often traced to the requirement in Article 3(2) Enforcement Directive that remedies for IP infringement be 'proportionate' (among other requirements).[53] There is a growing consensus that this means national courts must limit a patentee's entitlement to injunctive relief where granting an immediate and unqualified injunction would have disproportionate consequences, as is now also codified in §139 German Patent Act. But what does 'disproportionate' mean? Many

[49] See, for instance, Hoge Raad 21 April 1995, ECLI:NL:HR:1995:ZC1705 *NJ* 1996/462 (*Boehringer Mannheim/Kirin Amgen*) para 3.7. Landgericht Düsseldorf 9 March 2017, 4a O 28/16, BeckRS 2017, 104662, para IV.2.b.

[50] Compulsory licensing provisions differ across European jurisdictions. In some jurisdictions, such as the Netherlands, 'public interest' is interpreted strictly in the sense of policy goals pursued by the government: Minister of Justice 9 January 1980 «Weidepomp» *Bijblad* 1981, 185. Other jurisdictions, such as Germany, seem to have acknowledged aggregated individual interests, even of a relatively small group, as capable of justifying the grant of a compulsory licence 'especially if this group would be exposed to a particularly high risk if the infringing product … was no longer available': M Stierle and F Hofmann, 'The Latest Amendment to the German Law on Patent Injunctions: The New Statutory Disproportionality Exception and Third-Party Interests' (2022) 71 *GRUR-International* 1123, 1131.

[51] See generally Stierle and Hofmann (n 50) 1131 et seq.

[52] P Drahos, 'Intellectual Property and Human Rights' (1999) 3 *Intellectual Property Quarterly* 349, 367.

[53] *HTC v Nokia* [2013] EWHC 3778 (Pat), para 26.

authors suggest injunctions are disproportionate where they would overcompensate the patentee, on the theory – derived from patent law's utilitarian justification – that overcompensation harms innovation because it causes social losses 'with no clear corresponding benefit'.[54] Fair enough. The legal basis for the proportionality defence, however, is an EU Directive that, while mentioning the encouragement of innovation (eg Recital (3)), is primarily concerned with the attainment of a 'high, equivalent and homogenous level of protection in the internal market' (Recital (10)).[55] The Enforcement Directive thus strives for a high degree of protection for IP rights not so much because of their specific justifications, but primarily out of concern over fragmentation of the internal market, as is also evidenced by Recital (8). Indeed, when the ECJ has interpreted the Enforcement Directive – thereby deciding on the remedies the holder of a European Patent is entitled to and consequently giving shape to that right's effective scope – it made no mention of fostering innovation or other considerations relatable to patent law's utilitarian justification.[56] This is important because the Directive must be interpreted in light of its purpose 'in order to achieve the result sought by the directive'.[57] The result sought by the Directive is not increased innovation or the public good but a 'high, equivalent and homogenous level of protection' and if *that* is *to* be the guiding principle for the proportionality defence, its application may be guided by considerations quite different from concerns about patentee overcompensation. One might instead expect an emphasis on a uniform, workable, and predictable test to limit a patentee's entitlement to relief in appropriate cases, rather than an open-ended balancing exercise that creates substantial legal uncertainty.[58]

In sum, just as happened with the EU's internal market law and competition law, courts will need to theorise the interface between (national) patent laws on the one hand, and EU constitutional law and the Enforcement Directive on the other. This process is further considered in the next section.

[54] T Cotter, 'Patent Holdup, Patent Remedies, and Antitrust Responses' (2009) 34 *Journal of Corporation Law* 1151, 1179. In Europe, see eg R Sikorski, 'Permanent Injunctions in Patent Law – in Search of Flexibility' in S Frankel (ed), *Is Intellectual Property Pluralism Functional?* (Edward Elgar, 2019) 385; A Ohly, '"Patenttrolle" Oder: Der Patentrechtliche Unterlassungsanspruch Unter Verhältnismäßigkeitsvorbehalt? Aktuelle Entwicklungen Im US-Patentrecht Und Ihre Bedeutung Für Das Deutsche Und Europäische Patentsystem' (2008) 57 *GRUR International* 787, 791; C Le Stanc, 'L'abus Dans l'exercice Du Droit de Brevet: Les "Patent Trolls"' (2010) 10 *Propriété Industrielle* 63.

[55] For its part, the ECJ has consistently emphasised that this is the Directive's overall goal: see eg Case C-44/21 *Phoenix Contact* ECLI:EU:C:2022:309, para 37; or Case C-688/17 *Bayer Pharma* ECLI:EU:C:2019:722, para 42.

[56] *Phoenix Contact* offers a great example. Here, the ECJ ruled that the Enforcement Directive precludes a national rule under which interim injunctions are unavailable unless the validity of the patent enforced was confirmed in first instance or opposition proceedings. It would be easy to justify this decision by reference to patent law's goal of fostering innovation, as the Dutch Supreme Court did in 1993: ECLI:NL:HR:1993:ZC0986, *NJ* 1993, 659 (*Vredo v Veenhuis*) para 3.4 (interim relief especially important in patent cases because the period of time when the right is commercially valuable is limited). The ECJ, however, was completely silent on this and instead justified its decision by reference to 'the objective of a high level of protection of intellectual property' (para 40).

[57] *Phoenix Contact* (n 55) para 49.

[58] I develop this point at length in L Dijkman, *The Proportionality Test in European Patent Law: Patent Injunctions Before EU Courts and the UPC* (Hart Publishing, 2023).

II. The Search for a Common Language in the Crowded House

A. Judicial Dialogue as a Way to Overcome Fragmentation

Fragmentation of European patent law is nothing new as shown in two recent monographs that are entirely devoted to the overlaps in Europe's fragmented regulatory framework and its consequences.[59] Karen Walsh concludes that such fragmentation is ultimately unavoidable because it is 'inherent' in the European patent system.[60] It is therefore unsurprising that European patent courts have embraced a process known as judicial dialogue to reach consensus positions on controversial issues or open questions.[61] English courts have long openly adopted a certain degree of deference to the decisions of the EPO's Enlarged Board of Appeal, ascribing to them the status of 'commodore' among the convoy of European patent jurisdictions.[62] The German Federal Supreme Court has articulated a duty for lower courts to consider foreign decisions and if they decide differently, to explain why.[63] Citations of sister courts are thus a common occurrence in European patent law and through them something approaching a European law of patents may be traced. For instance, when the Dutch Supreme Court decided on the treatment of so-called Swiss-type claims under Dutch patent law, it noted that its approach was in line with that of the German and English supreme courts, as well as the EPO's Enlarged Board of Appeal.[64] In the same year, and almost 30 years after the aforementioned *Improver* decision, the UK Supreme Court abandoned the line of cases following *Improver* and explicitly aligned itself with continental European jurisdictions on equivalence.[65] It was repeatedly observed that the harmonisation of European patent law has come a long way because of these dialogues.[66]

Such dialogue will likely remain important (if not become more so) after the UPC becomes operational because, at least in its early years, it will contribute to fragmentation rather than resolve it.[67] Although the UPC will have the authority to decide on all issues relating to validity and infringement, it is not an appeals court whose decision formally binds national courts, even when it decides on European

[59] F Baldan, *Judicial Coherence in the European Patent System: Lessons from the US and Japan* (Edward Elgar, 2022) and K Walsh, *Fragmentation and the European patent system* (Hart Publishing, 2022).

[60] Walsh (n 58) 142.

[61] See generally E Mak, *Judicial Decision-Making in a Globalised World* (Hart Publishing, 2013). For various examples from European patent law, see K Walsh, 'Promoting Harmonisation Across the European Patent System Through Judicial Dialogue and Cooperation' (2019) 50 *IIC* 408.

[62] *Actavis UK v Merck & Co* [2008] EWCA Civ 444, para 48.

[63] Bungesgerichtshof 15 April 2010 *Walzenformgebungsmaschine* Xa ZB 10/09, para 14.

[64] Hoge Raad 3 November 2017, ECLI:NL:HR:2017:2807 (*MSD v Teva*), para 3.6.3.

[65] Walsh (n 58) 126 et seq; Baldan (n 58) 89 et seq.

[66] Walsh (n 58) 438; Arnold (n 28).

[67] Dijkman and Van Paddenburgh (n 8) 113.

patents with identical claims.[68] It is, however, worth mentioning that the UPC will offer advantages beyond a central court to rule on patent issues of shared concern for all European patent institutions. At least in the first years, most of the UPC's judges will have a part-time position and thus remain active as national judges. This institutional feature has the potential to create unique cross-fertilisation of European patent doctrine as UPC judges will be called upon to decide patent cases jointly with foreign colleagues, then return to their home state where they may decide cases in a similar vein. The influence of these types of institutional features on the development of European patent law is not to be underestimated.[69] Federica Baldan has highlighted and suggested a number of additional features which, if adopted by the UPC, may further strengthen its capacity to authoritatively decide cutting-edge questions of patent law.[70] These include the possibility for UPC judges to file dissenting opinions (Article 78 UPC Agreement), allowance for *amicus curiae* briefs, and institutional exchange with the ECJ in the form of *référendaires* with a patent law background.

In this way, a significant degree of harmonisation can be achieved even if no formal EU regime of patent law exists. As noted by others, this has been true of patent law in the past decades and it is expected that the UPC will further foster the joint, if decentralised, development of European patent law. Thus, while the UPC adds another layer of complexity to the system, it may simultaneously reduce fragmentation of the substantive law because of its authoritative voice in our crowded house.[71] It could even be argued that the EU is better off in this respect than the US, where patent jurisprudence is centralised in a single appeals court: the Court of Appeals for the Federal Circuit. Some American authors have argued that shared appellate jurisdiction with other courts (as is the case for other fields of IP law in the US) might foster creativity as lower courts become 'laboratories' for patent policy, with sufficient leeway to develop original solutions to common legal questions.[72] The structure of EU law, which relies heavily on partial harmonisation through directives to achieve policy goals while respecting national autonomy, seems to be particularly fruitful for this enterprise.[73]

[68] Arnold (n 28) points out that 'there are limits to what can be achieved through judicial dialogue and cooperation' in the absence of a shared appeals court. Because there will remain for a considerable time the possibility to opt patents out of the UPC's jurisdiction (*cf* Dijkman and Van Paddenburgh (n 8) 111) the UPC will not fully solve this problem.

[69] *cf* J Pila, 'A Constitutionalized Doctrine of Precedent and the *Marleasing* Principle as Bases for a European Legal Methodology' in A Ohly and J Pila (eds), *The Europeanization of Intellectual Property Law* (Oxford University Press, 2013) 238 (arguing that substantive European patent law 'will generally be the product of complex institutional dynamics as much as principled policy making').

[70] Baldan (n 58) ch 6.

[71] Pila (n 68) 234. At 239, Pila expresses the concern that 'one can have too many European courts' which might 'increase the influence of institutional dynamics and auto-legitimating tendencies at the expense of principled law- and policy-making'. In my view, the aforementioned unique institutional features of the UPC – authority, expertise, and shared membership with national courts – mitigate these concerns.

[72] C Nard and J Duffy, 'Rethinking Patent Law's Uniformity Principle' (2007) 101 *Northwestern University Law Review* 1619; L Ouellette, 'Patent Experimentalism' (2015) 101 *Virginia Law Review* 65.

[73] Ouellette (n 71) 105–106 refers to EU lawmaking as an example of 'experimentalist governance'.

B. The Role of Legal Scholars and Practitioners

As most of the literature so far focuses on the role of courts in overcoming fragmentation, it is worthwhile to briefly consider the role of non-court stakeholders in this endeavour. There is longstanding and interesting literature on the role of academia in the development of European private law. A particularly promising strand of this literature investigates the contribution of doctrinal legal scholarship as opposed to interdisciplinary work, for instance adopting an economic or sociological perspective of law, the former sometimes being perceived as under threat by the latter.[74] Jan Smits has argued for a new 'perspective' on legal scholarship that is less concerned with statements about what, judging from authoritative sources, the law is but rather what it ought to be through evaluating competing arguments. For Smits, case law and legislation become a mere 'source of information' from which relevant arguments 'for and against' are derived, which are then evaluated for fitness within a specific normative setting, such as a national jurisdiction.[75] It follows that doctrinal legal scholarship itself becomes a legal source in that it offers another 'source of information' that legal decision-makers draw upon for guidance on how to answer legal questions.[76] In a legal setting where a plurality of courts addresses the same issue without binding future courts, scholars can compete with courts to suggest compelling ways in which the law might move forward. Such suggestions become persuasive if they are convincing on two accounts: they must be coherent with pre-existing law and their real-world effects must be considered fair.[77]

Legal scholarship thus conceived seems to have a clear place in the fragmented European patent landscape outlined above. Courts may well be the most important institution driving the development of European patent law, but legal scholars have the time and freedom to speculate where it might go. Indeed, as any observer of European patent litigation knows, courts are rarely inclined to engage in doctrinal digressions for lack of resources if not out of institutional modesty.[78] At the same time, if my observations above on normative dissonance are correct, doctrine is indispensable as national patents become embedded in EU constitutional law and their remedies subject to a partially harmonised EU regime. Unifying theories are

[74] For instance, J Smits, *The Mind and Method of the Legal Academic* (Edward Elgar, 2012) 62 ('The present approach' to finding out what ought to be in law 'is to consult other disciplines outside the legal arena'); R van Gestel and H-W Micklitz, 'Why Methods Matter in European Legal Scholarship' (2014) 20 *European Law Journal* 292, 297.

[75] Smits (n 73) 76, 95.

[76] N Jansen, 'Making Doctrine for European Law' in R Van Gestel et al, *Rethinking Legal Scholarship* (Cambridge University Press, 2017) 233 ('… law is different from most other objects of human research in that it is not only the object but also the product of scholarship'). See also Smits (n 73) 79 on how legal academics can contribute 'to the making of a better decision'.

[77] Jansen (n 75) 235. It is unfortunately outside the scope of this contribution to provide the elaboration this statement deserves.

[78] *cf* R Posner, 'Legal Scholarship Today' (2002) 115 *Harvard Law Review* 1314, 1320 (judges 'do their best to conceal innovation, the better to emphasize continuity with existing law').

needed to reconcile national patent laws and EU law, each with their own rationales, because the chosen theory strongly influences the correct application of the legal framework to individual disputes and hence their outcomes.[79] Important work in these areas is already done by scholars. In my view, the need for this kind of unifying scholarship is too often overlooked in discussions on the fragmented state of European patent law and how best to overcome it.

The establishment of the UPC may prove to have galvanising effects when it comes to European patent law scholarship. The UPC will bring together, for the first time, the full range of patent doctrines in a jurisdiction that covers most of Europe. Whereas infringement, particularly, but also validity doctrines with their national idiosyncrasies used to be approached from a national perspective, there will now be a forum that brings together judges and practitioners from all over Europe, each with their own perspective, to craft a truly European patent jurisprudence. Perhaps it could go the way of European trade mark law, which has long operated on the basis of a dual system of national and unitary protection and today is the subject of EU-wide monographs and handbooks as well as exchanges among scholars and practitioners from all over Europe. By contrast, scholarship on issues of substantive patent law is often published in national journals in the jurisdiction's language, making access by outsiders and a dialogue difficult. Academics publishing in English in international journals are not always drawn to this type of doctrinal scholarship (and there is much of interest to say about the patent system from a variety of non-doctrinal perspectives), but it is often what is most useful to courts and practitioners.[80] That may be true especially in the UPC's early stages when the various practical issues it raises need to be ironed out.[81] While not writing entirely on a blank slate, the UPC will formulate pan-European positions on many issues of patent law. As past experience shows, legislative intervention will be a rare and difficult achievement, so Europe's unitary patent regime will likely be judge-made to a significant degree.[82] There is every reason for scholars and practitioners to join the courts' dialogue and suggest useful ways forward.

Thankfully, there is an increasing number of European journals with good international circulation and devoted to the practice of IP law, such as the *Journal of Intellectual Property Law & Practice* and *GRUR International*. One could even imagine a quarterly or half-yearly journal devoted specifically to the UPC and its

[79] Jansen (n 75) 238.

[80] Posner (n 77) 1322.

[81] L Petherbridge and D Schwartz, 'The End of an Epithet – An Exploration of the Use of Legal Scholarship in Intellectual Property Decisions' (2012) 50 *Houston Law Review* 523, 545 found that the US Supreme Court's reliance on legal scholarship increased following new statutory enactments: 'statutory changes can create ambiguities in otherwise mostly settled law. When the Court confronts these ambiguities for the first time, it is likely to be writing on more of a blank slate in terms of its precedents and other formal, legally acceptable sources of decision'.

[82] Petersen et al, 'The Unified Patent Court (UPC) *in Action*: How Will the Design of the UPC Affect Patent Law?' in R Ballardini et al (eds), *Transition in European Patent Law* (Kluwer International, 2015) 41.

patent law jurisprudence, modelled after the *Federal Circuit Bar Journal*.[83] Either way, European academics and practitioners alike should not be shy and embrace their role in the development of European patent law. Their insights are needed not just as inspiration for the UPC to draw on, but also to limit the risk of biases in the Court's case law which is inherent in a specialised judiciary.[84]

III. Conclusion and Outlook

This chapter has analysed European patent law through the lens of regulatory fragmentation. It is a promising subject for such an analysis, because as we have seen, the law governing patent disputes in the EU is found in a patchwork of national, international, EU and regional legal instruments. Connecting the analysis to the questions driving this volume, we can state that patent law is characterised by a high degree of regulatory fragmentation and that numerous complementarities, gaps and tensions can be identified in this legal framework (many more, in any event, than this chapter has been able to address). My suggestion in this chapter has been that one specific form of tension, here referred to as normative dissonance, deserves special attention because patent law's gradual submersion into EU primary and secondary law has made it particularly acute.

A surprising degree of consistency nevertheless exists in the application of the fragmented framework by patent law's various adjudication bodies. With regulatory fragmentation being what it is and unlikely to be overcome soon, those bodies do an exemplary job of creating through judicial doctrine something approaching a 'European' law of patents. The remarkable proclivity of Europe's patent courts to engage with the decisions of their foreign counterparts is no doubt born out of necessity as regulatory fragmentation is not a new phenomenon in European patent law and possibly even inherent to it, as some have argued. The trick is to avoid 'standing up and walking out' on colleagues we think 'sing out of tune', to paraphrase the song that lent its title to this chapter. Although it is tempting to think that the UPC will immediately become something of a band leader now that it is finally here, I have argued that at least in the short term the UPC will actually add to fragmentation and the search for harmony will remain necessary. Luckily, their experience with judicial dialogue makes European patent judges tuned in to this process and I believe there is still plenty of room in the chorus for non-judicial actors, especially patent law scholars.

[83] After this chapter was written, but before it went to press, two journals with just this ambition were launched: *GRUR Patent* and *European Patent Litigation in Practice*. The author is hopeful that these and other journals will provide a unifying forum for patent practitioners across Europe.

[84] Petersen et al (n 81) 55.

PART V

Lessons Learned and Future Perspectives

10

Conclusion

INGE GRAEF AND BART VAN DER SLOOT

This book has analysed the legal consistency of technology regulation from the perspective of the interaction between: (1) the EU and Council of Europe (CoE) frameworks, (2) the various EU frameworks, and (3) EU and Member State law. It has become clear from the eight substantive chapters that ensuring legal consistency is a challenge in each of these areas.

The interaction between the EU and CoE frameworks points at different underlying priorities with the EU being more focused on internal market integration and the CoE prioritising civil and political rights. Different legislative objectives influence the interaction between EU frameworks. And finally, the level of harmonisation determines to a large extent how EU and Member State law relate to each other.

The insights from the different chapters show at least three common trends.

I. Legal Consistency is not Black or White

The different chapters have illustrated that legal consistency comes in degrees and that complementarities and inconsistencies are not inherently 'good' or 'bad', although it is surprising that while the EU's overarching legislative aim is harmonising the internal market, it seems only marginally successful.

For example, although the use of similar concepts across legal regimes is usually seen as a way to establish useful complementarities and to align substantive protections, chapter four has shown that the overlap between the prohibitions of consumer manipulation in the Unfair Commercial Practices Directive and the proposed Artificial Intelligence Act can have the adverse effect of creating legal uncertainty and undermining each other's effect. Catalina Goanta coins the term 'regulatory siblings' to illustrate how the use of similar or identical legal rules across legislative instruments can increase coherence in fragmented legal systems, but may also lead to undesirable overlaps in scope in the case of 'mere duplication' of concepts that do not have an independent meaning within a particular instrument.

Inge Graef pays attention in chapter eight to how the co-existence of EU and national legislation targeting digital platforms can allow for useful experimentation and learning-by-doing as long as the application of the Digital Markets Act and national competition regimes is streamlined to prevent diverging outcomes on the same issues. By leaving scope for Member States to have additional rules in place at the national level beyond the Digital Markets Act, other relevant concerns or problematic practices may be identified that are not yet taken up at the EU level. Experimentation in the Member States can thus be a mechanism to keep the overall framework of economic regulation for digital markets future-proof. This does require that national divergences are closely monitored and that their effects are evaluated in order to inspire future interventions at the EU level.

Following a similar approach, Mark Cole and Christina Etteldorf explore in chapter seven how to determine whether different choices regarding the implementation of the General Data Protection Regulation (GDPR) in Member States constitute negative regulatory fragmentation or positive regulatory diversification. Some margin of manoeuvre at the national level is desirable to take into account different traditions and beliefs. For instance, there is no European-wide consensus on issues such as how to balance the protection of the processing of personal data with journalistic freedoms and at what age children are considered capable of giving consent for the processing of their personal data. At the same time, legal consistency can be ensured in the context of the GDPR through the cooperation mechanisms within the European Data Protection Board and through interpretation of data protection concepts by the Court of Justice.

II. Legal Consistency Requires Clarity about the Overall Policy Objective

A common challenge to legal consistency is when legal regimes that apply in parallel to a particular issue do not have the same normative basis. Establishing legal consistency in such situations requires clarity regarding the overall policy objective. The discussion in the various chapters of the book shows that the legislator rarely thinks through how different legal regimes relate to each other. Having clarity regarding the overall policy objective can help find ways to reconcile conflicting concepts and rules. In many cases, legal interpretation can address such uncertainties in the longer term.

Laurens Naudts and Ana Maria Corrêa illustrate in chapter two that the European Court of Human Rights and the Court of Justice of the European Union each take a different approach to assessing data-driven inequality and discrimination. While the former predominantly protects civil and political rights, the latter has traditionally focused more on socio-economic aspects. Although this can sometimes create divergences, it also provides opportunities for complementarities when inequalities that are not addressed in one system can be remedied in the other.

Chapter five pays attention to the interaction between the need to open up public sector information and the need to protect personal data. Maria Lillà Montagnani and Laura Zoboli discuss how the Data Governance Act complements the Open Data Directive and the GDPR in providing public sector bodies with a set of instructions regarding how they can open up public data in compliance with data protection rules. Technical tools deserve to be considered as well, including anonymisation, differential privacy and the use of synthetic data. Integrating legal and technical approaches could further support the opening up of public data without compromising data protection.

Andreas Wiebe discusses in chapter six the complicated landscape of regulating machine-generated data where data protection, intellectual property protection and the promotion of innovation and competition come together. This leads to overlaps and frictions, which are not all addressed upfront by the legislator. Recourse to legal interpretation will thus likely be needed to successfully apply new legislative instruments in this area, such as the Data Act and the to be established European data spaces.

III. Managing Legal Consistency is a Joint Responsibility

When the legislator does not set a clear hierarchy or does not clarify upfront the relationship between legal regimes that apply in parallel, it is up to those subject to the rules to interpret them. Regulatory authorities can also play a role by adopting guidelines to explain how they understand the scope of the rules they are competent to enforce. Ultimately, it is up to the courts to decide on disputes. At its discretion, the legislator can codify the outcomes of court judgments or adopt new rules to substitute or complement existing outcomes. Through this cycle of lawmaking, the different actors within a legal system can jointly manage legal consistency.

Bart van der Sloot points out in chapter three how the two European courts have contributed to ensuring consistency between the right to privacy and the right to data protection in the absence of proper harmonisation of data protection legislation by the EU legislator. The fact that the two European courts often either choose to take the same path or follow each other's lead has resulted in a minimum level of clarity in the area. In particular, the European Court of Human Rights played a key role by including principles developed under EU data protection law into its own case law about the right to privacy. However, in other areas where the European Court of Human Rights is not competent, the level of legal certainty is lower and it is up to the Court of Justice or the EU legislator to act.

In the area of patent law, Léon Dijkman shows in chapter nine that fragmentation is inherent in the patent system due to the existence of several layers of applicable rules at the international, regional and national level. Nevertheless, through judicial dialogue the fragmentation is managed by the courts. He argues that there is a role for legal scholars and practitioners as well, in particular now the Unified Patent Court has become operational and ways forward need to be established in this new context.

IV. Conclusion

This book has pointed out that legal consistency is challenged in different ways. Legal regimes may have different legislative objectives, underlying beliefs or priorities as a result of which there is no immediate alignment between concepts and rules. This is a challenge that is inherent to any legal system and it is therefore not specific to technology regulation. What may be unique about technology regulation is how the increasing use of data, AI and platform regulation is permeating different spheres of our lives that are each regulated in their own manner. This has increased the complexity of the regulatory landscape and the degree of interaction between legal regimes that previously could be applied largely independently. Now that is no longer the case, we need to adapt to the new reality and reflect on how to ensure consistency in a regulatory framework that is becoming increasingly fragmented. While the chapters illustrate that scholars can find ways to reconcile different interests and objectives, we should avoid reaching a stage where the situation becomes unworkable in particular for those subject to the rules.

Legislators, regulators and courts therefore carry a responsibility to maintain a sufficient level of legal consistency in the increasingly complex field of technology regulation in the future.

INDEX

www.ingramcontent.com/pod-product-compliance
Ingram Content Group UK Ltd.
Pitfield, Milton Keynes, MK11 3LW, UK
UKHW020810290926
15470UKWH00003B/1064